W

Shoot
Khawajas

'We that are young
Shall never see so much, nor live so long.'
King Lear, Act IV, Scene III

We Don't Shoot *Khawajas*

Chris Price

To my Mum and Dad, who must have gone through armchair-hell wondering if their son was dead or alive, while I sauntered through Africa ... oblivious.

First published 2023 by DB Publishing, an imprint of JMD Media Ltd, Nottingham, United Kingdom.

ISBN 9781780916569

Printed in Latvia

Contents

Author and Acknowledgements

"Where are you from?" It's a frequent question. Your author often gives a somewhat flippant answer: "I can't remember ... here?". This means the boondocks of Japan. I'm 65 now, but I was originally from leafy Surrey in England. After boarding school and university, I took a brief sabbatical on a North Sea oil rig. In 1980 I fled the UK in search of adventure, and in search of myself. I've lived so far in England, the North Sea, Johannesburg, Perth, Kobe, various parts of Tokyo, Singapore, Hong Kong, and Bali, never spending more than 2 years in one place. After traveling extensively in Africa and Asia, I ended up in Japan. I spent 20 years in banking. These are known in the family as "the school fee years". I then moved to Karuizawa for 10 years, which is a record for me, hence the answer "here?". Apart from writing travel books, I own and run Hotel Wellies. Think Fawlty Towers of the Far East and you won't be far wrong. I plan to travel South America next.

I owe most to **Dr. Ralph Pettman**, my mate, my neighbor, and most importantly my editor. Ralph is a retired academic who has written more books than I've had hot dinners. Crucially, he knows me well and has visited many of the places I've traveled through. I was dyslectic before the word was invented, and he's done a great job of making order out of chaos, and deleting the gibberish. I would also like to thank my friend **Krishan Gupta**, a Nepalese student at the local international school, UWC-ISAK. He edited the photos. I would like to show my appreciation

I think you can work out who is who!

to **Steve Caron** of JMD Media for publishing this, my first book. I would also like to thank my kids, **Mia and Alec**, for growing up to be great people. I should also thank the wonderful **people of Africa** for allowing me to travel through their great continent, without "let or hinderance" (as it says in my pompous British passport), almost always with a beaming smile, despite their sometimes difficult lot in life.

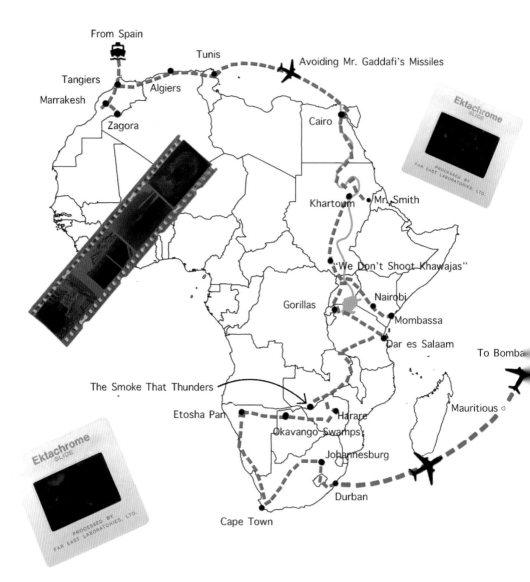

Prologue

Britain and Spain

It's 1982. Southern Sudan isn't flush with hotels, so I'm staying at the local police station. It's a secure compound (sort of) on the edge of Yambio, with barbed wire, a few cells, and rudimentary breeze-block barracks. Coming down from Khartoum, I've taken the most southerly route from Wau to Juba. I'm now close to the border with the Congo and the Central African Republic.

Yambio really is a tiny dot on the iconic Michelin map I picked up in a Moroccan *souk*. The map's made of paper, and it's been through various stages of hell, but it's still in good nick.

It's the police station and the market that define Yambio as a town rather than a village, since it's mostly mud huts and tribal people. I'm in the market area, sitting on a large, upturned cooking-oil tin, under a tatty tarpaulin, and eating *foul* beans. Yes, *foul*, but pronounced 'fool', which perhaps refers to the consumer. They're blackish, mashed up, and far from tasty, but they're a good source of protein. The sun is setting. Its rays are pushing through the motes of dust, slowly losing their battle to prevail. Dinner's eaten early here because the electricity supply is so unreliable.

The shadows lengthen. Then gunfire erupts close by.

I find this rather disturbing, particularly as it continues. I scoff the remainder of the beans with the twisted old spoon that I carry. It sounds like high-pitched small arms fire, and it sounds like it's intensifying.

I beat a retreat to the supposedly safer police station – my impromptu hotel. Approaching the fortified compound, I find a variety of ancient and decrepit

Two elegant ladies taken a few hours before the shoot-out at the bean pod corral.

firearms aimed at me by the local constabulary. Most are old Lee Enfield 303s. They look like they belong in the trenches of the Somme. I raise my arms and shout, 'Foreigner, foreigner.' An order is given, and the guns are lowered. The captain strides out. He's the epitome of decorum in a white shirt and peaked officers cap. 'We don't shoot *khawajas*,' he shouts back to me.

This is jolly good news, and seems to have been true so far. I've had a few guns pointed at me in my travels, but nobody's actually pulled the trigger – yet. To date, I've survived pretty well. On the whole, human nature seems to be, if not benevolent, then far from evil.

It occurs to me that this vaguely empirical (I'm still alive) confirmation of the essential goodness of man would make a fine name for my tale. So there it is, *We Don't Shoot Khawajas*. (I should also note that I've had some run-ins with boisterous wildlife as well. They've also let this *khawaja* live.)

In Egypt and the Sudan *khawaja* means foreigner, though in the local Dinka language, I think it probably means 'scruffy idiot coming from the direction of the gunfire with a belly full of *foul*'. The logical corollary of not shooting *khawajas*, though, is shooting other things. More of that anon.

The captain tells me there are bandits in town. He says to keep my head down, and shows me a deep concrete culvert – a storm drain. I clamber into this concrete trench, lie down, and somehow manage to nod off with the crackle of gunfire in the background.

This probably seems an odd thing to do, but real travel is tiring work. I'm also in my early 20s, and suffer from the belief that I'm bulletproof.

The twilight is gone now. I open my eyes to see stars twinkling against the black, velvet night. I think I might have been woken by the silence, since the gun fire has ceased, too.

The police are filing back into the barbed wire compound – my impromptu hotel and refuge. I clamber out of the drain and approach the captain.

'Did you catch the bandits?' I ask him.

'No,' he says.

'Did they escape?'

'No.'

I'm a bit stumped. Perhaps they shot them all.

I ask him, but the captain says no.

Now I'm really stumped.

'What happened?'

He refuses to tell me.

'Please,'I beg. When he eventually relents, he asks me to keep it to myself.

Sorry Mr Captain, but I've told a few people over the last 40 years.

The story unravels. When one of his junior officers hears shots going off, he thinks he's under fire. It seems to be coming from the tree line on the edge of town. He returns the fire enthusiastically, and shouts for reinforcements. A right royal exchange ensues. Then the bandits stop firing. Our heroic young policeman cautiously approaches, creeping forwards, wary of an ambush. The bandits are nowhere to be seen, dead or alive. A mystery.

As it turns out, the bandits were huge, dark, bean-pods, each one exploding with a loud crack, as they do at this time of year. They're probably activated by the sharp drop in temperature from day to night in the early evening. They sprinkle their seeds far and wide. There never were any bandits.

The Captain shakes his head. He's a stoic. 'At least none of the men shot each other,' he says.

I go to my room, which is actually a cell, and lie my sleeping bag down on the stained, dusty, concrete floor. The door stays open. They've lost the key.

So, what happened next? Plenty, as it happens, though very little of it comfortable. My subsequent rambles took me through much of Africa and Asia, until they were rather unceremoniously – and to my mind tragically – ended by an innocent-looking pot plant in Kobe, Japan.

But I'm getting ahead of myself. How the hell did I end up in Africa, in a shoot-out between the police and a bunch of exploding beans?

Chris Price stepped into the adult world in 1980 from a red brick university with a degree in economics and industrial relations. His degree was not very practical, but at least it wasn't based purely on numbers, as economics seems to be today.

His grounding in economics was actually laid at school by a superb teacher called Mr Chubb. He was superb precisely because he didn't teach. He left his students to learn. He set essays that they had to research themselves.

One of my fellow students was called Harry El-Erian. His real name was Mohammed, and his dad was an Egyptian diplomat. He eventually went on to Cambridge, where he earned a first. I happened to bump into him just after he'd graduated. We'd always got on rather well, and we discussed development economics.

He subsequently became the chief investment officer for PIMCO, a massive US fund management firm, where he was in charge of over \$1tn. His decisions moved world markets, and political leaders cowered when he fiscally chastised them. Mr Chubb's rather novel techniques had clearly worked on one of us.

At the time I was wondering what to do next. The Berlin Wall was still up, and Britain was in a mess. The coal miners seemed better at striking than mining. And the future looked not only bleak but also, to be honest, somewhat dull.

I was at one of life's singular crossroads – the one which defines what you become. What transpired was all surprisingly random. I was your standard, middle-class, English chap, with little idea of the real world, a 1970s boarding school education, and some reasonably rigorous tertiary training. My friends were all off becoming lawyers, accountants, or surveyors. This scared the living daylights out of me.

I won't bore you with the details of my childhood, or any of the adolescent stuff, though my hair was embarrassingly long, and my jeans were embarrassingly flared. I'll just say that I used to write from the bottom right-hand corner of the page towards the left in mirror style, though not in the genius fashion of a Leonardo da Vinci. It was more in the fashion of someone with a learning disability. This was in the years before dyslexia had been invented, so it was simply assumed that I was a bit thick, and that I should try harder. I survived by doing more sport than study, which means that if my grammar today is poor, I do have an excuse. My mother's maiden name was Larkin, like the poet Philip Larkin. He was a distant relative, so obscenity is in the genes. His famous poem *This Be The Verse* begins with, 'They fuck you up, your mum and dad'. I never even came close to understanding his work, and the poet-relative thing was a very closely guarded secret during my school years. God forbid that someone should have found out, and insisted I write and recite a poem in class. That would have really fucked me up.

Anyway, I decided to earn some money so I could travel the world for six months. This was at a time when Britain, as I said, was not functioning very well. There were strikes, three-day weeks, and all the rest of it. Thatcher's magic, neoliberalist mace was yet to come. It was still grey, miserable, and more than a little stuffy. How to earn a quick buck?

I hitchhiked to Aberdeen. Hitching seems to have been binned these days, but it served me very well in odd places like the Sudan. (At university, I'd once hitched around Ireland for the summer holidays with my best mate, Tom, who was 6ft 4in tall, and our flat-mate, Gail, who wore tight shorts. As a 65-year-old grandma in a Mercedes said, 'I decided to stop for you as nobody is going to stop for three, especially two boys with long hair'.)

Aberdeen was in the middle of a boom. I naively planned to get a job on an oil rig off-shore, but I had no experience. Catch-22. First I had to get past the secretary. Then I had to decide whether to lie about being completely wet behind the ears, or tell the truth and hope they were nice people, or trust to luck and hope someone had just been fired for showing up drunk, and they needed someone on a chopper in two minutes.

I somehow landed a job with a subcontractor on Shell's Brent Delta platform. In professional terms, I was the lowest of the low – the equivalent of grunts in the US military. Expendable. The absolute bottom of the pile were the cooks, who seemed to be mostly gay guys from Newcastle. Then there was me, fresh out of university, with my vaguely socialist ideals, and a complete lack of practical knowledge about what to do with valves and the like. I was pretty hopeless with a mop and paintbrush, too.

There was a lot of technical mumbo jumbo to learn. Have you heard of 'Christmas trees'? These are the large lumps of pipe and stuff at the top of

The North Sea - Chris on Brent Delta oil rig.

wellheads. They're superheated. When you dab paint on them there's a burst of noxious fumes that enters the atmosphere and hence your head. It's far stronger than any substance I came across at university. Painting things like that, while greasing nipples, cleaning floors, and dealing with poisonous chemicals, became my daily routine.

The guys I worked were what's colloquially known as the 'salt of the earth'. This meant they all had criminal records, drank like fish on-shore, and were incredibly kind – at least, to me. I was expecting to be bullied, or at least to have to suffer some sort of initiation, but there was nothing like that at all. They were, in fact, gentlemen.

There was Doddy, for example, a Glaswegian, who spoke a totally different language from the rest of us (though we didn't dare tell him). He had numerous convictions for assault and grievous bodily harm. Background checks seem to have been a little lax in those days. He was a very small, sinewy guy, with a thin evil moustache.

The North Sea, my bus to work; a survival craft that someone ironically fell off; flaring gas; Paddy and dangerous Doddy.

Then there was Irish Harry, who really had done time for stealing the lead off church roofs. He had a mop of black hair, a thick black moustache, an infectious laugh, and a razor-sharp mind that, unfortunately, was pointed in the wrong direction.

And there was Pat, the other member of our team, who'd run away to sea when he was 16, got his trawler licence when he was 17 or something (a record), and drank so much on-shore that he was literally crawling up the walls when he came off. The rigs were 100 per cent dry. Well, dry, so long as you didn't drink the duty-free aftershave, which I saw Pat do once. He could also do *The Times* (of London) crossword in about ten minutes. This made him an invaluable resource on quiz nights, when us grunts got to humiliate the teams from the upper echelons of rig society – the management, the engineers, and the rest of the social and professional hierarchy. Harry was also surprisingly knowledgeable. Doddy did not contribute much beyond 'menace'. At one stage Pat had to disappear for a couple of weeks. 'I've an appointment at Her Majesty's prison in Durham,' he said. I don't know what he'd done wrong, but he did actually have to sew mail bags there.

We lived half the time on flotels, which were floating hotels, like oil rigs, but just for sleeping on. The production platform itself was full of the people with more important jobs to do.

We travelled around by helicopter. There were the Boeing Vertols, which were monsters with two sets of blades. There were the Sikorskys, which were also big. And there were the Bell 203s. These were called Hueys in the war movies we watched about Vietnam. (I once saw *Apocalypse Now* on my own on the rig, changing the big rolls of film myself in the middle of the night. It was spooky.) Smaller than the Bells were things called Messerschmitt Bolkows. These were glass bubbles, with a lawn mower engine behind the seat.

Apart from movies and cigarettes (the latter a bit surprising, since we were sitting on a huge, hydrocarbon bomb), it was the food we looked forward to most. The Geordie cooks made vast quantities for us. Breakfast might be two steaks, a couple of lamb chops, three eggs, some bacon, and baked beans. We could squeeze in four meals a day by staying up for the night shift lunch at midnight. I remember calculating that I was eating 10,000 calories a day. And yet, I was still pretty skinny.

Out on the rigs the rain never seemed to fall from the sky. It came at us sideways. It could blow a man right over, even after one of the supersize-me meals.

Before starting the job we had to take a safety training program. It was late September. We met down at the beach in Aberdeen and were told to strip off to our swimming gear and run into the water. I don't know what the temperature was, but it was somewhere around six to eight degrees. It was agony. We stayed in there for five minutes. Once out of the water, one of the guys screamed at the instructor, 'What was the fucking point of that!' He replied, 'So you know how cold the water is, and won't do anything stupid on the rig. Without a protective suit, you're dead in ten minutes. With a protective suit, you're dead in 40.'

After our cold dip, we were loaded into survival craft. These were large, orange capsules, totally self-sufficient, and impossible to sink. They turned the right way up automatically. Unfortunately, they were also pretty unstable. One man was sick, which set off a rapid and revolting domino effect.

Another guy, who'd missed the cold-dip bit of the training, fell into the sea from the rig because he wasn't wearing his safety harness. He thought it wasn't cool. At the time there was a force eight gale blowing. Sirens went off, a flare was fired, and spotlights danced over the ugly, black swell. The tops of the huge waves were flecked with white spray. Each rig had a big trawler ready for emergencies, that constantly circled the rig. It tried to pick the guy up by dragging nets over the side for him to catch, but failed. A rubber Zodiac was lowered from the trawler, with its brave crew crouching in the tiny, buoyant craft. The guy was being pulled away by the wind and currents. The Zodiac crew couldn't see him and were being given instructions by walkie-talkie from high up on the rig. Somehow, they did rescue him, though after that he and his two best mates quit. The Shell press release said he was in the water for five minutes. It was closer to ten – the death point. The news is seldom right when you actually know what happened, which makes nearly all news either inaccurate, or just plain wrong.

I guess I earned my money out there. I also grew up a bit.

For example, Avon turbines are amazingly noisy and big. They're made by Rolls-Royce. I was cleaning and painting what's the equivalent of a huge aircraft engine from the inside, while it was running at full power.

A red alert went off due to a gas leak in my area. Everyone mustered on the helipad ready to evacuate. Lights were flashing all over the place, except in my area where they were all broken. Sirens wailed, though to no avail in the turbine hall. I wandered out for a tea break 20 minutes later, and found the rig strangely empty. Luckily, it turned out to be a false alarm.

This was when the Irish Republican Army was in full cry. At one point, we had a bomb alert, and were told to 'search the rig'. Those things are huge. It was hopeless, unless you considered the whole thing to be a bomb. We gave up. Later we found out that a bomb had gone off two hours before at the oil terminal on the mainland.

We worked one week on and one week off. In the off week I would get the train down south. The other option was to stay in Aberdeen with Keith, Paddy, and Doddy, get slobbering drunk, spend all my money, and probably get a criminal record to pin on the wall next to my mediocre degree.

I usually went to my parents place in Surrey, or the area around my old university in Kent. One time I hitched rather than take the bus or the train. I soon struck it lucky, and got a lift from a Tampax salesman. He took me right down to Coventry. My next ride took me to Canterbury, which was my destination. Awesome.

Harry met me at the airport one morning for our chopper ride out. He said, 'Can you lend me a tenner for some fags?' He'd won £700 on the horses, and then bought everybody in Aberdeen a drink. At the end of the week he had to pawn his watch.

After a few months I'd earned some cash and was getting itchy feet. I went down south for a week of rest and recreation. My mum was going shopping in a small country town called Horsham, so I went along to buy the Lonely Planet guide to India. It was a small place, and they didn't have it. They did have one called *Africa On The Cheap*, though. So the answer to the question as to how the hell I ended up in southern Sudan is because a book shop in Horsham didn't have the guide to India I wanted. Such is life. Of course, now I'd sit on the sofa, go online, buy the India book, and just go to India. All very easy. And all very unpleasantly predicable.

Before leaving, my mood switched between joyous anticipation and animal terror. I could feel the two emotions in the pit of my stomach. My earnest lawyer dad felt it his duty to put the fear of death into his son (or *pro-bono* client – I think he sometimes got confused). He repeatedly told me, in his most serious voice, that 'foreigners are not like British people'. This profound insight proved to be a source of great relief. To have discovered that the people of the North West Frontier Province, or the Mountains of the Moon, were just like Aunty Vera, would have been, well, dreadful. Dreadful for me, and dreadful for them.

Dorking railway station was a tearful place as my loving parents receded into the past. I didn't see them again, or my friends, for four years. There was no Skype then. Just thin blue airmail paper, and the occasional crackly phone call. The latter were very emotional, and filled with awkward pauses.

Sir Francis Drake set off from Plymouth in the *Golden Hind*. I was not such a swashbuckling adventurer (though I did have my aspirations) when I climbed aboard a nondescript ferry that also departed from Plymouth. Unlike Drake, I was bound for Santander, in the Basque region of Spain. The other travellers included an Iranian chap, whose name I forget, and two British girls, Lyn and Babs.

My metamorphosis from a rooted person to a nomad began gently enough. Mum's sandwiches ran out pretty quickly, but my Barclays traveller's cheques lasted a remarkably long time.

The train ticket from Santander to Madrid was more than I wanted to spend. I was determined to be an austere traveller, however, the Spanish were not as keen on hitchhikers as the Brits. (The Sudanese were the gold medal winners in this regard, along with the Ugandan Special Forces, the People's Liberation Army in China, and the kind-hearted Irish.) I stood around for ages with drivers staring at me like I was from another planet. I wondered if having my thumb up had some more sinister meaning to them. I made 20km in two and a half hours before deciding this was not going to work. So I got a lift back to where I started from – with some English tourist. Sometimes you have to know when you're beaten. I took the train.

That night, I woke up in a terrible panic. Where was I? Where was I? I wanted to crawl into myself and die. Then it finally clicked. I was in a hotel room in Madrid. I'd been away for two weeks. The problem was I was still tied to the idea of home – of having a place where I belonged. I seriously thought of getting the next plane out. Thankfully, thoughts of Aunty Vera set me straight.

The relief of working out my location was enormous. After all, I was still a lonely, novice traveller. Forty years on, I can still remember those few seconds of fear. They were really deep. I did, in time, grow to love the power of aloneness, but that brief moment was truly terrifying.

Waking up in a totally dark room, and not having a clue where I was, happened quite a lot on the road. It eventually grew into a kind of game. I'd wait to see how long it took to click. Ultimately there was no fear, just amusement that I had no clue which country I was in.

Another special thing about travelling was how quickly I got to know other travellers. This was particularly gratifying for Brit like me. It had something to

Classic Brit with a hankie on his head.

do with knowing that time was short before I turned left and they turned right. People became very open and honest then. They didn't know my friends and family either, and vice versa, so there was nothing to lose. This became a recurring theme, and it was fantastic. For example, at one point I travelled with Louise for less than 40 hours. It felt like we'd known each other for ever. Because time was short, we dispensed with the build-up and the background, which for someone English can take months or years. I'd no idea where she came from, or where she was going to, but in those 40 hours it was like we had a whole lifetime together. This was a regular experience, whether the encounter was a few hours or a few weeks. Further south, I met a South African university student, Gerda Visser, who was travelling on her own around Europe. She'd almost run out of money, so we slept on the beach together (separate sleeping bags). We became fast friends in the 24 hours we spent together, and before she turned north to West Germany.

My next move was to look for friends of my parents from the Capel Tennis Club. They owned a yacht, that was moored near Alicante. Once I'd found it, and been duly welcomed, I indulged my by-then desperate need for a shower, a Pimm's, and a croissant. Miraculously, Gerda showed up. She'd put her Youth Hostel Card in my backpack, and had forgotten to retrieve it. How she'd found me, I don't know. We slept on the deck. I was a bit worried about her on her own, but she was fine. I saw her next at her parents amazing Cape Dutch house in Stellenbosch, near Cape Town, almost a year later.

Re-reading my travel diaries today is a struggle considering my atrocious handwriting, my scratchy pens, the yellowing paper, and to be honest, the large amounts of drivel I wrote. One recurring theme, which played a central part in my life on the road, was the state of my bowels. These had managed to withstand the gristle and the overcooked vegetables of an English public school in the 1970s, the pasta and beer and no sleep of three years at a red brick university, and finally a year working on a North Sea oil rigs eating three steaks for breakfast. But the fountain water in the Alhambra in Granada was a whole new experience for them. Their response lasted for, well, the next three years. There's a wonder drug called Lomotil that stops you actually having to go. It doesn't cure you, but if some bright spark hadn't invented it, I might still be in Spain.

It was in Granada that I met Hywel, a young South African who was only 18, but very mature. His dad had been some kind of a businessman in Morocco – it's a profession that covers a multitude of sins. He'd fallen out with someone important, and the whole family had been booted out of the country. Crucially, his father still had bank accounts there. He was *persona non grata*, though, so Hywel had armed himself with a British passport, and had set off to try and get some of the money. (His South African passport was no good. These were still, after all, the days of apartheid.)

Chapter 1

Morocco

Morocco's formal name is the Kingdom of Morocco. I'd suggest renaming it the Kingdom of Hassle.

After a few days of having drugs planted on us (I swear, officer), of haggling over cups of tea, and of the most desperate bowel movements, my thoughts turned towards the future. If little, relatively developed Morocco, just south of Spain, was this much trouble, then how was I going to survive in the rest of Africa? The answer turned out to be very well, actually, because everywhere else was easy by comparison.

One small example of what I mean. We went into a shop (first mistake) where the owner tried to sell us a blanket. Its unique selling point was that one side was smooth (for summer), and the other was rough (for winter). In the end we could only grudgingly admire his creativity and persistence.

We registered at the British Consulate in Tangiers, so the Brits could come to the rescue if Hywel was ever mistaken for his dad. At the front of the British passport was this wonderful message to anyone who found it, or found its owner, 'Her Britannic Majesty's Secretary of State requests and requires [yes, it says REQUIRES] in the Name of Her Majesty all those whom it may concern to allow the bearer to pass freely without let or hindrance, and to afford the bearer such assistance and protection as may be necessary.' No wonder they're so sought-after and cost so much to renew. To all intents and purposes, It's a global get-out-of-jail-free card. I do love the 'requires', though, as if Britain was still an all-knowing, all-seeing, invincible superpower. If it was a US passport, where they could call down a drone strike, or a splash out with a bit of the old Agent Orange, it might have been different. But, quite frankly, we even struggled a bit against the Argentinians. I was in Uganda at that time. Apparently, our supply lines were stretched, and our blue water capacity was not really up to snuff. The thought of Her Majesty, or the British Secretary of State, coming to my aid anywhere in Africa seemed highly unlikely.

The other problem with what Britain 'required' was that the lower-level security forces wherever I was would occasionally give me a hard time, but they often couldn't read. This seemed to me to rather defeat the point. If they could have, they'd likely have just laughed. The test was to pass them my passport upside down. If they turned it around only when they saw my photo, then I knew they couldn't tell what it said. This was a little bit risky, but it was fun. To look at my passport they usually had to put their AK-47s down, too. That was another step in the right direction.

There was a further problem with the passport I should mention. My parents christened me Christopher Andrew John Price. Having to write that in triplicate at every remote border post was enough to keep a man in leafy Surrey.

Yet another hassle was that they speak Arabic in North Africa. This had not been on the syllabus at school, where they seemed to think we'd only ever meet French people, or talk to Catholic clergymen in Latin. The Brits failed to colonise Morocco and Algeria, so my English was of not much use.

Much to my surprise, it was my schoolboy French that came to the rescue. I'd been to Paris, and come away convinced that French was a completely different language from the one I'd struggled to learn for years. They didn't seem to use words there. It was just one long noise. This made it impossible to discern even the first letter, let alone the meaning, of whatever they were saying. What bliss in North Africa, then, where it seemed we all knew the same thousand words, and spoke them like leisurely drips of water from a tap, rather than in an overwhelming gush, as if from a broken mains pipe. I actually enjoyed speaking French there.

Most of my travels in Morocco were by bus, with the occasional shared taxi out in the boondocks. My backpack would be tied to the roof rack along with assorted goats, chickens, and sacks of vegetables. It was always a great relief to see it again. We had to pay a dirham for the privilege of having it passed down. *C'est le Maroc.* It was a hassle, but it was one I came to enjoy.

A tannery, the photo does not do justice to the smell.

Bus stations in richer countries are drab, lifeless places, with bad hamburger outlets, vending machines, coin lockers, and a sign that says the bus has just left. I often fail to understand the convoluted timetables, or that today is the third Friday of the month after the introduction of summer time. The passengers look sad and harrowed because they can't afford the train, a plane, or petrol.

By contrast, bus stations in poorer places are fascinating. Even if I'd arrive two hours late, I'd probably be still one hour early. Morocco was my first experience of this.

The one at Meknes was a good example. The place was buzzing with flies and life. The smell of grilled lamb and liver wafted through the dusty air. People loaded the buses with pots and pans, a menagerie of domesticated animals, and suitcases. There were screaming matches between drivers and passengers. Grimy mechanics fiddled with critical bits of engines. A man in the shade sold yoghurt from big tin buckets. Occasionally, an ancient vehicle, belching smoke, lurched forward and moved out, with its uneven load wobbling. My shirt was soaked and sticking to my back. These places were the life and soul of every town, the heart that pumped people around the country.

Once out in the desert, a huge Arabic script in white paint appeared across the side of a mountain. I assumed it was something to do with Allah. 'No', I was told. It says, 'Attention! Beware of Mirages.'

We went through the magnificently named Gorge of Ziz and out into the desert. The trappings of western commercialism began to drop away. There were no more Coca-Cola signs (which look great in Arabic. I'm surprised the 21st-century mullahs haven't banned their alluring, female-shaped bottles.)

As we went deeper into the desert, all that was left were Camping Gaz signs. For some reason I found it ironic that the people used Camping Gaz for their everyday lives, and not as it might be on a Boy Scout trip.

The nights were bitterly cold and my cheap-as-chips sleeping bag, lined with some kind of ineffective baking foil, was possibly colder inside than out. Innumerable trips to the toilet didn't help. My stomach was still veering strongly towards the 'very upset'.

The stars were shockingly bright, though. And so close.

The sun took a long time to rise and to warm me up. As it did, I once again praised the Great God Lomotil. A dodgy-looking local approached me, and asked me to help him. My guard was up immediately, but it turned out I'd misjudged him. He wanted me to help him write a letter to his sweetheart in Glasgow. I hope she spoke better English than Doddy on the Brent Delta.

Soon afterwards, Hywel began scheming how to smuggle the money that he'd managed to get out of his father's bank, out of Morocco. He hit upon the idea of buying silver. There seemed to be a lot of willing sellers. Rather too many. The silver he bought turned out to be tin with burnt candle rubbed into its nooks and crannies. There's a lot of 'not silver' in this world. And he was only 18. It was a cheap lesson, since he'd only had to pay for it with his dad's, possibly ill-gotten, gains.

We eventually got to some decent dunes. Rather unexpectedly, in the valleys they grew carrots, onions, and turnips. Coming from England, I considered these to be English vegetables. It seemed incongruous to find them in the Moroccan desert.

I bought a small radio and tried to listen to the BBC. This was in the days of knobs and manual tuning. I never really worked it out. I'd tune in to a station and started listening. For example, I'd hear 'This is London calling'. Or I'd mistune and get 'This is Moscow'. They both had BBC accents, which made it tough to tell the difference until I heard 'comrade' or 'capitalist pigs'. In my imagination there was someone old and serious in a dark suit in front of a huge microphone at Bush House. 'In Morocco today …', he'd say. Then there was a whole lot of crackle, and nothing. How could that happen? It was perfectly tuned three seconds before, for Christ's sake. I thought there was probably a prankster out there who waited until

Chris in the desert

we were all huddled up in our sleeping bags in the sand dunes about to hear a little bit about home. Then he'd give a big dial a small nudge. Asshole.

I also began to wish I liked Arabic music. This was a hassle, as well. Life would have been made a whole lot easier if I had, since almost every twiddle of the knob produced it. There was no escape until the Sudan, when Carlos Santana's acoustic brother came on.

Speaking of hassles, what follows is a story about hitching a ride for 170km to Zagora. It took 24 hours.

The vehicle was a Peugeot pickup. We first stopped to pick dates and drink water from a well (via a goat skin – not hygienic). Then cars coming the other way

Ancient desert town of Ait Benhaddou over the Atlas from Marrakesh on our way to Zagora.

started flashing their lights to signal that there was a roadblock ahead. Since there were seven of us in a vehicle with a permit for three, we decided to wait for the police to move on. Hywel fixed the car radio. We had some soup. Time passed. But they were still there. Many hours later we had a brainwave. Four of us took a taxi past the roadblock, and we all met up on the other side. Bloody obvious really. (A similar thing happened on the Rwanda/Tanzania border, to slightly more dramatic but still amusing effect. We met a guy who'd just come back from working in France. His accent was terrible. I couldn't understand a thing, which fairly translated probably means he spoke proper French. We still hadn't got to our destination when we had to stop and bleed the clutch, whatever that means. The truth is, who cares about the destination? That's not the point. It might sound like a cliche, but it isn't. The bit between A and B is the point. Not A, and not B. It's all in the state of mind. Now, that really does sound like a cliche.)

When we pulled into a garage we changed three of the tyres. (For those unfamiliar with Peugeot pickups, there are only four!) We washed the brake shoes, and changed some other fluid. That took another three hours. The engine finally conked out 300m from Zagora's imposing city gates.

Salah was one of the local cool guys in Zagora. He was dressed in brown platform shoes (it was the '80s), blue and white Adidas tracksuit bottoms (too

30

short), a yellow cardigan, and a blue flowery shirt. We'd agreed to meet him at 2pm, but he didn't show. An hour later, we bumped into him. He'd been in town all the time, but hadn't got around to coming to meet us. He'd meant no harm. As far as I could tell, it was more that the Arabs I'd met just didn't get time as I understood it. (I later learned that the Indonesians have a marvellous term to describe duration. They call it *jam karet*, which translates as 'rubber time'. Very Einsteinian.)

We went with Salah to the town square to watch some Berber people dancing. If I remember correctly, they're not Arabs. I enjoyed their music. To my ears, it wasn't what I'd come to call 'mosque music'. A sign said we were 52 hours from Timbuktu, though I think that was by camel. We took some photos of the dancing, and the Moroccan army took exception. A hassle again, but Sahel jumped to the rescue, and there was a big shouting match. He seemed to win since we kept our cameras and films.

On the bus to fabled Marrakesh we managed to do 5km in the first hour. It was extraordinary. We left the bus station, and 200m down the road we stopped to let on a man and his goat. There was ten minutes of shuffling around on the roof, deep discussion, far-reaching negotiations, and much catching up on local gossip. Then 200m down the road, another chap got on with 20kg of dates, and the whole process was repeated. A few minutes later, the driver must have been exhausted, since we stopped for mint tea in small glasses that burned our hands unless we held the bottom with our fingers and the top with our thumbs. I know I said getting from A to B wasn't the point, but I was getting rather annoyed. An Indonesian would have handled it much better, with a murmured *jam karet,* and a few *Insha'Allah*s. (The Muslim concept of Allah being willing is used across large swathes of the world. In my experience, though, Allah is often NOT very willing, especially when it involves long bus rides on hot days. He actually doesn't seem to give a damn.)

As we climbed up into the Atlas mountains there were lots of hairpin bends. These were taken at speed. Allah could have sent us all to a fiery, roly-poly death at the bottom of a gorge. Maybe he'd decided to wait. Once we came over the top, we left the rain shadow, and were confronted by trees.

In Marrakesh itself, the Djemma El Fna was where it all happened. We hung out there at the Café de France, which had a great view of the square. (A recent check on TripAdvisor suggests that it's gone downhill these days, but we probably

Marrakesh Jemaa el-Fnaa, cool place to hang out.

had no choice. There was certainly no TripAdvisor to consult then. Just out-of-date guide books, and word of mouth, and following one's nose, so to speak.) I bought a relatively recent copy of the *Sunday Times*, and had a salad, an omelette, chips, carrots, yoghurt, a Coke, and a coffee. It was well served, and felt a bit safer than what had caused the gut ache I'd had the night before.

Another hassle was what it took to take photos of people. This was because of the steal-my-soul belief (though King Hassan II didn't seem very bothered. There were pictures of him everywhere we went.) My rugged Pentax required me to focus and get the right light settings. I rarely managed to do both, and was a terrible photographer anyway. I tried to take a picture of some women all covered up (I was not really taking a photo of them. It was more a picture of a lot of black material. They waved their arms wildly, and ran away.)

Because Hywel was at that stage planning to go back to the UK to start college, we made our way up to Rabat. In one of life's lovely coincidences, he bumped into his best friend from when he was a boy in Tangiers, before his dad had been expelled. The friend's dad was now the governor of the Rabat prison, so we stayed with them (as guests, not inmates).

I said goodbye to Hywel soon afterwards, and headed for Algeria. The main border crossing was at Oujda, near the coast, but it wasn't letting people through due to the simmering border war. The good folk at the tourist information office told me to go south into the desert, and cross at Figuig. As they said, 'They don't care there.' It was another eight-hour ride, but it was very practical advice, much more so than telling people when to see the changing of the guard at Buckingham Palace, or how to visit the Cotswolds, or what time the next talk about Pollock at the Museum of Modern Art might be.

Prior to crossing into socialist Algeria, I needed to lay my hands on some dinars at a decent rate. The official one was eight for £1. I got 16 at the same tourist information office I mentioned above. Splendid entrepreneurs, those tourist information Moroccans. (For those of you who aren't foreign exchange wizards, getting a decent rate meant that stuff I bought in Algeria cost me half of what it would have cost if I'd changed it at the official rate at a bank. I put the dinars in a secret pocket in my backpack.)

Chapter 2

Algeria

Once I was in Algeria, I noticed that the hassles Morocco had represented soon began to recede. The Algerians proved to be really nice. There was an additional factor, though. As the weeks passed, I was becoming more hardened. The hustlers could sense that my skin thickening. I was no longer such easy pickings.

In Figuig I'd met some fellow travellers and we'd hired a donkey and cart to take us the 5km to the border crossing. This was so much better than the tube to Heathrow, or the Narita express, or those mysterious yellow cabs out of the international terminal in New York. (I say mysterious because they're the reverse of *Doctor Who*'s Tardis. They're vast on the outside and tiny on the inside. At least we could communicate with our donkey driver in rudimentary French. In New York he'd likely have spoken Afghani, or Russian.)

The man who issued the exit stamps at the final checkpoint in Morocco was out to lunch (a long lunch). That meant another three hours. The customs officer gave our backpacks a cursory inspection, and waved us through. At the last moment, he asked us for our currency declaration forms. None of us had them. He let us go, regardless.

Land borders are a blast. I crossed many in Africa. The smaller they are the better. This particular border area was a high-security one. It had roadblocks, spikes to puncture tyres, and plain-clothed guards who asked penetrating questions like, 'What is job your father?'

The border with Morocco was closed. Not if you go to the desert crossing 15km inland!

All the travellers had changed their money to dinars, so when the Algerian customs man asked, 'Do you have any dinars?' there was an unequivocal chorus of, 'No.' The banks were closed for the weekend, anyway. He must have known that. The Moroccans, bless them, would have used the opportunity to squeeze a few more dirhams out of us.

The hotel in the nearest village turned out to be very expensive. So the local policeman said we could sleep by the railway station. It was another freezing-cold night. I dressed in everything I owned, curled up in my joke shop sleeping bag, and prayed for morning. The local Turkish baths opened at 6am. If only the tourist information people in Oudja had told us about that as well.

Three years at Kent University in Canterbury, being taught by professors in ivory towers, and combined with sitting on the grass and trying to be intellectual with my fellow middle-class students, had left me with political sympathies that were vaguely socialist. One of our professors was not a socialist. He was a Keynesian. He'd even married an Italian ballerina, though Keynes had married a Russian one. In one lecture, our professor had given us the following variables, 'capital equipment [tractor], labour [a man], working capital [£100], and a fixed capital asset [a field]'. In front of 200 students, I foolishly tried to put my alternative perspective by asking if he could make this wonderful agrarian scene a bit more realistic. 'No,' he said. 'If you add more variables, the model doesn't work.'

Algeria was the first socialist country I'd ever visited. It immediately rid me of any thoughts of evolutionary socialism as being a good idea. Their model didn't seem to work either. The main variables missing seemed to be the drive and avarice the Moroccans had in abundance. Lovely people, the Algerians, but Christ Almighty, the country was a mess.

The shelves in one shop were totally empty except for three glass and steel contraptions on the top shelf. I got one down, but could not figure it out. 'Do you want to buy?' 'What is it?' After much discussion in schoolboy French it turned out to be an artificial camel insemination device! The socialist planners had overestimated demand for this item (not difficult), and underestimated demand for everything else.

Though Algeria was also relatively expensive after Morocco, I'd luckily done my dodgy black-market deals. I sat down in a restaurant and pondered the menu. Two quid for a meal was about ten times my normal budget. The old owner came over and asked where I was from. He also asked if I was short of money. I told him I was English, and Algeria was pretty pricey after Morocco. He then said the meal was free, *gratis*, a present. I immediately became very suspicious. In Morocco, a meal might have been free, but there would have been an expensive magic carpet attached to it, or the world's priciest cup of mint tea. But he absolutely insisted, so I asked him, 'Why?' He said nothing. At the end of a meal of excellent, albeit rather greasy, fried chicken, and a Coke, he absolutely refused to take any money. With hindsight, I wondered if an English person had done something for him in the past, or perhaps it was something to do with England in general. I came to the conclusion that perhaps it was not that I was English, or that I was me, but that I was not French. There was certainly not much love lost there, and an enemy's enemy is a friend. I might, of course, have simply come across a true, Fabian-style, evolutionary socialist. Or even a revolutionary one. 'From each according to his ability, to each according to his needs,' as Marx once said. He even gave me boiled eggs and bread to take away.

Third-class travel in Algeria meant wooden, slatted seats. I did that for 22 hours from the border on to Algiers, the capital. The indentations in my buttocks feel like they're still there, like the residual radiation left over from the big bang. The conductor was very jovial. That took some of the pain away. He explained that he had to retire when he was 50, because the government said it was a 'difficult job'.

Kids by the railway line.

I told him being a passenger was a lot harder than being a conductor. He had a nice little room with a bunk bed. The train was packed, and people were sleeping in the luggage racks, which was a neat trick I soon latched on to.

Socialism in Algeria meant that all the hotels had signs outside that said '*Complet*'. Ostensibly, they were full. This was because they didn't earn any extra money for having guests. In fact, having guests cost them money. Travellers had to break into places to stay there.

It was in Algiers that I finally got my Turkish bath, though. Coming from the English public school system, I was quite used to being naked with other blokes. I did find being pummelled by a fat Arab with a leering grin a little disconcerting. *Midnight Express* had just come out, and all the masseurs looked to me like the evil Turkish prison guard in the movie. This made it tough to relax. The good news was that I was able to steam off two months of accumulated grit and grime.

While wandering around Algiers, looking for the museum that had rock paintings from 6,000 years ago, I picked up an assortment of locals keen to help me in my search. In the end there were four of them. I felt like the Pied Piper of Hamlin. We finally found the museum, back near where we'd started from. They (the paintings) came from caves in the Tassili, deep in what is now the Sahara. Then it was a grassy savanna with lots of horses. In my diary, I mused how quickly we've managed to mess up the world with how far we'd spread, and with all our pollution. I wrote, 'The whole planet is going to be like the Sahara,' though it seems that I got that particular apocalyptic vision wrong. It looks like those on the coast are going to drown instead.

That evening I was befriended by a girl from the university. She wanted some exposure to the outside world. It was socialism with a Muslim twist. Naturally, we were stopped by the police. I behaved like I couldn't speak French (not difficult). Apparently, the locals were not supposed to talk to foreigners. I suspect they meant that foreign men were not supposed to talk to local women.

The train journey from Algiers to Constantine was a bit of a challenge as the station names were only in Arabic. This made it difficult to know where I was. Oranges cost five times what they had in Morocco, and the sheets on my bed were made of wheat sacks.

Constantine was dirtier than Morocco, which was quite a feat, though it was spectacularly sited on a large piece of rock with a river rushing around it. The cafes were closed at lunchtime, and the museum only opened at 3pm. I tried to buy some bread, cheese, and water, and only succeeded in getting the bread. I ended up in a grotty restaurant eating soup that tasted like soap powder.

I was looking forward to Tunisia. I'd had enough of smiling socialism.

The train left at 2.30pm. I got there on time and milled around for a bit before discovering that it left at 2.30am the next day. This meant that I had to use up some dinars. It was either that, or perform some magic with my currency declaration form. With a marker pen I'd picked up in Morocco, I did an admirable job of cooking the books.

I was down to my last dinar when there was a sudden bout of ticket inflation. This was now 64 dinars, not 55. Happily, the ticket officer took the 55. Maybe socialism did work. A perfect example of 'from each according to his means'.

Crossing the border, the customs guys (half) joked about hash and dirty magazines. All I had was my battered copy of *King Lear*.

Chapter 3

Tunisia

It took 15 hours to do the 600km to Tunis, the capital, and that was with train, customs and immigration. How does time manage to stretch so?

Back in the real world, the shops had lots of useful stuff to buy, as well as with being open. It was a winning combination.

The Hotel de Suisse even had rooms to rent for two dirhams (which I considered expensive). What's more, they were even happy to check people in. (The hotel is still there, though recent reviews are rather scathing. 'Don't leave valuables in your room, as it may not be secure.' Which is a dumb comment, really. True travellers always have their valuables with them at ALL times, even in the shower.) The comments I made in my own diary were, 'A good hotel, TV downstairs, wash basin though no plug, sit down bog (a major selling point for scatologists like me) and even hot showers. A bit upmarket.' In the morning I went to find a cheaper place.

The thing is when you're travelling, and don't have an end date in mind, spending $5 a day means you can travel twice as long as you can on $10 a day. That's simple, I know, but it's not so apparent to the average person behind an in-tray in an office. I not only chose the five-dollar option, but I was also gradually shifting my thinking to US dollars *per se*. It's the global currency, after all.

I couldn't find a cheaper hotel. They were full of Algerians, which made me laugh. They'd travelled all the way to Tunis for the night because their own hotels were *complet*. I'm joking. The Algerians came because the shops had things in them they wanted to buy.

To my mind, Carthage is a town from antiquity. It's even in the movie *Gladiator*. The cool thing is, you can still go there. I even bumped into Lyn and Babs, the two girls who were on the ferry with me from Plymouth to Spain. Africa can be a small place sometimes. It doesn't have as many roads as you think.

The town itself was a bit rundown but it's amazing to think that 500,000 Phoenicians once lived there. I stayed in a dodgy youth hostel, and met some real English tourists who kindly took one of my completed diaries back to England.

But I digress. Back in the capital, Tunis, the great challenge of applying for a visa for Libya had begun. This was prior to the Libyan Embassy siege in London, that resulted in a policewoman being shot. But we were still not on friendly terms with mad Gaddafi and his stooges. The thing is the embassy only accepted applications on Thursdays and Saturdays, and the passport had to be translated into Arabic. I hoped they'd do a good job with the first page, and stress the 'requires' bit. Despite my washing my hair to look good, the whole application process wasn't going well. The Embassy didn't accept my passport on Thursday (I don't remember why). So I did a whirlwind tour of Tunisia in order to get back by Saturday. One old guy I met on a train claimed to have four wives and 20 children. I personally found that hard to understand. What the hell could it be like with three more? Not far from Tunis are the Punic ruins at Kerkouame. I had a view of the sea there from the Maison de Jeunesse (the youth hostel), and a hot shower, too. I walked the 2km to the ruins to find they were closed. So I jumped the gate and had the place to myself. There was nothing grand to see, like a coliseum. But there were houses and streets, and all the houses had baths. Cool.

As there was a train strike on, I switched to hitching. A Libyan guy gave me a ride who was big fan of Gaddafi's. There had recently been an incident in the Gulf of Sidra where two F-14 Tomcats had used Sidewinders to take out two Libyan Sukhoi Su-22s. He was adamant that one of the F-14 jets had also been shot down. Ah, the state media. Those North African leaders certainly had staying power.

I don't think I went to the Tunis suburb of Ben Arous. This was where, in 2010, Mohamed Bouazizi burned himself alive, and became the spark that set the Arab spring ablaze. I did go to El-Djem, though, which has one of the best Roman coliseums in the world. 'It was like a UFO planted there in the middle of a normal town,' I wrote at the time. 'Like the black slab in *2001: A Space Odyssey.*'

Amazing Roman amphitheatre at El Jem.

Hitching requires some improvisation. At one point I left town on a tractor with six other people on it. I kept getting hit on the head by date palms. We stopped at a cafe for a break, and to watch the old, toothless men play dominos. The younger ones played cards. A couple of them had towels on their heads, but most were in Tommy Cooper hats (that is, the basic red fez).

Back at the Libyan Embassy, I queued for 45 minutes in numbing cold rain, with my backpack getting soaked, and my mood spiralling downwards. I eventually gave up.

I had nowhere to sleep that night, and it was dark and miserable. I hadn't managed to get the visa I wanted, but I was strangely at peace. I was already a far cry from the panicking new-boy in Madrid.

The next day the sun shone, I'd found a place to stay, and I was sitting at Café Dinar – my favourite. (It's still there selling mint tea. And it's still a good a place to sit.)

I spent the day running errands around Tunis, getting a letter of recommendation from the British Embassy to give to the Sudanese, and tracking down the Sudanese Embassy. This wasn't easy. In the end someone from the Greek Embassy took me there, though it turned out to be the Sudanese ambassador's house. I never found the actual embassy, but I did buy some shoes and a scarf for my dad.

Chapter 4

Egypt

Egypt Air lifted me over Libya. The plane made a rather wise detour out into the Mediterranean to avoid Gaddafi's missiles before landing in Cairo late in the evening. (Travelling lesson number one, 'Try not to arrive late in a big city without a budget place to stay. Apart from the hassle, it means ending up at a middling priced place.')

A Greek guy on the flight to Cairo suggested that I try the Golden Hotel near Tahir Square. Apparently, there was a Mr Pepper, who sat outside. His claim to fame was that he could find the right hotel for anyone.

The Golden Hotel was not very golden. In fact, it was rather manky; that is, dirty and disgusting. I slept in my sleeping bag to give myself one degree of separation. (It's still there, too, though these days it looks a lot less gross. The rooms have free wifi and mini bars and are no longer cheap.)

Tahir Square was the centre for political dialogue in Cairo. It still is. Anwar Sadat had been assassinated a couple of months earlier, and two young Egyptians told me it was better that he was dead, because power had gone to his head. One of the assassins had said, 'I have killed a Pharaoh.' (Ironically, Cairo built a metro in the 1980s, and the closest stop to where I was had the name of Sadat on it.) Mubarak, a Sadat protege, seemed popular. He'd been in power for only two months. No one thought it would take another 30 years to dislodge him.

While researching this book I found out, or more accurately I remembered, that there were two versions to my life. There was the 'all the stuff that happened'

Tahir Square, Ramesses II seems to have been bumped and replaced by an Obelisk now.

version, most of which I wrote down and sent people in letters, like my mate Tom. Then there was the version my parents received. This was rather tamer. It not only left out the racier incidents, but also the references to pointed guns.

On a related issue, I wish I had decent handwriting. The round, perfectly formed, loopy stuff. Instead, I have a spiky, crabby, cramped hand, which is an absolute pain to decipher. Dyslexia, or just a plain inability to spell, doesn't help either. As a result, I cheat. I write so small that it's not clear if I've written 'ie' or 'ei' in the middle of 'thier'. Sorry. Their.

My writing materials were also a problem. Later in life I was able to write in beautiful Italian notebooks purchased in Florence, bound in leather, and using a nice Mont Blanc, or at least a Pilot rollerball 3-G (I've hundreds of them). By the time I had the money for a posh leather-bound book, though, the rich experiences I wanted to write about had come and gone. The truth is, proper travel diaries aren't written in nice books. They're written on anything you can lay your hands on. They're written on nasty paper with nasty pens. I economised on paper in my travels by also buying stuff with narrow lines. I'm presently trying to read notes written on squared maths paper. The absolute nadir was the Ugandan school exercise book, though it did have the 12 times table on the back. They didn't sell moleskin notebooks in Africa when I was there – the ones that have the sexy little back pouches, and the connections to Hemingway and Picasso. Even if they had, I wouldn't have bought one. Expensive notebooks were the equivalent then of an extra three days of travel. For me the travel won out. At least, until I got to Firenze, that is, and then my life circumstances forbade three extra days of travelling anyway.

Back in Egypt, the train from Bab al-Louq, in Cairo, to the city suburbs, was extremely crowded. It was one of those hanging-on-the-sides-for-dear-life numbers. It was also one US cent for a 10km ride.

Maadi was a foreign enclave with a lot of sandbagged military guards, whose bayonets glistened in the sun. They carried their magazines in their hands. Perhaps there'd been some unfortunate, friendly fire incident in the recent past.

I was going there to stay with people who a contact had told me about, though I needed to find them first. They were friends of friends of friends. They also, as it turned out, hadn't received the letter telling them to expect me. Once I did find them, they said, 'Oh.' There was an awkward silence before they said, 'Come in anyway.' As it happened, Cathy and Donald were marvellous. As was their washing machine, the milk from their cartons (not goat), their Scotch whisky, their hot water, and their proper sheets. They'd moved from the address I was given, which was probably the cause of the confusion, and of their not getting notice of my arrival. They'd never heard of a foreigner catching the train before, or more accurately, hanging on to the sides of one before. They gave me porridge for breakfast, and all the creature comforts, and they even had a driver, for goodness sake.

For those of you not so up on the Sudan, it's a big country to the south of Egypt. To get, though, I needed a visa.

The Sudanese application process was protracted. It took a minimum of three weeks. This was tricky, since my Egyptian visa was only for one month. With my application submitted, it was time to see Cairo and the rest of Egypt. I ended up meeting the director general of antiquities who gave me a free pass to the museum, though his power didn't seem to stretch to the provinces. They didn't recognise it in Luxor.

On the weekend Donald and Cathy rented a *felucca* (a traditional triangular-sailed river boat) on the Nile. I sat there musing that if things had turned out differently, I could have been an estate agent in Epsom instead. Everything's relative. We found the ruins of Memphis (no sign of Elvis), which had been the capital of the 'Old Kingdom'.

The Egyptian museum was a shockingly disorganised place where priceless pieces collected dust in the corners. When I went back to Egypt in late 2006 with my family, not much had changed, except that I could afford a guide who knew which corner to look in for the priceless pieces. There was actually rubble in some of them, which was also probably priceless. Five-thousand-year-old rubble.

The Tutankhamen collection was usually on the road overseas raising foreign exchange. Happily it was home when I visited (and again when I visited with my family). The mask was the most beautiful thing – animal, vegetable, or mineral – I'd ever seen. The Egyptian civilisation lasted thousands of years, but the basic style didn't seem to have changed much. Not like us, with our fashions coming and going in the blink of an eye. A postcard of Tutankhamen's mask is stuck to the front of my current diary. Its gorgeous, *lapis lazuli*, blue and gold is simply stunning. And to think that in soccer parlance he was second division. The premier league stuff all got nicked, except for the magnificent pyramid mausoleums. These were essentially nick-proof, though someone did take all the marble facings off them. Not Harry from the Brent Delta, though. He only nicked lead.

Cheops, the biggest pyramid, was the tallest man-made structure for 3,800 years. That's how long the rest of the world took to catch up. I can't really compare the style, form, and grace of the pyramids with the nouveau riche, penis-envy towers in Dubai, either. They'll fall over in a few years, or get pulled down, anyway.

Cheops was perfect. Of course, Pink Floyd and the Louvre couldn't both be wrong.

In those days a traveller could clamber all over it, though each block was so huge I quit pretty quickly. It was better seen from a distance, preferably perched on the top of a petulant camel. This is easy to do, since there aren't any unpetulant ones. (They're the most ridiculously awkward things to ride. I know this because I later spent four days on top of one in Rajasthan in the Tar Desert. They're bastards.)

That evening I bumped into a chap I'd worked with in the North Sea. We watched *The Awakening* together, which was a dreadful film starring Charlton Heston and Suzanna York as mummies that 'awaken'. This said, Egypt was certainly the place to see it in.

The Son et Lumiere at Giza was also mind blowing, I bought loads of postcards and wrote one to everyone I knew. The Sphinx polished up well in the evening, too. It was a bit like an old car under a light. The blemishes caused by the Marmadukes and Napoleon, who used it as target practice for their cannon, were hidden at night.

Obligatory shot, you could climb them in the 80's.

My cushy life was coming to an end. I had to get back on the road. Which is why I found myself at Rameses railway station. This was the epitome of chaos, particularly when the tickets went on sale for the Luxor train. I got there early – my bid at strategic planning – as I was aiming for my very own luggage rack. But when they opened the booth, there was mayhem. Old, toothless guys bashed each other (perhaps that's why they were toothless), and I failed miserably, even though I launched myself through a window. I didn't even get a seat. For the first part of the journey I ended up on the floor.

I haven't looked up the definition of 'window', but it probably includes something about the ability to be closed. I'd launched myself though one of the many symmetrical holes in the side of the train, but it had no glass, no shutter, and at night-time it was dusty and cold. Two weak and bare electric bulbs hung from the carriage roof. They cast a dim glow through the gloom. Passengers drifted in and out of the light as they swung lazily with the rocking of the train.

Plumes of white came out of my nose as I breathed. No wonder ancient people prayed to the sun. I totally got it now. In fact, praying to the sun makes a lot more sense than praying to the various bearded fellows that a lot of the world consider to be their gods. The sun gives us everything. The Egyptians hedged their bets by having multiple divinities, that mostly had sculpted human bodies and birds' heads, which was a bit odd. They also had a thing about scarab beetles, which was even odder. But they built the pyramids. And if religion is true, and there is reincarnation, please god don't make me a donkey in Egypt. I'd prefer to be a scarab.

I talked with a vet who was sitting opposite me until it was too cold to think. The carriage was a plethora of headdresses that were constantly being rewound and rearranged. I did actually have a Yasser Arafat head towel, but I didn't wear it because I was too embarrassed. Stupid me. 'Here lies Chris Price, who died of hypothermia on a train in Egypt, because he was too English and embarrassed.'

Luxor was tranquil in comparison to Cairo. Then again, the roaring Avon turbines on the Brent Delta were tranquil compared to Cairo. There were towering columns against a thick blue sky, and I sat there for two hours pondering I'm not sure what. Karnak is a truly great temple.

The overnight 17-hour train journey had knackered me, which made the Son et Lumiere that evening extremely interesting. Sleep kept overwhelming me. This resulted in a bizarre mixture of fact, dream, and a sort of mishmash of the two. Unfortunately, the place was huge, and we had to get up and walk around while strategically placed spotlights were shone, and mysterious and majestic scenes were played out, on all the ancient stones.

A vicious dose of the runs stopped me moving around much the next day. I sat by the Nile, ate Lomotil, and read *King Lear* (again).

Luxor wonders.

Over on the Karnak side of the Nile, the hassle was quite severe, and I was reminded of Morocco. The brakes on my rental bike didn't work, and I got ripped off for the ferry, though to put this into perspective, I only paid about eight cents more than the locals.

Coming back I passed the Colossi of Menon (Colossi is plural). These were two really colossal statues. They were guarding something that seemed to have long gone. They looked so lonely and sad, out there on the plain, still doing their duty, long after what they were supposed to protect had left.

Back on the Luxor side, I sat on the banks of the Nile with a Dutch guy and a German girl and smoked dope. A few policemen were lounging around with large guns 20m away, but they ignored us.

Around this time, it seems that I used to press-gang travelling girls into cutting my hair. Looking at old photos, this clearly didn't happen often, and after I'd left Luxor and reached Hurghada on the Red Sea, it seemed there were no suitable girls left to pressgang. This is why, I suppose, I risked a trip to the local barber. He not only cut my hair, but he then whipped out a cutthroat razor, sharpened it on a leather strop, and proceeded to give me a great shave.

Afterwards, to steady my nerves, I went to a tea shop that had lots of hubbly-bubbly pipes. These are probably common in Milton Keynes by now, but at the time they were considered exotic and somewhat edgy. They only contained tobacco soaked in fruit juice, but they did conjure up images of fiendish drugs, and wild-eyed addicts. In fact, most of the smokers were just more of the toothless old men. There was also *helba* tea, though it tasted stale. It turns out that *helba* is fenugreek. I still don't know what fenugreek is, but it doesn't make tasty tea.

To get from the Nile to the Red Sea coast meant crossing 150km of nothing-desert. Just dry *wadis* (stream-beds) and rocks. No pretty dunes, or date palms, or oases. It was a lunar landscape with not much life in it, except for five army checkpoints. The sides of the road were mined, as well so there was a strong incentive not to stray. I took a shared taxi.

Hurghada is a popular Egyptian diving town with wonderful reefs. The contrast between the dead desert, and a place with water that's piped in from the Nile, that has a profusion of technicolor life and death under the waves, was extreme. I say death, because the place was apparently a magnet for sharks. I sat down on a rock, and fell into conversation with a couple of army types, who turned out to be a colonel and the chief of police. They said in their immaculate English that they were 'just killing time'.

A couple of Germans, Rolf and Mienhart, were staying in the same cheap place as I was. One of them was studying religion and sport. So much for economics. There was also an odd-looking Swiss chap there called Urs, who did manage to spot the waiter cheating me on the change at dinner by slipping low-value notes into the pile of high-value ones that was supposed to be my change. It was all part of the game, but thanks Urs. And sorry for calling you odd-looking.

We organised a boat out to the reef to do some diving. The colonel and the chief of police had told me about the sharks, and about Captain Mohamed, who took people swimming. 'It's safe,' they said. 'Nobody's ever been attacked, except for Captain Mohamed's brother. He went out three times and was attacked each time. On the last occasion, only his wetsuit held him together.'

This was my first experience of the colour and variety of life on a reef. Everyone should see it at least once before they die. I tried to describe it to myself afterwards but utterly failed. 'The coral was very beautiful,' I wrote. 'White, blue, and red. Some like trees. Some like sheets. Yellow fish with black stripes. Fish with long noses, purple fish, etc. etc.' None of it did justice to what I'd seen.

In the evening I got some *baksheesh* (a tip) from the hostel owner for bringing some gullible tourists to stay. They paid him the non-negotiated rate. My payment came in the form of having my room rate dropped to half for the night.

Christmas Day was approaching, and I wanted to get back to the luxury of Maadi. The coach to Cairo had reclining seats, but the barren landscape was shocking. There was not one bush or shrub that I could see.

The novelty of having Christmas away from drizzle and snow was extreme. I sunbathed on the balcony. I spoke to Mum and Dad on the telephone (it still amazes me). I not only had Christmas Day in Cairo, but I had Boxing Day in Alexandria. Cool.

The City of the Dead in Cairo is big. I stumbled on it by accident. It's a town full of graves rather than a cemetery, all designed so the inhabitants feel more at home in the afterlife. There's a strange community of caretakers who maintain it, otherwise, it's eerily quiet. There were no tourists there, which is always a good sign. Most of the houses didn't have roofs, either, since rain isn't a thing you worry about in Cairo, especially if you're dead. The place was dotted with minarets, Coptic crosses, and even the odd synagogue. There weren't many landmarks, even

The City of the Dead in Cairo, much more fun to visit than it sounds.

though I was trying to pay attention so I'd have an exit strategy in case Michael Jackson and his zombies suddenly burst out of the earth (*Thriller* came out in November the following year).

The City of the Dead would have made a great stage set. The people there were pretty friendly, too. I stopped for *chai* (tea) at a small stall, where a few old men sat around in the dusty street (toothless as usual). The proprietor made me a cup after clearing his nose of excess mucus with an elephantine roar, and wiping it on his stained *djellaba* (cotton dress). I did drink the tea, but I declined a refill. I also checked my pocket for my emergency Lomotil.

Speaking of tea, I was subsequently writing my diary in the Nile Hilton on Zamalek island, while nursing an expensive cup of it, when I began reflecting on the two worlds in front of me. There was the Hilton. There, I was sitting in the US. And then there was the seething mass of Cairo. There were all its blocked freeways, donkeys pulling impossible loads, people hanging off buses, car horns blaring, and filthy air clogging the lot.

The coffee table was unstable, which is one of my pet peeves. I'd spent a stupid amount of money on a flash-sounding beverage, and I had a wobbly table. I was ultimately distracted by a big Arab in a suit next to me, erotically stroking the waiter's hair.

Me and a Sphinx.

The first-class ticket I'd bought to Alexandria carriage gave me access to reclining seats and free tea. Very nice, but I resolved to take second-class next time.

The Alexandria youth hostel was a bit of a step down, though I did meet a Kiwi there who'd also worked on the rigs. He had long blond hair and always wore a bandana. We bumped into each other all over Africa, first in Alexandria, but then in the Sudan, in Kenya, and finally in South Africa. In some ways Africa is the smallest big place you can imagine. Or it was in those days.

Alexandria is on the Nile delta. This is where the water that hasn't been used to feed, wash, and sustain the whole of Egypt and the Sudan, finally pours into the sea. It comes originally from Uganda and the Ethiopian highlands, before ultimately making its way to the Mediterranean.

The Nile makes for life and civilisation. This said, my mum told me that one of her relatives had died nearby in the Second World War, fighting under Montgomery against Rommel and his Afrika Corps.

The cemetery at El Alamein was not far away so I took the train there, sitting by the door in the sun with my legs dangling over the side. And yes, I was drinking lots of small glasses of sweet tea.

El Alamein hit me quite hard. There was line upon line upon line of neat graves stretching far into the distance. Thousands of young men, just like me, buried in the desert. It made me cry. 'In loving memory of our dear son, he gave his all that we might live.' And, 'He will never be forgotten.' I wish that were true. My dad could have been resting there. Then I'd never have been born. I wouldn't have existed. It was a both deep and a penetrating realisation.

The place is quite well maintained. The wind removes any footprints, so it seemed like I was the only person who'd ever been there. I was quite alone that day, surrounded by the young dead in the desert, thousands of miles from their homes. I was the lucky one. It was a much sadder place than the chaotic, grimy, City of the Dead in Cairo, where the dead really are at home.

I hitched back to Alex, which was pretty hard work, and I also left my sunglasses in a water truck. I lost loads of pairs of sunglasses on the road. Where did they all go, I wondered? I wrote a card home as well (number seven). I numbered them so the recipients would know if any of my correspondence had gone missing. Smart!

I had dinner that evening with a chap from Yemen. I ate stuff that would have flattened me in Morocco. My usual diet in Egypt (excluding the T-bone steaks I was given in Maadi) consisted of *falafel* sandwiches and *foul* beans. *Foul* are actually fava beans, which was one of Hannibal Lecter's favourite foods. He thought they went well with human liver and Chianti. I stuck to the vegetarian option. I never saw Chianti in Africa.

He (the Yemeni) took me to see Pompey's pillar, which apparently has nothing to do with Pompey, but does roll off the tongue rather nicely. My bowels were not completely out of the woods yet, so I bought 60 more Lomotil for a dollar. They were my life insurance policy.

The second-class trip back to Cairo proved more than adequate. There was waiter service, the tea was cheap, and the seats reclined. The other passengers were decidedly middle class, which is to say that there were no Egyptian soldiers in the luggage racks. I hazarded the guess that it was probably more comfortable than the first-class carriages on British Rail (which would probably, at that time, have been on strike anyway).

Charcoal-grilled corn tastes great, and the high temperatures zap any unwanted microbes from the soiled hands of the vendors. I was munching on a cob as I took the mad ride again to Maadi. Due to a technical problem on the line, only half the usual number of trains were running. (The technical-problem-on-the-line thing seems to be endemic to trains around the world. It's impossible to find out what's happened since they're even less forthcoming than airlines. 'The engineers are testing the turbines as there's been a minor malfunction,' the ground staff say, which translated into plain English means, 'A pelican smacked into the engines. The dumb flapper was not only shredded, but it totally stuffed the turbine blades. Hence the dodgy landing that we blamed on wind shear.' Trains don't have that excuse. Usually, the worst that happens is that the thing stops. But they're still cagey. They still blame it on leaves on the line.)

I joke about having guns pointed at me, but I was actually at far greater and more frequent risk on public transport than I ever was of being shot. Tumbling off a hairpin into a gorge in a bus, or falling off a train, were regular possibilities. (I describe later how I once had to tie myself on to the roof of a train in the Sudan with my belt. There were no safety demonstrations by air stewardesses for that one. I had to do it myself. And I had to pay very close attention, as it really mattered.)

On this occasion I was encumbered by my Berghaus backpack. I felt like a tortoise. The platform was jammed with humanity, and everyone was bustling for the best position. This wasn't the 5.37 to Surbiton, or to White Plains, New York, or Kichijoji, Tokyo. I had the pole spot in the front line, but making it into the carriage while the train was still moving was like playing rollerball.

Back in Cairo I wanted to visit the Citadel. This was closed to the public, and had been for three months (coinciding with the assassination of Sadat). It was a massive stone structure was built by Salah Al-Din, who was the bloke with the large curved sword, and matching nose, who fought the Crusaders. We usually get his name wrong and call him Saladin. Near the Citadel is the bulbous and magnificent Mohamed Ali mosque. It's to Cairo what the Eiffel Tower is to Paris, and Tower Bridge is to London. It's iconic.

I needed to get back to the centre of town and do some wheeling and dealing on the black market. The Cairo buses had Arabic script only on them, so I asked a local, in my stuttering Arabic, if this was the bus to Miden Tahir (Tahir Square). The response was a nod of the head; an affirmative; a yes. With a belch of carcinogenic smoke, the bus lurched off, but it did so in exactly the wrong direction.

I immediately got a second opinion from a guy who did speak English. 'Oh, sorry, this is the wrong bus,' he said. 'So why did the other man say yes to Miden Tahir?' I asked. 'He didn't speak English,' he said. 'But Miden Tahir is Arabic,' I said. Dah. Down this road lies madness. Don't go there. Just accept. I think what happened was that a pink-faced monster approached a local, blabbering a question, and he panicked. He said 'Yes' but what he actually he meant was, 'Yes, I heard you babble something (while butchering my language), but I've no idea what you were talking about.' The trick was to move on to the next local, and the next, and after a few, to seek a casting vote.

Wheeling and dealing on the black market was not quite as complex as it might sound. It was a lot easier than getting a bus in the right direction. Unlike the banks, the black market didn't close. You could also shop around. You went up to a kiosk in Tahir Square, for example, and asked for the rate for US dollars. Then you went to the next one, and asked him. You did your final exchange with whoever offered the highest rate. There was no rubbish about commissions. It was fast and efficient, though it did make me a bit nervous. I wasn't happy until it was done, and I was around the corner, deep in the crowd.

I spent the new year period in Cairo, whereas the previous year I'd spent it on Brent Delta in a frenzy of mopping and painting with Irish Harry. We'd pulled the night shift.

I didn't seem to incur much of a hangover. This was evidenced by the way I wrote ten pages in my diary of absolute drivel about development economics. I also wrote something about the nations I'd encountered so far. I described the Moroccans as bandits and robbers, greedy with vitality, who could also be perfectly friendly if they weren't able to rip me off. It was a big game. Moroccan shops were tiny, but they were packed with the stuff you needed. Tins of sardines. Lomotil. Cigarette rolling papers. Algerian shops were, by contrast, huge and almost empty. If I wanted to buy toilet paper, they'd only have huge syringes for artificially inseminating camels for sale. The state controlled everything. Prices were fixed. And the people couldn't be bothered. The Tunisians got a big tick by comparison. The Egyptians were a sort of cross between the Moroccan bandits and the Algerian sleepers.

When my Sudanese visa came through it was finally time to get back on the road. Maadi was in danger of becoming a home away from home. I needed to move along.

I happened to bump into the Kiwi guy at the Sudanese Embassy. I learned from him that the Sudan-bound ferry left on a Friday. This gave me a couple of days to visit Aswan. (I didn't need too many visas further south due to the British Commonwealth. This roughly translates as a large group of ex-colonies that remarkably don't hate the Brits).

It felt strange to have everything once more on my back, or secured in a money belt around my waist. I knew that the next place I was likely to have all the lovely stuff I liked to take for granted was in South Africa, thousands of kilometres to the south.

I bought a second-class ticket to Aswan. This put me a few days over my 30 days on my Egyptian visa, but I suspected they wouldn't care too much down there. I also went shopping for one specific item, before diving deeper Africa. This might sound a bit odd, but my class of hotel never had plugs in the basins. I hadn't seen a plug in a hotel since Essaouira, on the Atlantic coast of Morocco. The Moroccans nicked them all, the Algerians forgot to produce any, and goodness what the Tunisians did with them. The Egyptians couldn't afford them. The trick was to get one with a flat bit of rubber that fitted all basins. Having a personal plug was one of the marks of a seasoned traveller, as opposed to someone who takes a few weeks off and flies in and out. I took a certain pride in being a traveller of this sort – one with a battered passport full of odd stamps, dreadful diarrhoea, a small, beaten-up backpack, and of course, a plug. I think I actually got laid on the back of lending my plug. I wrote to Hywel, telling him proudly about my purchase.

The train south to Aswan left at 8pm (well, that's what it said) from Rameses Station. I stocked up for the journey with ten *falafel* and *foul* sandwiches, and a bar of plain chocolate. It looked like fruit and nut as it had two dead flies squashed into it. I ate it anyway.

I was moving into malaria country, so I started taking a cocktail of drugs. I popped a Paludrine each day, which apparently stops the malaria parasite from reproducing inside the red blood cells. Nice, though the side effects could include a feeling of sullenness. I also dropped two Chloroquine tablets a day. This stuff was quite nasty. It was initially considered too toxic for humans, since it could result in blindness. Fortunately, I can still see, and I didn't get malaria.

I actually slept for most of the journey to Aswan. This was as opposed to nearly dying of hypothermia, which is what I'd done on my previous trip, where I'd wanted to a pittance for what was only half a day's travel. There are times when it's worth splashing out. This was one of them.

Chapter 5

The Sudan

I'm not a creative writer. Coleridge and those chaps used to take copious amounts of laudanum to help them, and they probably had some raw ability as well. I only have my stories about what happened to me before I got a job.

Writer or not, at that time I felt truly free. I felt powerful. I felt like I was in total control. If I wanted to turn left, I did. If I wanted to turn right, I did that instead. After Egypt, this meant travelling to the Sudan.

The ferry on Lake Nasser from Aswan to Wadi Halfa was something of a watershed. I was preparing for a three-day journey, and the chance to see the magnificent temple of Abu Simbel, but everything was already starting to feel different. Where Egypt had generally been poor and squalid but still part of the 20th century, the ferry was loaded with tribal men in flowing white gowns, who had impressive knives strapped to their arms. I immediately wanted one. I could feel that we were on the edge of Africa proper now.

A third-class ferry ticket gave me space on the roof, which meant I was out in the elements if it rained. But this was a supremely arid area, which meant this was very, very, unlikely to happen. Being frozen stiff at night was pretty much guaranteed, though.

In Aswan I'd stocked up on bread, honey, fruit, olive oil, cheese, and a bottle of medicinal brandy. I wondered how long it would last.

Apart from Catherine, who came from the Haslemere tribe in the south of England, there were no women. The fairer sex was confined to the hold. I liked

The ferry on Lake Nasser, Bandana Duncan putting in another appearance

Catherine, but that was rather difficult to do anything about on the crowded deck of a boat surrounded by fierce-looking men with knifes on their arms. She'd worked in the Sudan for a year, and was just back from hitchhiking to Jordan. She clearly had true grit. The Kiwi-without-a-name-but-a-perpetual-bandana-round-his-head was also on the ferry. So were two equally nameless Aussies.

The ferry was actually two passenger boats lashed together with some sort of tug thing to pull the whole thing along. One of the locals caught his foot between the two boats, and it was badly crushed. There was blood everywhere. He immediately went into shock because of the massive pain. I had my medicine chest (the boat had nothing) which meant I had the choice of giving him Lomotil, malarial prophylactics, or something called Mogadon. A little knowledge being a dangerous thing. I selected the last and immediately became the ship's doctor. In a world of the blind, the one-eyed man is king. Mogadon is a sedative and an anti-insomniac. It can also help epilepsy. Its side effects include rage, violence, and impaired motor movement. It was the best I could do, along with putting some antiseptic on what was a gaping wound.

The boats uncoupled, and one of them took him back to Aswan. Going forward to the Sudan would have been suicide, or rather, slow death from gangrene. I was forcefully reminded that an emergency in the middle of Africa really can be the end. There are reasons why the average lifespan of many of the countries I went through was in the forties.

We stopped in the evening at what was called a port. It was actually a hut and four dogs. People got off to wander round for a bit, but Catherine and I stayed on the roof and had a good meal (everything being relative). In an attempt to woo her, I even cracked open a tin of sardines from my Moroccan stash. Everyone came back on board, and then drifted downstairs, except for us two. Don't get excited. It was romantic, but nothing happened. The moon began to eclipse – literally. As the shadow of the Earth consumed it, the stars came out. They were like diamonds in the sky. They were beautiful. After half an hour, the whole disc was covered, and the edges glowed a deep orange. Small clouds drifted in front of it, which gave the impression of it rolling towards us. We'd also smoked some weed. That probably helped. Then the show ended, and the moon re-emerged. It was dazzling.

I'd worked up the courage and common sense by then to wear my Yasir Arafat headgear to keep warm. We fell asleep in our respective sleeping bags, and in the morning, Catherine cut my hair.

The great temple of Abu Simbel was moved, stone by stone, to higher ground before the Aswan dam flooded the Nile valley to make Lake Nasser. Waiting to pass the great temple was like a 48-hour version of *Waiting for Godot*. We had no idea where it was, and neither did the locals. We did finally pass it (which was notably different from Samuel Becket's famous play.) I'd pre-purchased a postcard and wrote on it to send home. Number 13. In a strange way, Abu Simbel reminded me of Mt. Rushmore. So stony, and so stuck out in the middle of nowhere.

We were down to our last loaf of bread. This sounds very biblical, but no miracles transpired. We started to eat the local food instead. This consisted of freshly slaughtered chicken, in a bean stew, with macaroni. It seemed out of place, but it had been quite popular in Egypt. We added another tin of my Moroccan sardines, some of Catherine's mackerel, and some of Duncan's cheese (Aha. That was the name of the bandana-wearing Kiwi). I've no idea why we made this concoction. It tasted really strange.

As the steamer pulled in to our destination, some goats were eating a cardboard box, and others were climbing in the trees to eat twigs. Wadi Halfa was a harsh place. The foreigners were taken to the front of the immigration queue. The locals had to wait, with their pots and pans, their carpets, and their new electronic goods still in their boxes.

A local gave Catherine and I a ride on his horse and cart to town. There we did have some bread, and some fish. It sounds rather biblical. It certainly tased better than the concoction on the boat.

There were four classes on the 36-hour train ride to the Sudanese capital, Khartoum. I bought a fourth-class ticket, perhaps because I had a short memory, or perhaps because I was masochistic. There was no glass in the windows. There were wooden slatted seats. And there were no lightbulbs. I was not looking forward to the trip since the 12 hour one to Luxor had nearly killed me. I was also Catherine-less. She'd taken the slower, but more comfortable, road route by truck. Clever girl.

The journey looked to be about eight hundred kilometres on my Michelin map. Lake Nasser is over 300km long, so the three days by boat was actually pretty quick. This was before the long civil war between the north and the south of the Sudan, though. It was already simmering.

The Sudan is large. It's about 2.5 million square kilometres. This makes it something like the ninth-biggest country in the world. If I discarded kilometres, and just thought in terms of the hours or the days or the weeks it would take me to get from one place to another, it was probably the second-largest country in the world after Russia.

Looking back, I think going fourth-class, eating the cheapest local food, and staying in the cheapest hotels, was all part of being a member of the true travellers' tribe. You couldn't sit in the legendary Thorn Tree Café in the Stanley Hotel in Nairobi and hold forth about train trips from hell to goggle-eyed, fly in tourists, and wannabe travellers with new backpacks, if you'd gone second-class. Fourth-class got respect.

The nights on the train to Khartoum were very, very long. I took Mogadon tablets to no effect. Bandana Duncan and I went out to sleep on one of the flatbed trailers. It was noisy and bumpy, but it was a change from being cramped up in a dusty carriage. My rubbish sleeping bag let me down again, so I clambered back, frozen, over the slumbering, groaning bodies, on to the carriage floor. (I was chilled to the bone in Africa far more often than I was too hot.)

There was not much to look at in the daytime. The Nubian desert was very barren, though we occasionally saw eagles. Or maybe they were vultures. The train stopped everywhere. Once again, I had to remind myself to think of travel not in terms of A to B. In reality, I was always where I was. I was always in the moment.

We got out at most stops. The Sudanese women were far more involved in life than the Egyptian women. We bought grapefruits from them, and tomatoes, and cups of tea. Sadly, this all changed when chauvinist Muslims came to power and implemented of Sharia law. (There are quite a few places where the world was a better place in the 1980s than it is now. The Sudan is arguably one of them, and being a woman in the Sudan even more so. Having to take such a massive step backwards seems to me to be very sad.)

Everyone was brightly dressed. It felt like we were leaving the dourer Arab world and entering an Africa of primary colours. We also seemed to pay the same for produce as the locals. This was a novel experience, though I sort of missed the challenge of the commercial push and pull.

Then dusty, tired, and rather relieved, we finally arrive in Khartoum.

The Royal Hotel was a great place to relax. All the beds were in the garden under the trees. There were no doors, no keys, and all of our possessions were accounted for at the end of our stay. Remarkable. Since we were all out in the garden, working out who the other guests were was pretty easy. Half were members of the traveller tribe. A quarter were Sudanese from the provinces. And a quarter were wealthy Ethiopian refugees.

I extended my visa for another two months as there was no way one month was going to be enough. I also got a permit to go on the road up to Port Sudan. And another permit to take photos.

When I changed money on the black market it was in an office. And my Sudanese pounds were presented in a crisp white envelope. Cor.

There was a long, quite decent, tarmac road from Khartoum, that went down south a little and then looped up beside Ethiopia to Port Sudan. When I was there it was the only road that could really stand up and say with a straight face, 'I'm a road.' The other ones were either mud or rock or something else uncomfortable that made the 100km journey from dawn to dusk something that rattled me to pieces.

Hitch hiking in the Sudan was also surprisingly easy. I was aiming for Port Sudan, and Iranian truck drivers gave me a lift. We made good progress, though even with a good road, there were still plenty of reasons to stop. There were innumerable tea breaks, prayers-to-Mecca breaks, meal breaks, toilet breaks, change-the-wheel breaks, change-the-other-wheel breaks. It went on. And on. It was 1,200km to Port Sudan. I got as far as Gedaref on the first day. This only was about 80km from the Ethiopian border. It was swarming with Eritrean refugees.

One thing that always surprised me was the depth of knowledge of the people on the street about world affairs. Though poor, and devoid of a free press, I could chat with my fellow Sudanese residents about Margaret Thatcher, and the local dictator, Gaafar Nimeri, quite freely and openly. And what's more, they knew what I was talking about.

Another day, and I was riding on the top of another truck in the baking hot sun. My head was wrapped in a turban-like arrangement *a la* Lawrence of Arabia. Camels lolled by water holes, herded by members of a fearsome tribe called the Hedenduar who carried enormous swords and spears. The latter had steel points on both ends. Breaking one off on a lion's head meant there was still another to fight with. I don't know if my credulity was being tested when I was told this, but at least I didn't have one tested on me. The men also had curved wooden throwing sticks that didn't seem to come back.

It was semi-desert country, which made it all the more bizarre when we drove past a line of smart, green and yellow John Deere tractors. I guessed they were part of some well-meaning, but misguided, foreign aid package.

The truck pulled into the ubiquitous truck stop at a town called Kassala. It was already dark and all the hotels were full, but a local kid offered to find me a place for a small fee. We haggled, and I ended up in a place with a couple of other *khawajas*. The next morning the same kid came back. When he heard I

Camel herders at a water hole while hitch hiking towards Port Sudan and met Mr. Smith.

was British, he suddenly went bonkers. 'Our English teacher, you know him, Mr Smith, he also British, you know him!' he said. I guess he thought the British were all one tribe (which is not far off, actually, with sub-tribes depending on the soccer team people support). I just wanted to rest, but he insisted on taking me to meet Mr Smith. I refused, but he was so insistent I eventually gave in. He marched me off down several dusty alleys, turning left and turning right. The buildings were all low and flat roofed, like Mogadishu in *Black Hawk Down*, but without the nasty militia. Eventually we came to a compound door where the poor deluded kid began to rap furiously, yelling, 'Mr Smith, Mr Smith, Britishman, Britishman.' The door finally opened and there stood a tall bloke with blond hair.

'FUCKING HELL. SIMON??' I screamed.

'CHRIS!!' he screamed back.

We immediately hugged each other. It was an emotional and awesome moment. As it happened, we'd gone to the same school together. He was in South House and I was in West House, but we recognised each other at once. It was a real Stanley-and-Livingstone moment. The kid said, 'I told you so. You know him. Same British.'

Simon provided me with a bed, which was in the garden, just like in the Royal Hotel, and I spent a few days with him. I never did make it to Port Sudan.

As a break from *King Lear*, I tried to bone up on where I was. I read a copy of *The White Nile* by Alan Moorehead, where I noticed that he was quite complimentary about General Gordon (who may have met his Waterloo at the end of one of those double-pointed spears). Moorehead was less complimentary about Earl Kitchener, and the Ma'di tribe he fought against (not to be confused with the posh Cairo suburb). It seems that Kitchener wanted to decapitate all the Ma'di's and make their skulls into teacups. According to Mr Moorehead, it was Queen Victoria who put a stop to that.

There were a lot of Eritreans in Kassala, and they had a lot to say. One fellow spoke immaculate English, and had been a freedom fighter against the Ethiopians. We shared a cup of tea in the market. He thought the two sides were roughly equally matched in terms of military hardware, but the Ethiopians had got a hold of a load of helicopter gunships from the Russians, and the Eritreans had had to beat a hasty retreat across the border into the Sudan.

The *souk* was full of really colourful tribal people. I asked a few if I could take their photo, and they enthusiastically agreed. They clearly didn't have the Muslim superstition about having their soul stolen. Indeed, they wanted the actual photo. Mr Polaroid must have been through before me. I eyed their double-pointed spears and huge swords with trepidation, but the tension quickly eased, particularly when one very proud old boy wanted to show me his curved British cavalry sabre.

My films from this time seem to have got lost. I sent things home by a wide range of decrepit and dodgy-looking mail services, as well as with people I'd met in the street. Pretty much everything made it. My films were an exception.

My postcard fetish also got stymied in the Sudan. All I could find was pictures of night scenes of mundane high streets with cars, electric lights, and concrete buildings on them. Then it dawned on me. There were only a handful travellers. There were no fly-in tourists. And if there were foreign businessmen, they didn't buy postcards. It was not commercially viable to produce postcards just for people like me. These postcards were for the Sudanese visitors from the provinces to send back home. Electric lights, and concrete buildings, and cars on the street, were what was exotic. They were much more interesting than pictures of tall, proud, naked, Nuer tribesman with spears. The Nuer were two a penny. (The poverty of decent postcards was to reach its nadir when I sent one home from Uganda with a faded photo of two characters from the then-popular TV show, *Dallas*. On the back it said 'The Murchison Falls game park'. At least my mum got a laugh.)

I needed to get south and out of the country before my permits expired, so I made my way back to Khartoum on the top of more trucks. Once there, Bandana Duncan and I headed off to the Ugandan embassy to get travel permits. As Commonwealth members, I didn't think we needed visas, though what we did need, as it turned out, was courage. That or stupidity.

Khartoum then was really a big village of two million souls. Gaafar Nimeiry was the resident dictator. He'd closed his Ma'di Palace, scared that he would get assassinated the same way Sadat had a few months earlier. The palace was where General Gordon had been killed, so it had a certain pedigree. Nimeiry had a pretty good innings. He died of natural causes in his Omdurman home. A few days before, students were shot dead protesting about the rise in the price of sugar.

It was in the Sudan that I also saw dervish dancing done for the first time. It was pretty cool, since it was done for real in the dust of Omdurman (the most populous city in the Sudan). The huge orb of the sun was rolling towards the horizon, and I probably had a bit of weed in my system as well. It was out by the

Omdurman market was a lot of fun

old graveyard, where there were tombstones in the desert, for heaven's sake. Talk about dust to dust. It took place every Friday, which was the local holy day.

The dancers were mainly in ragged flowing green robes. I initially wrote performers, but they were not performing. In fact we were very lucky to be allowed to experience such a deep religious ritual. They literally whirled themselves into a mystical trance.

They had large swords, jangling beads, big beards, and happy faces. This was the sort of Islam I couldn't understand, but really liked. As I wrote at the time, 'They're a poor Islamic sect that worships Allah by dancing wildly instead of praying.' This seemed pretty good to me. Some of them looked like Rastafarians from across the border in Ethiopia. They were similarly spaced out. Looking back, I couldn't ever see guys like these getting all bitter and twisted and crashing planes into the World Trade Center.

We met a Sudanese-Moroccan chap there who spoke good English and worked on a building site for 50 cents a day. We had dinner with him and he told us about the relationship between the political elite, the army, and the dissidents. The petrol stations all had armed guards, though strangely the Omdurman Bridge was unguarded. Perhaps the guards were there to deter common criminals. It's tough to steal a bridge.

Sufists in Omdurman about to start their trance dance.

I bought some more malaria tablets in the market and had a cholera injection. They didn't have disposable needles, so I was literally taking my life in my hands, though I didn't know it at the time. Cholera or AIDS, spin the wheel.

Sudan's National Museum was nowhere near as big as the Egyptian one, but it was still impressive. The Pharaohs of Egypt were actually the Pharaohs of Egypt *and* the Sudan. At least most of the exhibits had labels.

I also got to sit at the confluence of the White and Blue Niles. You can sort of see two different colours merging, but the White and the Blue must have been descriptions by an explorer with a sense for the dramatic. I suppose the Muddy Nile from the Ethiopian highlands and the Very Muddy Nile from the Mountains of the Moon in Uganda would have been too confusing.

Lyn and Babs showed up yet again, and I went swimming in the Nile with Lyn, who was in a bikini and looked rather fine (to use an English understatement). They were flying back to the UK, so she gave me her mosquito net. I thought girls travelling like they did were amazing. They pretty much had to do it in pairs for safety. They might not shoot *khawajas*, but girls were vulnerable to a lot more.

Water melons in motion.

And so I headed south, though as the train pulled out of the Khartoum station, I was unaware of what an epic trip through life and death was about to unfold. I was later to describe it as the 'dreaded journey to Wau'. It was no little jaunt for a few hours. It turned out to be large part of my life. I'd already had plenty of experience of hard wooden benches, and sleeping in luggage racks, but this was extreme, even for me. The carriage windows were glassless, which meant dust swirled around to fill my eyes, my nose, my ears, my camera, and my food. Children defecated on the floor. People coughed and spat. I moved to the roof to get air and to admire the view (see cover photo).

We chugged along, pulled by an old black warhorse of a steam engine that had probably been around for so many years it didn't know how to stop. It was no doubt built in some miserable, dank, Scottish foundry, by gruff men in flat caps, when Queen Victoria was still strutting her stuff in black. The only other *khawaja* on the train was German Peter. He had his camera stolen on the journey, as well as one of his shoes. I think he was an amateur. Somewhere we crossed the divide between the severe, white, billowing, cotton *djellabas* of the Arab north, and the minimalist, at least partially naked, Black South. This was Livingston country, *par excellence*.

The thing was that I had no idea in the rainy season things got to be slower. Though we eventually made the 1,500km in a relatively spritely seven days, the

Another delay in the 7 day 1,500km odyssey. By comparison Apollo 11 went 1,500,000 km, but it took them 8 days. Also they did not get to ride on the top or eat foul beans.

Hanging on to the train for dear life, with that inevitable big smile.

conductor said two babies had been born on the way, and one person had died. It was a steam-powered village of humanity, puffing through the bush.

For example, by 8pm on the first day we'd been in the same place for about six hours. There were also far too many cockroaches in my carriage for my liking.

They dropped off the luggage rack, scuttled across the floor, and disappeared under the seats. They also poured out of a hole in the wall at the rate of a few a minute. (Here's another tip, 'Don't take the compartment next to the toilet on a Sudanese train. A local man told me I should stay, since they wouldn't hurt me. He was right, but they were really gross. I did get used to them later, but it took a while to learn to tolerate them crawling over me in the night, or crashing into the walls.')

Up on the roof it was warm for a few hours. The real problem was the risk of falling off. The roofs of trains are convex, and the natural tendency is to roll down. To stop myself doing so, I tied myself to the centre of the carriage with my belt. I eventually made arrangements (it took a bit of *baksheesh*) to sleep in the corridor of the first-class carriage. My choices were, after all, pretty stark – the cockroaches, freezing to death, or dropping over the side.

Kamel, the ticket inspector felt sorry for Peter and I and allowed us to eat in the first-class buffet car. This, rather remarkably, had leather armchairs, and Mappin & Webb silver cutlery. There was also a rather prominent service button, that didn't work.

You get to know people pretty well after a few days on a train. Kamel was a 6ft 5in giant from Dongola, the capital of the old Nubian kingdom. He invited us to his compartment where he 'fuddled' us with *foul* beans. I've since searched the web for the meaning of 'fuddle'. It means to intoxicate, though nothing of that sort took place.

At this point my letter from Egypt about the war cemetery at El Alamein had managed to make it home, and my mum had answered it. I'd picked up her reply at the Khartoum *poste restante* before I'd left. I sat on the roof of the train (tethered) where I read and re-read it. She was very grateful and emotional that I'd gone to Alamein. Her stepfather, Ted, had died in the North African campaign. She'd wanted to go after the war, but it hadn't been possible. (When my son, Alec was 18 and about to set out on a gap year, I tried to give him some pointers on being aware of what was around him. I travelled alone a lot of the time. When I did, I felt I was the most omniscient person on the planet, unencumbered by mortgages, work, friends, relatives, TV, newspapers, or consumer choices. In the movies you sometimes see someone approach a sleeping man, and in a flash he's awake with a knife out. That was me (without the knife). Alert. One hundred per cent aware of my surroundings. Always reading people and situations. My son

Shame the guy in the 70's t-shirt got in the way of the cool naked dude.

was planning to travel in Europe, which in my view was much more of a risk than Africa in the 1980s. I bought him a pouch to hang around his neck.)

As we slowly headed south, the scenery become more and more stereotypically African. The women were bare-breasted, and Peter got told off for snapping away at them with my camera. After travelling for four months, something was finally stolen from me, or rather, from Peter, since I'd lent him my Adidas trainers, and they'd disappeared in the night from right beside him in the first-class carriage corridor. The police did search the train, but there were no shoes. I thought that Adidas trainers must have been gold dust, but actually, no. Most people hadn't heard of them, and most didn't even bother with shoes. Later on, neither did I, though I paid for it by getting a huge thorn in my instep. It found its way out six months later via my ankle.

I made some small, very crude drawings of the main features of the various tribes we came across. Many of them shoved tiny stones under their skin to make patterns. It was a sort of Braille tattoo. I recorded the markings of the Dinka, the Shiluk, the Herdendeur, the Rachida, the Jibine, the Dongola, and the Shiga. Regrettably, my sketches all looked like the work of a five-year-old.

We arrived in Wau after spending a whole week on the train. I'd gotten to hate Peter.

Wau, just after the epic 7 day train journey.

At the hostel in Wau, I slept on the floor. Sometimes there was water, and sometimes there was electricity, but more often there was neither. Most importantly, it wasn't the train.

The diet in the south certainly seemed to lack variety. There were the inevitable *foul* beans, and there was *kibder* (liver). Apparently, the weed was pretty good, and it was certainly dirt cheap. Meals were often washed down with Sudanese sherry, whatever that was.

Since we'd left the Muslim north behind, I sometimes heard church bells ringing, which was pretty incongruous. The wailing Mullahs had also been replaced by a police bugler, who woke me up at 4.30am.

I bought two handmade spears in the *souk*. My fascination with weapons resulted in a few ridiculous impulse purchases along the way. I still have a box of pen knives and the like that I never use, but refuse to relinquish. There were even market stalls that sold deep-fried doughnuts. That made a change.

Travellers tended to gravitate to the same shops, stalls, hostels, and bars. Our local favourite (goodness knows why) was run by a couple of ugly old hags, who roasted their own coffee beans, and fried their own doughnuts. The one who served us had a terrible, terrible smell, but at least the place had character.

That night I heard movement in my room. The bare lightbulb went on and there stood a 6ft 7in Dinka tribesman, with his glistening, pitch-black skin, dressed only in a pair of brief red Speedos. He was towering above me with a spear, his eyes bulbous and manic. As he looked down at my disorientated, feeble, pale, prostrate figure, he launched his spear and skewered a frog that was sitting in the corner. What a nightmare. And to think I'd woken up in Spain in a cold sweat just because I didn't know where I was. He was actually a great guy, who came running out of his room at the slightest sound armed either with his spear or with a huge axe. In a fight, he was another one you'd want to have on your side, a bit like Doddy.

I also got to know the police quite well. Their station was the local jail. They had an almost naked man there manacled to the floor, his two front teeth sharpened to two sharp points. They were open and friendly, and it was clear they were trying to do the right thing. Pretty much everyone in the Sudan was tribal, but they were sort of educated-tribal. They'd been shipped in from other areas to provide some neutrality. They told me about the problems with the Arab north, and how the south was always being ripped off by corrupt officials. Petrol, for example, was ten times the price it was in Khartoum.

A man making me a couple of assagais, which I sadly threw away (responsibly).

There were two ways to travel from Wau on to Juba – the northern route and the southern route. The latter was my immediate choice because it was really remote, though there were rumours of a mail truck that took passengers. It was run by the Ministry of Youth (there was no explanation for this delegation of duties) but the driver hadn't been paid for months, and so not much was happening. I had less than two Sudanese pounds left, which was not much. I needed to find a black market again. The hostel manager promised to do a deal, but he hadn't been paid either, and couldn't give me any local cash. I ended up getting a dismal rate from a friend of the two old hags. That's finance. You get absolutely killed when you need liquidity. (Another hint, 'Change all the money you think you'll need in the capital city. Though one drawback is then having to cart it all around. In Uganda, I once changed 50 bucks, and I ended up with a carrier bag of local notes covered with pretty pictures of elephants, and flattering shots of the president, Milton Obote. This said, trying to change foreign currency can get pretty tough in the provinces.')

At some stage I seemed to have moved out of the hostel and into the police station. This certainly had logistical advantages. Every vehicle going by the southern route had to get a permit from the police. This meant I knew who was coming and going.

I think I owe a paragraph to the humble toothbrush. I left the UK with a standard Boots-issue one and promptly broke it in half, discarding the handle end as a waste of space. Somewhere in the southern Sudan it disintegrated. They don't sell conventional toothbrushes in much of Africa. They do however sell special sticks. You rough up the end of the stick and hey presto, a toothbrush. You don't have to break it in half as it gradually gets used up until there is just a stub left, then you buy a new one, or cut one yourself. It must be fresh green wood and roughly the dimensions of a pencil. Simple, ecologically sound and effective.

This brings me on to the subject of African teeth. I never saw one dentist office until South Africa (no doubt they have them in the cities), but I never saw anyone with bad teeth (before old age). All bright gleaming gnashers that a Hollywood A-lister (or anyone from California) would be proud of. Why? I am guessing they only had enough money to buy maybe one Coca-Cola a year – I think that's the secret. India was a different matter; I saw street dentists there performing things with pliers but no anaesthetic that would make the Khmer Rouge cringe. I had to cross the road to avoid the horror. Indians eat a lot of sugar and drink dreadful cola called Thumbs Up. But that's a story for my next book.

A rare shot of an unhappy guy. He probably wanted some baksheesh payment.

To kill time, Ian (the Kiwi partner of another Kiwi called Donna) and I went across the Wau river to a village that had a pub. The Wau is a tributary to the White (Muddy) Nile. The bar consisted of a mat on the ground under a tree, and a cauldron of *marissa*. This was a grey, opaque liquid with the texture of ,milk of magnesia. It tasted vaguely like home-brew gone wrong, but we drank rather a lot of it.

The Kiwis were staying at the Catholic Mission. I visited them in the evening, and there must have been a curfew, since I had to leave by climbing over the wall.

The visit to the Catholic Mission somehow resulted in a ride being fixed up for the following morning. Hurray. I was back on the road again. It was due to come at 5.30am, but by 2pm it still hadn't arrived. I went off to the market to stock up on mangos and peanut butter instead. A different truck driver told me, in French, to wait at the El Nileen Hotel. He never showed up either. I finally left on yet another truck which was transporting bags of food-aid flour for the European Economic Community. It left along the rather grandly named A44, which for those who know the south of England has considerable significance (it's a major road that goes from Oxford to Aberystwyth). This A44 was a rough track that consisted mostly of dirt, stones, and bedrock. We weren't able to go over 30kph.

We stopped when it got dark to eat dinner and sleep. Those on board mostly slept on the ground. I didn't like to because of the ants. I preferred the flour bags.

The countryside gradually changed from savannah and semi-desert to equatorial rain forest. Everywhere became very green. There were bananas, and palm trees, and huge mango trees, as well as cassava, coffee bushes, and tobacco plants. Throw a seed on to the ground here, and I swear it'd become a plant overnight. We saw small, duiker antelope near the road, too. It was my first sight of African wildlife.

It seems to be one of the world's great mysteries that where there's vibrant growth, the villages are mind-numbingly poor, and the kids have distended stomachs and spindly limbs. In one village of four sad huts, I gave the kids my supply of peanuts. They didn't say anything. They just took them, gazed at them, ate some, and wrapping leaves around the rest for later. One of the houses had a large mural of a copulating couple on the front wall. We'd obviously left the Arab north well behind.

The passengers on top of the truck were a mix of Sudanese, and travellers like me. One Sudanese chap had three watches on his arm, none of which worked. A German girl had her shoes stolen. What is it about the normally efficient

I still don't know what he was selling.

Germans, and not looking after their shoes? I made a note to be more cautious myself, then I reflected that my shoes weren't worth stealing. On deeper reflection the local people were mostly so poor that everything was worth stealing, though it was not necessarily the locals who stole the German girl's shoes. There were other trucks around, which is why I slept on high alert. Where was the giant Dinka in his Speedos when I needed him?

I bought some local tobacco leaves and attempted to create a cigar or cigarette with them. There was definitely a skill to rolling them that I didn't have. I probably ate more than I smoked. It was remarkably strong

We sat by a big fire on a hollowed-out tree trunk with four legs. I'd seen the same thing in the Ethnological Museum in Khartoum. I felt like I'd gone back 1,000 years. Or 10,000. The good news was the music, which was bouncy and comprehensible and a bit like calypso. The locals would dance to it in the streets.

We were heading for Yambio, which we hoped to make by nightfall. The problem was that the suspension leaves (those long, curved pieces of steel that absorb all the shocks) had been taken off the bottom of the truck. There was a lot of loud hammering going on. The driver had been hitting the rocky outcrops too hard and fast. We were still planning to make Yambio by nightfall. But the nightfall of which day? That night a rat ate a hole in my food bag. I sewed it up while eating a breakfast of fried liver.

When I finally arrived in Yambio (famous for the raging gun battle with the bean pods) I didn't do so on the lorry, though. That didn't make it. Like an old donkey, beaten too hard, it'd given up the fight 15km short. The truck driver arranged for us to take a bus the rest of the way. The bus was an ancient Bedford lorry, with seats. From there, it was another truck that took me on towards Juba – the Sudan's southern capital.

I should say that when Julius Nyerere's Tanzanian army pushed Idi Amin out of Uganda in 1979, in a move similar to the Vietnamese ousting Pol Pot and his crazies from Cambodia, rogue troops had remained that were still loyal to Amin, or at least, not loyal to the new government. They roamed the lawless north of Uganda, murdering, pillaging, and terrorising the area along the Sudanese border. This was where I planned to cross. The other option was to cut across to Lake Turkana and enter Kenya direct. But that was for sissies.

My next border adventure started mildly enough. I woke up in the Malakia police station on the outskirts of Juba, close to the lorry park. As I was running out of Sudanese pounds, I walked the 4km to the immigration office in Juba to get an exit stamp in my passport and an exit permit letter. The Sudanese authorities had now filled up two pages with permits for this and that. A shortage of cash had forced me to switch from coffee at ten cents to tea at five cents. In typical Sudanese fashion I was 'fuddled' by a fat officer (there's that word again). He appeared at just the right moment to give me a great meal of liver, *foul* beans, cheese, and bread. On reflection, I must say the police were really great. It's a shame there was so little cross-pollination with their Ugandan counterparts.

Chapter 6

Through Uganda to Kenya

This crossing was rather scary. There are moments when I did feel powerless, and this was one of them. If it hadn't been for the two Kenyan lorry drivers from Mombasa I was with, I don't think I'd have gotten through.

I was with another traveller. We figured that if one of us didn't survive, the other could report back to his respective parents where their son was buried, and which one of the local bullies had eaten him for breakfast. Mike was also English. We'd already fixed up a ride, but at the lorry park the Kenyan driver said we'd have to find another one because his lorry was having mechanical problems. We found two other drivers and they agreed to get us to Nairobi for $25 dollars.

The East African coast around Mombasa and Zanzibar has been a trading *entrepot* since the time of Marco Polo. Slaves, Chinese pottery, spices from Indonesia, and opium resin from the Golden Crescent – they've all, in their time, come through here.

I sat under the truck waiting for it to leave, and smoking some of the latter. Nothing seemed to happen. It was 44°C. If I'd landed here directly from Britain, I really think I'd have died. The wind was like a tumble dryer. Mind-altering substances weren't really necessary to liven up my life. The reality of my environs was already too weird.

Once the tag team of two Mercedes trucks had roared into life, we rolled out of town with dust from the dirt road pluming out of the side. I was in the cabin, which was quite a novelty. The trucks had come up from the coast with food aid (beans) from the United Nations High Commission for Refugees (UNHCR), and were leaving the Sudan empty, except for us itinerants. We passed rows and rows of UNHCR tents. These were for Ugandans who were too scared to go home. Not a good sign. After driving into the night, we camped at Nimule on the Ugandan border. It was important to get an early start to get passed the vagabond armies along the no man's and before they got too pissed off and trigger happy. (Traveller's tip, 'Never cross on a Sunday. That's their day off. They get even drunker and more trigger happy earlier then. It was Saturday morning for us, which was OK.')

Typically, there was a mechanical problem, and much tinkering under the hood. Large bits of oily metal were removed, and then reattached. This took all day. With night falling it was too late to leave. Damn. We'd have to cross on Sunday morning. The border area would be populated by gun-toting soldiers drunk by 9am. It was just what we didn't want.

We left early on Sunday. At the final border post in the Sudan, it turned out that Mike didn't have the right papers and had to go back to Juba. A few Kenyan shillings sorted that out. The huge trucks then edged gingerly over the rickety bridge separating relative order from anarchy.

The road immediately deteriorated. Ugandan irregulars in camouflage ran towards us. Some were young men. Some were kids, scampering down the dusty road. Others appeared out of the bush. Uganda's Artful Dodgers and Fagins. Bands of child warriors humping AK-47s. It was apocalyptic.

All our valuables were tied to the engines. It made them too hot to get close to and steal. This was not great for my camera, but it was the lesser of two evils.

The irregulars waved their Kalashnikovs around. They had extra, banana-shaped magazines taped to their standard magazines. We stopped, and the Kenyans plied them with packets of cigarettes. I could smell the booze.

Somehow we got through, with some of them now riding on the two trucks. They were clearly menacing, callous, juvenile, random, and mad. Gloucester's lament on the nature of life, and the malevolence of the divine, came to mind, 'As flies to wanton boys are we to th' gods. They kill us for their sport' (*King Lear*, Act IV, Scene I).

They called themselves the Liberation Army. It also reminded me of Colonel Kurtz, up the river in Frances Coppola's *Apocalypse Now*. The madness there was an adaptation of Joseph Conrad's *Heart of Darkness*, which was set, unsurprisingly, in the once-Belgian Congo.

At the first official army outpost, the Kenyan drivers sprayed the soldiers with cigarettes, and near-worthless Ugandan shillings. My backpack was searched and kicked making even more holes. My torch and medicines produced a lot of 'I wants'. I was surprised to still have my stuff left at the end of the day. I was jabbed by AK-47s, and there were lots of shouts of 'money, money, cigarette, cigarette'. The Kenyans did an amazing job, combining diplomacy, crowd control, and strategic bribery. One flash of anger from us and that would have been the end. It was useful, I discovered, to know by sight the position of the safety lever on an AK-47. Up was off. The middle was semi-automatic. Down was fully automatic.

Once we were able to move on to the next army post, we passed deserted, burnt-out shells of buildings, and scenes of general desecration. A soldier came up to me, sweat glistening on his forehead, saying, 'You got food?' His breath reeked of alcohol. I shook my head. 'You got no food?' He asked again, louder. Again, I shook my head. He disappeared, at which point another guy took over hassling me. The original one came back holding something behind his back. 'Oh fuck,' I thought. He then produced a tin of baked beans. 'What is that?' I asked. 'It's for you,' he said. 'You said you had no food.' There I was, thinking I was going to die, and here was this drunk soldier giving me a tin of HP baked beans with 'Made in England' printed on the side.

It's pretty easy to misread people. I'm pretty good at that. Not everybody is bad. It seems that even these guys didn't kill *khawajas*, at least, not this one. Another one of the soldiers paid our driver for his ride. That even surprised the Kenyans.

We were eventually able to leave for the immigration office at Atiak. On the way we passed wrecked, western-style houses. They were semi-detached, mock Tudor places, and yet they were in equatorial Africa. Bizarre. They'd also been blown up and burnt-out by the war and the general mayhem. Local huts had sprouted up around them as the whole place had begun to revert to the local norm.

Border control consisted of another shakedown, with demands for money and non-existent documents. I had all of mine, but Mike was deficient again. Once enough money had changed hands, it was all smiles once more. The officials even issued us with a letter similar to 'Her Majesty requests and requires …', which they said we could show to other police along the way.

Customs was another few hours of haggling, though the trucks were returning empty. While the Kenyans were dealing with that, we met a 14-year-old boy who spoke perfect English, and whose dad was a teacher. He told us a little about his life. The army had tried to enlist him, but his dad had managed to prevent it. Even ten-year-olds were being conscripted, and the nights were always interrupted by the crackle of gunfire. Life wasn't easy in the West Nile province of northern Uganda. I sometimes wonder if he managed to survive. What with the violence, the AIDS epidemic, and the poverty, his chances were slim. I hope he did.

We still had troops riding with us. One guy told me he had gonorrhoea, and demanded I cure him. I didn't think my Lomotil was likely to help.

The lorry was really hot, and we had more mechanical problems. Only one differential was working, whatever that meant. At full revs we could only do 50kph. I retrieved my camera, which was too hot to handle after its time next to the engine. It still worked. Built to last, it had gone through hell. It was a great advert for Pentax. No in-built obsolesce there.

The country itself was intriguing. It was clear that at one time it had been far more developed than the Sudan. There were telephone poles, with wires strung between them (though I assume they were no longer live). We drove through communities that looked like model English villages, with small, lush, grass parks in the middle of them, like village greens. Some even had duck ponds. The roads were still tarred, though they were in an advanced state of disrepair. Travelling at night was difficult because of the holes and not just, as in the Sudan, because you could get robbed or killed.

That evening we all got drunk to celebrate. We ate the tin of beans, laughing and laughing about how we could have died. One of the drivers told us a story about how he'd once had trouble at a Ugandan checkpoint, and had decided to make a run for it. He'd accelerated in his truck and hit one of the Ugandans soldiers. He'd driven on and later (surprisingly) reported the incident to the police. They'd understood, and made him pay only a small fine. The commanding officer had said, 'Many people die in Uganda. It's unfortunate, but what's one more?'

The Kenyan truckers were a pretty worldly, albeit self-educated lot. The conversation was diverse and never dull. It shifted from Darwinism to fundamental Christianity and Islam and to development economics (their view was simple; the Sudanese had the resources and worked one hour a day while the Kenyans had nothing and worked 12 hours a day as well as helping the Sudanese). We also discussed arms versus food, and the current standoff between the (then) USSR and the US. They could fix trucks, deal with crazy, drunk mercenaries, cook chicken stew, and hold their own in debates about world affairs. They truly were the Renaissance men of East Africa.

Something similar seems to be true all over the world. It's only in the most developed countries, where the real world is wrapped in cotton wool, and CNN provides the reports, that the conversation becomes dull.

The world was very real to the Kenyan truck drivers. Of course, they knew about development economics. They were ferrying food aid for the UNHCR. Of course, they knew about the US and USSR. They'd stared down the barrels of too many AK-47s not to. Of course, they knew about fundamental Christianity and Islam. They lived in a country that was half-and-half, and had travelled all over it. I was surprised that university-educated Mike and I could keep up with then. But then again, perhaps we didn't.

The next day, we got up at 5.30am to get to Nairobi by nightfall. I had the worst splitting headache imaginable – the result of bad alcohol. I felt like there was someone in my head with an ice-pick trying to hack his way out. It was the reverse of Trotsky. And it lasted for a week.

The Kenyan truck drivers earned about US$250 per month, and they really earned it. To supplement his income, one of them filled his wheels with hash. His net income was a bit higher (sorry about the pun?). The cash paid for the ride by passengers like ourselves helped, too.

At the border of Kenya proper, the Ugandan officer looked at my passport. It seemed there was no proper entry stamp. I showed him the letter we'd been given coming in. He raised his eyes to heaven and shook his head as if to say, 'YOU CAME THROUGH THERE!' He obviously knew that the whole area was a hell hole.

We walked the kilometre to the Kenyan immigration and customs. They were efficient, and had smart uniforms with brilliant white shirts. I felt I was in Germany. Our Kenyan lorry-driver friends met us at the other side. By this time, we'd fallen in with a couple of Irish girls who worked for a charity called Concern. They were on their way to Nairobi in a 4x4. The truck drivers (who I'm ashamed to say, didn't seem to have names) gave us knowing looks, and waved us goodbye.

The Irish girls were on holiday. They were also going to post some letters and collect their mail. Because Uganda didn't function, their charity was in the process of pulling out. The place was a mess, and was getting more dangerous daily. To buy the basics, like sugar and flour, it was necessary to buy a T-shirt with the president, Milton Obote, on it. After my sojourn in Kenya I went back through Uganda, where I ended up with a few Obote T-shirts myself. In one election the opposition got 80 per cent of the vote. The radio then went silent, and Obote was president the next day. Idi Amin was his protege.

We stopped at a cheap roadside cafe at a place called Eldoret, and feasted on chicken and chips, cans of Coke, and a bar of Cadbury's chocolate. Heaven. The toilet even smelt of disinfectant. They not only had a toilet, but it was clean.

We were approaching the equator – my first time ever. Images of palm trees, warm waters, tropical jungles, and stupid drinks with parasols, came to my mind. Not so where we crossed, since it was about 2km above sea level. We were in a southern version of Scotland, with pine trees. It was bitterly cold and felt really strange.

We stopped for coffee at a hotel in the Rift Valley above Lake Nakune. The place was famous for the huge flocks of flamingos that pinked the water in vast swathes.

At around 10pm we arrived at Nairobi's Iqbal Hotel, just off Tom Moboya street, near the River Road. It had washbasins, sheets on the bed, and mirrors even. I felt like Crocodile Dundee, when he arrived in New York. A 21st-century reviewer described his stay at the Iqbal as 'a little on the scary side'. I don't think he'd just come through the West Nile province.

I was knackered from hard travelling. My head was still hurting from the alcohol poisoning. I had some sort of virus, so that my ribs ached when I coughed. Being, and still being poisoned, I decided to keep a low profile.

When I finally got out to the *poste restante* in the Nairobi central post office, I found a record nine letters waiting for me. It was a feast of home and nostalgia. There were four letters from my parents, packed with the addresses of people dotted around the world where I might drop in for a meal, a washing machine, and a bed. Mum was great networker, resourceful and relentless. I think I had the address of every remaining white person in Zimbabwe. There was also a letter from Betsy, who I'd met in Aswan.

The *poste restante* was a wonderful system. It was very simple. It worked. And it was a lifeline to home. The whole thing relied on trust. If I saw a letter to someone I knew was on the road, but had left already, I'd take it and try to get it to them. E-mail and texting have killed it now, which is such a pity, since there was something magical and uplifting about getting those crumpled, airmail envelopes, edged in red and blue, the Queen's head on a whole bunch of stamps, and the letters themselves written on translucent, onion-skin paper to save weight. If I'd wanted to communicate with people every day, as we can now, what would have been the point in leaving home? High-speed communication has made life more convenient, but also more difficult. When later in life I had to send an email to head office to order paper clips, or to sit in on ridiculous conference calls at midnight and listen to other people's problems, some of whom might delay their call to pop out for a mid-morning latte in New York when it was midnight in Asia, I began to think I preferred the East India Company, when I could have raised a native army, taken over a new country, planted the flag, bought all the local natural resources for a bottle of rum and some coloured beads, and reported back to headquarters in a letter every six months that might or might not make it depending on whether the tea clipper survived the storms.

Nairobi was like being in London, Tokyo, or Paris. They had supermarkets, and they put stuff in brown paper bags for you. Coca-Cola was freely available, and they had newspapers and TVs. Moi Avenue, funnily enough named after the eternal president, was clean, had pavements, had working drains, and flowers. There was even a Barclays bank where I could buy more traveller's cheques, and US dollars for the black markets coming up in Uganda, Tanzania, and Zambia.

We were close to the birthplace of mankind. Just across the border, in Tanzania, Richard Leakey (actually his wife Mary) had discovered the fossil bones of our ancestors, and mapped how humans had evolved in the East African savanna over a million years ago.

This made it all the odder when I overheard an elderly western gentleman in a white linen suit, with his wife beside him in a billowing, flower-patterned dress and a big floppy hat, complaining to the Barclays clerk about the local bank notes. They had an image of *homo erectus* on them. It seemed these two didn't believe in the theory of evolution, and didn't want banknotes that promoted it. They asked the employee if he had notes with other images on them. I detected a southern American drawl. Since the only notes suitable were very low denominations, they would have needed a wheelbarrow to carry them all. They settled for Darwin's bills in the end.

I wandered around Nairobi quite aimlessly. A friendly policeman showed me around the parliament, which seemed to be a carbon copy of the one in London. The difference (and it was a big difference) was the president's seat (or throne one might say). President Moi's face was everywhere. There were framed photos of him in shops, restaurants, hotels, and on the flip side to Mr Homo Erectus.

That day two girls I'd met in the southern Sudan showed up at the Iqbal. Ann and Ann (I thought of them as Tweedledum and Tweedledee) had taken the safer route via Lake Turkana, though it still sounded interesting. There were nomadic herdsmen who wore cool beads, and had the stools they sat on tied to their arms. We went to the reptile zoo together. We could squeeze our noses up against the plate glass and be 1cm away from deadly puff adders. Walking in the bush, they were the ones that freaked me out the most. If I couldn't see where I was going, or if it was night-time, I'd stamp my feet in the hope that the vibrations would inspire them to get out of the way. The problem was the ones that didn't move much. They were the dangerous ones. The fat, lazy bastards. This said, I hardly saw any snakes in Africa, though I'm sure they saw (or felt) me.

My seven-day hangover was wearing off, and my cold was receding, so I began to fancy a safari. The Nairobi National Park is just outside the city. I shopped around and chose a day trip. The minibus picked me up from the New Stanley Hotel (which is still there, though it's not so new now). Since it's possible to see the city from the park, I wasn't expecting much, but it was packed with game. There were elegant giraffes, absurd ostriches, wildebeest, impala, Thompsons gazelles, Grants gazelles, waterbuck, oryxes with their long horns, and lots of zebra. They all pretty much ignored us. The bus stopped, and we went on foot through the bush. We

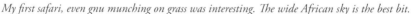

My first safari, even gnu munching on grass was interesting. The wide African sky is the best bit.

A half decent shot of a giraffe, most of my wildlife shots were rubbish.

came across some small monkeys, and there were some warthogs in the mud of a trickling river. And there were vultures circling overhead. When I deviated from the path, the guide came after me. He said I shouldn't walk on my own as there'd been a green mamba in one of the trees I'd just walked past. I think he was telling a fib, but I couldn't be sure. What I did realise is that I was beginning to get a real taste for foot safaris.

The highlight was a cheetah with her two cubs, half hidden in the long grass about 20m from us. Near the exit from the park, a black rhino stared at us through his dark, beady eyes. Not bad for a first go.

Donna and Ian (also a single unit in my mind) arrived from the Sudan, as well. The Iqbal Hotel was a real magnet. I'd last seen them in Wau, at the Catholic mission where I'd made my escape over the wall.

The retail price of beer was controlled then, which was great for me. I could sit in the Hilton, or the Thorn Tree in the Stanley, both very posh places, sipping a Tusker and making it last the whole evening. These were good places to swap travel information. 'Was it still possible to get into Uganda? What was the black-market rate in Tanzania? What was the cheapest flight to Bombay?' Usually, we didn't get to talk about Bombay. It was a real achievement just to get to the next village.

I could feel the lazy life in Nairobi making me soft. It was time to get back on the road. So, I tried to hitch to Mombasa on the coast (the hometown of the truck drivers I'd ridden with through the top of Uganda). I'd get about 200km, and then there's be a dearth of lifts. Which was fine, because off in the distance was the massive, snow-topped Mt. Kilimanjaro. This was Hemingway country. I was about 100km away, and it was still impressive, rising just under 6km. I stood on the side of the road with my thumb out, looking at it for an hour or two. Nobody was stopping, so what to do? It started to get rather scary. Ten meters away there were growls and grunts in the bush, and the sun was going down. Then a monstrous red Mercedes truck rumbled past and put on its air brakes. It came to a thundering halt, with the dust billowing up. I humped my pack on to my back, scampered in, and hauled myself up the cabin. The driver had recognised me from the Malindi truck park in southern Sudan. It was another one of those great coincidences – not as good as Mr Smith, but pretty useful for someone in the middle of nowhere, with what sounded like lions looking for their supper.

The road that connects Nairobi and Mombasa is the busiest in Kenya. It cuts through the Tsavo National Park, so we saw quite a lot of game. There was a herd of elephants, brown from wallowing in mud. They were only 10m from the road. We drove on, since the truck had to be off the road by 6pm. We raced to get to Mombasa, but we finally had to stop at 6.30pm, about 35km short. I paid for our dinner, tied up my backpack, and slept on the trailer under the stars. Nairobi is a high-altitude city, cool or cold, and quite dry. Here we were down near the coast, nearly at sea level. The trailer was hard, and it was steaming-hot, so not much sleeping got done.

The Hydro Hotel in Mombasa was another one of those places where travellers congregated like moths to a flame. It was recommended in the Bible (otherwise known as *Africa on a Shoestring,* published by Lonely Planet). It was a bit flash for me, but the fans worked, and they kept the place cool. They burned mosquito coils at night, and there was even toilet paper in the toilets. There were a couple of used needles in the bedside drawer, though, so it wasn't perfect.

Sharing rooms was a lucky dip – sometimes great, sometimes so-so, but seldom a problem. In the Hydro I was sharing with a chap from Croydon in south London, and Janis, a lovely Aussie. There was equality between the sexes, and you got to know people quite quickly and quite well.

Old Mombasa had narrow alleys with whitewashed walls and lots of mosques. The coastal areas of East Africa are mainly Muslim. In the hinterland there are various strains of Christianity, usually mixed in with the local animism. It seems the Muslims were not so enthusiastic about traipsing around the bush for years on end risking death, like the evangelical Christians. Perhaps wisely, the Arabs stayed near the coast and traded. They also painted everything white, sailing back home from time to time on their ocean-going *dhows*. When they did pop into the bush, it was to pick up a cargo of slaves destined for death or the New World, or to saw the tusks off elephants. As a consequence, the coastal dwellers are a mishmash of blacks, Arabs, Indians, a few colonials, and their many-hued offspring. They're mainly Muslim and they're mostly tolerant. They even put up with the Portuguese for a long time. Then there were the British, who admittedly treated their empire more as a business, and left people to pray to whoever they chose, and in whatever direction they chose, just so long as they kept working and didn't mutiny.

This mishmash of peoples speaks Swahili. The word itself is Arabic and means people who live near the coast. It's the *lingua franca* of East Africa, and is spoken inland as an alternative to English.

Down at the port, I met some sailors from two trading *dhows* just in from Lamu. They gave me some of their local speed, derived from a leaf that they mixed with bubble gum. It didn't seem to have any effect, but by then I was pretty drug-resistant. They used it to help them stay awake at night. The island of Lamu was then a left-over, hippie hangout. It was close to the border with Somalia. I was soon to head there myself.

Mombasa's harbour-front architecture was a mixture of Arab and British colonial. It was replete with stately white symbols of authority and power. The alleyways behind the front reminded me of Morocco. The Portuguese had built a chunky garrison appropriately named Fort Jesus. I wandering around, sweat dripping off the tip of my nose in the crushing humidity, stopping occasionally for a cooling drink.

The next day two big motor bikes came roaring into town with UK plates. The previous year I'd got very drunk with a guy called Luke Dugdale, in Dingwall's club in Camden, north London. He was riding one the bikes. Another coincidence. They tore around town with me on the back making lots of noise, before leaving next morning for Tanzania.

Just north of Mombasa is the beach resort of Nyali. It was my first experience of a tropical paradise. There was a crescent of pure, fine white sand. There were coconut palms blowing about in the stiff cooling breeze. There was a flat, calm sea that reached out to a reef. And there was thick vegetation beyond the sand. Being a pale-skinned Northerner, I got absolutely roasted in about 20 minutes. When sunscreen costs more than you normally spend in a day, you try (foolishly) to economise. The water was very warm.

Back at the hotel, I tried to have a bath in Nivea skin cream from the well-prepared and lovely Janis. I then went for a fish curry. This seemed to be the only thing I ate in Mombasa. It was a great step up from the *foul* of the Sudan, or the chicken and chips in Nairobi. I think when you're on a budget, and you find something good and cheap, you stick to it. Why change a winning game?

Not long after that I got some more dollars from the local Barclays bank and left for Malindi, on the coastal road towards Lamu. My Michelin map marked Malindi to Lamu with little blue dashes. These meant, according to the legend, that it was impassable in the wet season. It was not very passable during the dry season either, I can tell you.

Supplies came in by *dhow*, so I'm not sure why I went overland. Perhaps to see some wildlife, though I only saw a few oryx, a few baboons, and a family of warthogs. With hindsight it wasn't worth it, but at the time my idea of wildlife was a few grey squirrels, birds with dull plumage, the occasional deer, and hedgehogs flattened by traffic.

In Malindi we stayed (and by 'we' I mean Aussie Debbie, the girl I was then travelling with, and myself) at a local campsite. As ever, we tried to save money. I didn't have a tent, so I assume we rented one. The wind kept rustling it, and I kept waking up with my pen knife to the ready. It was steaming hot. A tent with no air movement is a disaster.

Lamu Island port - Dhows work the East African coast.

During the day we sat around and swam. We ate pineapples and coconuts and planned our next move. We decided to catch a ride on a truck going north towards Lamu. This took us through a particularly barren and arid landscape, with only a few brilliant and elegant birds on the telegraph wires to add bright their flashes of red and blue. They look like spray-painted swifts.

Near to Lamu, some cute local girls, maybe around ten years old, danced in front of us at one of the stops. They ran away screaming with delight and fear when I brought out my camera. Kids are the same the world over. Actually, they're not quite the same. I would say that so long as they're not suffering from malnutrition, no matter how ragged their clothes, or how dirty their skin, African kids have ear-to-ear smiles most of the time, and the air is rampant with their irrepressible laughter. They have bright, flashing eyes, and they seem to live for the fun of the moment, barefoot in the dust. They must come close to number one on the global happiness scale. They don't care about exams.

When the coast of Lamu island appeared, it didn't look very promising. It was protected by defiant, biologically diverse, but ultimately ugly mangrove swamps. We were on a 30ft boat with 100 others, mainly locals, approaching the harbour and blinded by the glare. The tropical sun was flashing off the waves, and off the white colonial-era and Arab-style buildings. I squinted at them with my eyes watering and my head hurting. Only the dark wooden *dhows*, tied up against the wharf, provided relief.

The slavers moved up here when they were forced out of Zanzibar. Though the place had a dark history built on misery, it'd been converted into a sort of paradise for travellers off the beaten track. It was one of those end-of-the-world places, or used to be in the 1980s. It has a bloody airport now.

Speaking about the end of the world, this was meant to take place (again) when a full moon and five planets lined up. I saw three of them with the naked eye – Mars all soft orange, and Venus harsh white, and the moon big and (ummm) round. This only happened once every 500 years. There was no Armageddon, but I did happen to fall in love, which felt like the same thing.

After some haggling, I checked into the Salama Lodge. I sharing a room with Aussie Debbie. Purely platonic. Behind the grandeur of the waterfront was a maze of narrow, whitewashed alleys, and houses with ornately carved doors. There was only one vehicle on the island, a Land Rover belonging to the district commissioner. The centre of town had a small square with a prison on one side and a market on the other.

Members of the traveller tribe usually walked the 40 minutes to the beach, or hung out at one of the vaguely healthy cafes. At the Yoghurt Inn my skinny, disease-ridden body sought sustenance from muesli, fresh fruit, omelettes, and other such wonder foods. It was there that I also met a lovely Irish nurse called Cookie.

One of the waiters there didn't seem to speak any English, or understand what finger-pointing at items on the menu meant. This led to many humorous mis-orders, and unusual food combinations. The place also had a good selection of tapes. It was a fine place to while away a day (or a week, or a month, or the rest of my life). The only problem was that they didn't sell booze. In fact, the only place that did sell alcohol, on what was a predominantly Muslim island, was a bar called Petley's.

The Salama Lodge was well fortified, but when Ann and Ann showed up they were burgled in the night. They lost their money, their passports, and sadly, six months of diaries. Their passports did come back. They were thrown into their room in the middle of the night by what must have been a thief with a conscience. Our room all had bars and shutters, but the bars were not enough. The thieves were very adept with fishing rods. The manager of the Salama told us that the police were part of the criminal gang, so there was not much point going to them.

A crap picture of a typical travellers hotel room. Note the bars are poor defence against innovative locals with fishing rods. I slept on literally everything important.

I wandered about what was supposedly a little piece of paradise with my knife in my back pocket. My valuable belongings were safe in my pillowcase under my head.

The daily routine for a chap like me was either to get up late and go to the Yoghurt Inn and get no further, or after breakfast, walk the 40 minutes to the beach and get burnt, eat and drink coconuts, and lie on your stomach and ogle the girls in their bikinis. When Bandana Duncan showed up, we went out on a *dhow* to snorkel. The sea was a bit rough, and with nausea coming on, one of the girls gave me some tablets. They didn't do much good, probably because they were for morning sickness. *Dhows* might look cool but they move badly. They sort of wallow around in the swell. A *dhow* back to Mombasa sounded good, but throwing up for 24 hours didn't. It was the boring old bus for me.

Lamu was not a late-night party town. The loudest noises after 10pm were cats fighting, though once we heard what sounded like a donkey being castrated. There was a little outdoor cinema where we sat on the floor because it was cheaper. This often resulted in spending a whole evening watching fat Indian girls rolling around being showered with flower petals, when we'd been expecting a Charles Bronson movie.

Cookie worked in Johannesburg as a nurse. She was a fly-in traveller. We talked about everything, which meant that we talked about more than bus timetables, or the best place to change dollars in Dar es Salaam (the capital of Tanzania. It means 'House of Peace'. Nice.)

Cookie asked extremely awkward questions like, 'Why do you travel? What are you trying to prove? Are you trying to escape from something?' Other travellers didn't ask these questions, either because they didn't like to think about them, or because the answers were self-evident. They usually stuck to black-market rates, the state of their stomachs, and the cheapest flights from Durban to Bombay.

The first question was very broad. My answer was that I viewed myself as incomplete after finishing university, and that I needed to grow up and become more worldly. Travel seemed to be a good way to do so. It seemed better than commuting to London to an average job that made me feel stuck. I was not a high achiever at school or university. I thought that if I didn't have the raw intelligence of my peers, then the best way to augment my ability was to experience more. To a large extent, I think this was true. And to a large extent, I think it worked, or at very least helped.

Tied to this was a general feeling of inadequacy next to some of the people I'd gone to school with, or grown up with. I was a good tennis player, and I actually taught for a year in Japan, but I was never going to make any money by competing. One of our closest family friends was a superb sportsman. He was a year younger than me, but I hadn't beaten him since he was ten. He ultimately failed on the tennis tour, but he got a gold medal for Britain at the Seoul Olympics in hockey. Not bad. Friends from school went to Oxford and Cambridge and were in the first 15 for rugby. They were also excellent in their house debating competitions. I was the captain of the tennis team at my school and university, but that didn't really count next to rugby, soccer, and Oxbridge. So, I think I did feel I had something to prove. My best mate Tom, from university, seemed to me to be more mature and savvier than me, but he'd stayed home. Travelling, and sending him letters and postcards from weird places while he slogged it out in a relatively tedious job, seemed to even things up a bit. My parents had spent a lot of money on my education. I hadn't been a disaster, but my school reports had never made for good reading: 'struggles with the basic concepts'; 'poor written work'; 'needs to contribute more in class'; 'occasional glimmer of hope, but mainly below standard'.

Of course, there were a lot of other Chris Prices out there. We were probably the majority. Muddling along. Getting through in the C or D streams. But I didn't see them. I only saw the high-achievers, like my friend Magnus. I think I wanted to do something where I could say that I did that, and that none of the other guys had. It wasn't dependent on intelligence, or on being a fantastic sportsman. But it was still somehow extraordinary, given what you had to go through, what you experienced, and what it did to you. You needed some courage, and it gave you more of a personality. The job on the oil rigs had been a good beginning. It got people's attention, and it impressed them. But it was only the start.

Cookie and I stayed up until 3am, talking and kissing, until we had to wake up Silus, the manager. We retired separately because, bizarrely, I was still sharing with Debbie.

When Cookie asked me if I thought about the future, I said I was very happy with the present. The relationship blew up a few days later. She accused me of being selfish. The affair was reignited later in South Africa, but I'd been meeting new people every day, and any relationship that lasted for more than a week had become a real strain.

Lamu Island: The photo does not reflect the terrible sea sickness and awful sunburn.

Lamu life continued. On the beach I was reading *King Lear* and *Journey to the East* by Herman Hesse. After dinner at the Yoghurt Inn it was Petley's, and waking up the ever-patient Silus. For a change one night, we all went to a private restaurant. Images of London pop-up place might come to mind, but they'd be wrong. It turned out to be a poor fisherman's kitchen, in a mud hut, where we sat on the floor and ate lobsters and fish curry. With rice and coffee the bill came to less than three dollars for the four of us. I hope we gave him a tip.

When it came time to leave this paradise of love, sand, yoghurt, and thieves, I took the sleeper train from Mombasa to Nairobi. Cookie was reintroducing me to civilisation. There were wood panels, and waiter service, and even cold Tusker beer.

I got my old room back at the Iqbal and tried to collect information on travelling on to Uganda. There was not much. Nobody had been. It was deemed too dangerous for the average traveller. Which seemed, to me, to be right up my street.

Chapter 7

Uganda

Let me tell you about George Ridley Barnley MBE. He was a field scientist in East Africa in the 1950s. Without any formal training or qualifications, he became head of the Entomology Division of the Ugandan Medical Service. His obituary, as published by the Liverpool School of Tropical Medicine, reads in part, 'Due to some misunderstandings about his scientific expertise, he was sent [during the Second World War] to Washington as a ballistics expert. He rapidly became an expert on small arms … when he left the army he sought adventure in the tropics … he will be remembered especially for his spectacularly successful elimination of *Silulium damnosum* from the Nile in Uganda … as a result millions of people have been relieved of river blindness and the intolerable skin and eye diseases which had made their lives miserable … releasing thousands of square miles of rich agricultural land for cultivation … his lectures on parasitic and vector-borne diseases were always rated very highly for both entertainment and instruction … he endeared himself to his staff by his ability as a marksman to protect them from dangerous game, and also because he was always the first to enter the rapids, thickets and swamps wherein lay his insect quarry … George was a man of many talents, 'in addition to his skill as a biologist he was a gunsmith, forensic firearms expert, engineer, gardener and photographer.'

When his wife was killed in a car crash, he came back to the UK to bring up his daughter. For his sins, he ended up teaching me biology. He was a fantastic teacher and storyteller. He taught lessons how they should be taught, and was a teacher as they all should be. If we asked to see his teaching certificate, we'd be met by lion-like roar.

If we would get him on to a red herring, whoosh, the class would be over. 'Doctor Barnley, did you ever encounter restless natives?' 'Young man, can you repeat your question. I'm rather hard of hearing.' The query would be shouted again. The doctor would begin a tale that took up all the time we were supposed to spend learning tiresome stuff about cell membranes or cross-pollination. It would culminate in a description of our intrepid teacher facing off against war-like tribesmen. 'You have to watch their feet. Their spears are sheathed in a small leather cover. If they put that between their toes, then it's time to shoot the blighters,' he'd say. His deafness increased when we asked exactly how many 'blighters' he'd shot with his howitzer of an elephant gun. Our guess was quite a few. He'd mellowed by the time he got to us. The obituary by the Liverpool School of Tropical Medicine wisely stuck to his prowess shooting big game. I remember him telling us spotty teenagers that there were insects he'd discovered that were named after him. Research hasn't turned up any, but a man like that didn't need to lie or exaggerate.

It was pretty easy to get him off course over reproduction too. 'Sir, could you tell us about sexual maturity?' 'Ahhhhhhh,' he'd bellow. 'I envy you young men waking up with erections. Me, I'm an old man. I can't even have a dirty thought any longer. Enjoy it while you can.' We all had dirty thoughts, particularly about his teenage daughter, which was probably not what he'd intended.

Sometimes we got him into trouble, too. A wise man like the doctor should have known that teenage boys and parrots don't mix. We'd taught his pet bird a few colloquialisms. Unfortunately, the headmaster was showing some snooty parents around when it decided to squawk, 'Fuck off, fuck off, fuck off.' I think it had to be put down in the end, if that's what you do to parrots. Maybe the doctor just took it home.

The front of the great man's tattered black teaching gown was usually smeared with yellow snuff. He was sometimes generous enough to share some of it at the end of class with the naughtier boys. I never got the snuff thing, but I kept on trying.

The British colonial army used to lend him soldiers when he was out in the bush. One corporal was a Ugandan man who the doctor described (we called him 'doctor' though this was technically incorrect) as a 'jolly efficient giant, and an excellent sportsman'. This paragon died in exile in Saudi Arabia in 2003. His official self-administered title by then was, 'His Excellency, President for Life, Field Marshal Al Hadji Doctor Idi Amin Dada, VC, DSO, MC, Lord of All the Beasts of the Earth and Fishes of the Seas and Conqueror of the British Empire in Africa in General and Uganda in Particular.'

Idi Amin used to be a gun-bearer for my biology teacher. He was also the reason for me having a tough time in his old stomping ground.

You might ask why I just devoted a couple of pages to my old biology teacher's biography. Well, I think he deserves it. The man saved millions (yes, millions) of lives, which puts Florence Nightingale into perspective. When I tried to research more about him on the web, I found nothing. That's tragic. Apart from my memory, the only information was from his daughter, and came via Dr Jones, the other biology teacher. Dr Jones taught the clever boys in the top streams.

The other reason I've spent some time writing about him is that he clearly made a big impression on me. His stories of Africa may have consciously, or subconsciously, inspired my desire to see the world in general, and to see Africa – and indeed Uganda – in particular.

But back to my travels.

Nairobi was making me restless. It felt like it was time to stop being a tourist, in a place where they had hot showers and cold beers and supermarkets and Irish girls called Cookie. It felt like it was time to get back on the road, and boldly go where no man had before, or at least, where not so many had.

I actually knew it was time to leave Nairobi when I walked into my local restaurant for breakfast and the waiter said, 'The usual?' That was sort of comforting, but it also felt totally wrong. I was in my early 20s. That 'usual' had struck a very false note.

Cookie had given me *The Covenant* by James Michener as some sort of ficto-historical introduction to South Africa. I was impressed by Michener. He wrote about all sorts of places. I didn't realise that he'd actually had an army of researchers, and just sort of sewed up the bits to make the garment after others had done all the hard work of cutting out the pieces of cloth.

I finished breakfast at 4pm after spending a couple of extra hours talking with some cool Swedes. Cookie was staying in a proper place, far away from the dodgy Iqbal Hotel. Later, she and I got a bit drunk at the Thorn Tree. We ended up as friends, and agreed to meet in Johannesburg.

I started out cold and a bit miserable on the morning train to the Ugandan border at Malaba. The night before there'd been a tropical downpour. These were new to me. I'd come from England where it sort of rains most of the time, but mostly in a light, misty way that hangs in the air. The rain in Africa was different. When it happened at night, it could happen very quickly. A few large drops would whack into the dust, like little mortar rounds. Then the rumbling thunder would get closer. An almighty flash might light up the cityscape for miles, and thunder would shake the glass in the window frames (if there were any window frames). The air would then metamorphose into a wall of water. The corrugated iron roofs would become percussion instruments. On the streets, people would scuttle for shelter under makeshift bits of plastic sheeting that were really a waste of time. It was total water. All life stopped. I was standing in my window at the Iqbal and my bed got soaked. I ended up sleeping in the far corner on the floor.

I was a bit apprehensive about Uganda. There didn't seem to be any other travellers on the train, and I'd found it really difficult to get useful information about the country. Nobody had been. There also seemed to be some good reasons for this being the case. They included anarchy, disappearances, and serious embassy warnings.

The train left on time just after 9am and climbed through the uplands. The Rift Valley was spectacular. We snaked our way along getting great views of the valleys below. From time to time, big banks of clouds let the sun through. The clouds always seemed bigger in Africa, whoever I was. The whole sky always seemed bigger.

Around Lake Naivasha the grass was being fired. Smoke obscured the view, and the midday sun became like a warm orange sunset over our heads.

The Thorn Tree drinks were catching up on me and I fell asleep, my foot throbbing because I'd cut it in Nairobi. I was worried it was becoming septic.

Kenyan Immigration and Customs were Germanic again in their efficiency, though I was pleasantly surprised by the Ugandans. The surprise I didn't like was their currency declaration form. This was unexpected, and the sort of local knowledge that I'd hoped to pick up at the Thorn Tree or the Iqbal. The problem was that when I changed money, I meant having the form stamped at a bank to prove that I'd done so. Then when I tried to leave, they could confiscate all my dollars, and lock me up in a cell with sex-starved criminals. As it turned out the tourist information office solved that problem for me. I had to know how much to declare, and how much to stuff in my secret compartment. The maths had to balance at the end. The amount minus what I declared, and any amount I'd changed at the bank, had to equal the amount that was left when I left. The trick was to smuggle in the amount I expected to change on the black market, and only declare the rest. It required a bit of thought and planning, but the basic rule was to under-declare.

I got something like seven times the government rate in Uganda. Looking back, I maybe should have had some moral qualms about using the black market. I was never ripped off, at least as far as I know. There is some honour among thieves. The problem was the way the government set a fixed rate that wasn't reasonable. People were desperate for dollars to buy imported stuff, or as a store of value. They were willing to pay a much higher rate to get it. No one in their right mind changed money at the government rate unless they absolutely had to. There was a problem, again, with storage, though. If I wanted to change $100, I'd get a carrier bag full of grubby Ugandan notes.

The Jinja area on Lake Victoria is the front-runner when it comes to claims to be the start of the great Nile river. I spent a while pondering how I'd now been to the source of the Nile, as well as to where it pours out into the Mediterranean at Alexandria. I'd also been to various other points in-between. This was not quite up there with Speke, Livingston, or Stanley, but it was an achievement nonetheless.

The Nile is around 6,600km long. Some claim that it actually starts in the Mountains of the Moon, to the south and the west, in Uganda. I went there as well, just to make sure.

We crossed over the Owens Falls Dam. It was supposed to generate electricity, but I found out later it was under repair, and had been for years. I snapped a photo, which was a little risky considering the number of Kalashnikovs around. It was still guarded heavily.

The approach to Kampala, the Ugandan capital, was through run-down low-level warehouses. I can only describe it as like entering a ramshackle farmyard. The downtown had a few skyscrapers, but on closer inspection they turned out to be mostly unfinished. They were like Hollywood sets. Just facades.

It was getting late, and there was a curfew. Kampala was not the place to be out and about after dark if you wanted to stay alive. Luckily, I'd seen the hotel I was planning to stay at on the way in. Unluckily, it was closed. As dusk was approaching, it was a bit of a scramble to find another place before the local werewolves arrived. After 20 minutes of fruitless wandering, accompanied by copious furtive glances over my shoulder, I managed to check into the 1980 Hotel. It was not the time to argue about the price. Water did come out of the taps, but electricity didn't come out of the wires. I made a note to myself to say HELLO to all the police I met in the daytime, with a big smile on my face, in case I bumped into them at some other time, and needed their help. (I think that smiling at people never hurts wherever I am, though one place it doesn't seem to work is when I'm faced with officious Brits, or US border officials. Smiling to them seems to raise a negative profiling flag, and results in more questions about the conference I'm attending.)

Many of the shops were boarded up. Most of the others were empty. The East African Asians had all been booted out by Amin and his cohorts, and they weren't coming back in a hurry. There was nobody left to do the commerce or import-export because there was no trust. Trade needs trust.

I looked out the window and darkness was enveloping the street. Shadows darted from doorway to doorway as the curfew began to bite. The power shortage seemed to be localised as there was rock music blaring out of the next building. I could hear, 'We gotta get out of this place, if it's the last thing we ever do.' The Animals' classic. The Blue Oyster Cult version. It was very appropriate, and kind of cool. I wrote by candlelight, which I soon got used to and rather liked. It created such a tiny world, and my concentration became phenomenal.

Out on the street the next day I started to analyse the police. They loitered in packs. There seemed to be two teams – the AK-47 team and the FN-7.62 team. The latter was the semi-automatic rifle that was then standard NATO issue. It was made in Belgium. I'd used it at school when I'd played soldier in the cadet force on Friday afternoons, instead of beating up the other boys playing rugby. My smile was broader to the AK-47 boys. I assumed the ones with the FNs were the good guys. I went up to one of the more senior-looking FN-touting chaps and introduced myself. I asked who they were defending, and why. He told me an extraordinary story about the army attacking the Central Kampala police station two weeks before to spring some of their mates. He explained that the police were taken by surprise and gave in. It didn't seem to be worth the fight. There'd only been a few shots fired. I'd heard about this in Kenya, but I'd thought it was Kenyan propaganda. 'Aren't the army and the police on the same side?' I asked. 'No, of course not, you're in Uganda now,' came the *realpolitik* reply.

The Ugandans' last gold medal at the Olympics had been at the tragic Munich event in 1972. It was won by Abako Akii-Bua, one of 42 children. He trained at high altitudes, running twice a day over extra high hurdles, with an additional 10kg strapped to his back. He got into the 400m hurdles final. His track shoes were two years old and had a spike missing. Coming around the final bend, he overtook the British and German favourites, increased his lead, and stormed home to rapturous bipartisan applause and an Olympic record. He was so happy, he grabbed a Ugandan flag and ran around the track once again, thus beginning an Olympic victor's tradition. Uganda had to wait for 40 more years for their next gold, when Stephen Kiprotich won the marathon in London, beating out the favoured Kenyans. He came from the same tribe as the Kenyans across the border. The Kenyan Kiprotich came third. Then in 2021 they won two more in Tokyo. It is heartwarming when little countries with a tough story to tell do well.

After learning about the war between the army and the police, I went to the British High Commission to register my presence as a precaution. While there I read an old copy of the *Financial Times*. I might as well have been reading about life on planet Zhor. It felt so strange. The lady there told me about the frequent carjackings and break-ins, and about the Korean ambassador being shot. I didn't have a car (or much else) to steal, and I wasn't Korean or an ambassador, so based on this logic, I figured I should be safe. She told me the official policy was to tell me to leave immediately. I smiled. She resigned herself to the fact that she was dealing with another young man who thought he was bullet proof. She did say to be careful of the 'Special Forces', though. She described them as wearing blue camouflage uniforms.

I also visited the Rwandan Embassy, where I got a visa for 30 cents. They'd wanted five bucks in Nairobi.

I changed $60 at a small shop and was given a huge pile of notes. It was too many to count so I measured it by inches. They didn't have any tourists, and apart from one Japanese chap and I, there didn't seem to be any travellers, either. They did have a good tourist information office, though. They told me there about the game parks, and suggested I head for Chobe Lodge at Murchison Falls. They also said there was not much chance of seeing gorillas in the south. 'Ugandans have been bad,' they said. 'They cut off their hands and penises. The gorillas know this and they go to Rwanda.' I questioned them about the currency declaration form, and they said, 'Go to the bank, change five dollars, go back outside, and add some zeros. No problem.' They were right. It was no problem, though as it turned out, this was for a rather different reason.

Uganda being a coffee producer without anyone to sell it to, combined with the currency black market, meant I could buy 2kg of coffee for next to nothing, and mail it home to England. Buying coffee, however, meant I was forced to take possession of two Milton Obote T-shirts. Obote was the dictator before and after Amin. One shirt I sent to Tom. The other I kept as a bargaining tool to demonstrate my patriotism if I ever got hassled by the police or the army.

The Ugandans seemed to be fans of Thomas Hardy. One street seller had quite a collection. I bought *The Mayor of Casterbridge* for next to nothing. I was reading a surprising amount, both in my room and at meal times.

The person in the next building only seemed to have two albums, The Blue Oyster Cult and Neil Diamond. Unfortunately, it was Neil night.

The next day I went to the market to buy some fresh food. Avocados were in season and they were excellent. I also needed to plan the trip to Chobe, so I went to the bus park to sort out the transport. This turned out to be rather complex since the buses didn't go there, and the people who went on safari in Uganda were expected to be posh and have a car. I got the times for those buses that went as close to the park as possible.

I seemed to be on a roll so I decided to go to Entebbe, on the shores of Lake Victoria. It was the site of the main airport. It was also infamous because the Israeli military had pulled off a daring commando rescue mission there in 1979. They'd extracted over 100 people after a plane had been hijacked by Palestinian and German extremists. In under an hour they'd flown in, freed the hostages, blown up the Ugandan air force, killed all the baddies (including a lot of Ugandan soldiers), and left. A Ugandan electrician on the bus next to me roared with laughter when he told me what the official newspaper had said. 'The Ugandan commander decided to let the Zionists leave,' was the official line. He was also in tears telling me how Amin had invaded Tanzania, and how he claimed to have annexed a huge amount it, despite this being clearly impossible. 'Another world record by Amin,' he said. He was clearly a realist.

The ability of Africans to take rubbish from their rubbish governments and still look on the bright side of life never ceased to amaze me. When the Tanzanians invaded Uganda and kicked out Amin, there was a lot of looting in Kampala. I'd heard this was done by Tanzanian troops. He said it was actually angry Ugandans.

'I saw it,' he said. 'I was there.' The Tanzanian officers had controlled their troops very well, he said. Amin had one of the strongest and best-equipped armies in Africa when he fell, but the soldiers had dropped their equipment and fled. 'This is why there's so much violence now,' he said. 'Many people picked up those weapons.'

There was not really all that much to see in Entebbe. I went with the electrician to the Lake Victoria Hotel and bought him a coffee and an excellent beef curry. The botanical gardens were right by the lake. The trees were all named in English and Latin and the place was surprisingly well kept. Somebody cared. The broad tarmac paths put most so-called roads in the Sudan to shame.

My electrician friend also had something to say about the frequent carjackings that the High Commission had mentioned. 'Yes it can happen,' he said, 'but usually the driver just sells the car and goes back to his village to lie low for a few weeks, or tells his boss it was stolen at gunpoint.' He explained the economic drivers. The minimum wage was 1,000 Ugandan shillings per month. Even at the government rate, that was only $50. If a car cost about 3,000, then who'd prefer to work for 60 weeks rather than sell the boss's car? Some drivers had been held up at gunpoint several times. There seemed be a pattern there.

He'd done part of his training in the UK, and had a soft spot for the British. 'Would you British consider coming back? It was much better with you around,' he asked, in a way that implied I might have some say in the matter. People said the same to me, in all sincerity, several times in Uganda.

My electrician friend had some work to do in Entebbe the following day, and so we said goodbye. The zoo was quite good. Unfortunately, the black bear had got into the lion's cage the previous week and ripped out its tongue. It had then killed it, a turn of events I wouldn't have predicted. They had also had to shoot the elephant as they couldn't build a structure strong enough to hold it. The great, grey hulk had kept escaping and mangling the other animal compounds. The remaining animals looked surprisingly well fed, and had large, clean cages – better than the locals.

Coming back into Kampala on my own was a hassle. I'd underestimated the time-consuming roadblocks. The curfew was fast approaching, and I didn't want to be turned into a perforated pumpkin. As I couldn't find any transport, I asked a group of policemen. They were overly interested in my bag (the one that now had a few inches of Ugandan shillings sitting in the bottom). This was uncomfortable, so I gave away a lot of cigarettes. They offered to change dollars for me. I declined. Luckily, a minibus showed up just then. A fellow passenger said, 'I wish you'd seen our country 12 years ago. We had everything then.' I felt sorry for him. I still do. If you're a venture capitalist, or an investor thinking about Africa, give some consideration to Uganda. There's something special about the people there.

The next morning, I overslept. Luckily, so did the bus driver. The 7am bus to Masindi left at 7.30am, with me on it.

The countryside was hilly and lush, but the roadway was littered with the scars of war. There were burnt-out tanks, and torched buildings, and a lot of roadblocks. At the military ones, young guys lounged around with rocket-propelled grenades between their legs, smoking. We were moving towards the lawless north, which was the region I'd come through from the Sudan, with all its child soldiers, and the national resistance army. The intensity of the roadblocks increased. At the police ones, the young guys lounging around had automatic rifles. Everyone had to get off the bus except me (some sort of ex-colonial privilege?) It all took time. At one stop I got searched, and the guy was close to my stash of shillings (it was now about an inch deep). I distracted him with my Swiss Army knife. He wanted to keep it. 'I would like to give it to you,' I said, 'but it was a present from my mother.' This wasn't true, but the Ugandans respected mothers.

I changed buses, and got as close as I could to the park. This was still about 20km from the entrance.

I was in the middle of nowhere, so I started to walk in what I hoped was the right direction when a vehicle came hurtling along behind me. I stuck out my thumb as a sort of reflex. It was a Land Rover, and it squealed to a halt and backed up. A guy in blue and black camouflage fatigues and Ray-Bans, with a packet of Marlboro on the dashboard, asked where I was going. I was in luck. He was going past the entrance to the park, and told me to get in the back. I pulled away the tarpaulin to find it full of guys in blue camouflage, with AK-47s and more Ray-Bans. Jesus. The woman at the High Commission had told me that whatever I did I should avoid the Special Forces. And there I was in the middle of nowhere getting in to the back of their bloody Land Rover.

It must have been the sort of vehicle full of soldiers that went tear-arsing around the country and causing havoc. The Stallone-wannabe drove very fast, which meant he covered the 20km in double-quick time. A relief, I suppose. They dropped me off intact at the entrance to the park, and left me there with a smile and a wave. Nobody would have known if they hadn't.

The walk into the park was a lot more threatening than the Special Forces. It was late afternoon. I had my backpack on, and I was gripping my silly little penknife in my pocket. Should I take on the lion with the 2in blade, the corkscrew, the toothpick, or the tweezers? Male lions are usually too lazy to kill. So, it was likely to be my 65kg of skin and bone, with my Swiss Army knife, against a female. All 150kg of finely honed killing machine.

The road was decent but not made up. There'd been some rain, the bush was solid green, and there were noises and crashing sounds. I was walking really quickly. It was another 20kg to the camp, and I had about an hour of daylight left. It wasn't clear what my plan would have been if the Special Forces hadn't stopped. That would have made it a 40km walk.

My back was soaked with sweat – a mixture of heat, exertion, and animal fear. I spent a lot of time looking over my shoulder.

Luck arrived once more, this time in the form of a Toyota Land Cruiser. Some Ugandan politicians gave me a ride to the camp. They were extremely annoying, coming out with lots of socialist, anti-imperialist claptrap. At least it was better than being dinner for a big cat.

I made the mistake of telling them I was British. I should have said I was a Kiwi. Or better still, Irish. One of the previously oppressed.

'The BBC are lying when they say Kampala is not safe at night. London is much more dangerous,' I was told. It was that sort of stuff. Smile, nod, don't respond, count down the miles while trying to make small talk about antelopes. Don't mention that your biology teacher was Idi Amin's boss.

Things looked up a lot when we got to the Chobe Lodge. Built on the banks of the Nile, it was heaven. Churchill visited it. Hemingway saw it by mistake, his light plane having clipped a telegraph pole and cartwheeled into the bush (he survived). Humphrey Bogart and Katherine Hepburn's classic movie, *The African Queen*, was filmed nearby. And Chris Price had a nice room with a balcony and a view of the river. Hippos were snorting in the water. The whole scene was bathed in late afternoon sunlight. The air was full of the noises of birds, insects, and reptiles.

At the reception the man told me the room was 20-seven dollars a night. I showed him my cash-stricken currency declaration form. After much negotiation, and pleadings of poverty, we settled on four bucks.

I had a writing desk, a telephone, an en-suite bathroom, taps with water, and (some) electricity. The main thing, though, was the view. I kept a candle close at hand, and had both a bath and a shower, just because I could.

Apart from the annoying government people, I was the only one there. One hundred rooms and six guests. Dinner was a bit of a challenge. Potatoes, cabbage, and cow stomach lining. The latter just didn't want to make the trip down my oesophagus. It was very school dinner, and completely defeated me. 'Please let us know when you will be retiring,' I was told. 'Then we'll turn off the generator.' The whole bloody place was lit up just for me. I felt quite bad. The moon was out, so I told them it was OK to power down now, and went down to the river for a walk. Which was pretty stupid, actually, but I survived.

A *hippopotamus amphibius* weighs up to three tonnes. Its closest relatives are whales. It can charge on land at 30kph. After dark they come out of the river to graze, and they're famously cantankerous. As an idea as to what I mean, Usain Bolt, when he was really trying, could average 37kph over 100m, wearing nice spikes on a perfect track. Chris Price was not so well endowed.

It was wise to steer clear of the crocodiles, too. Wandering down by the river between the thorn trees in the moonlight, I could see lots of them in the water. At least, I could see their black backs, their beady eyes, and their gaping nostrils. They were like tropical icebergs, 90 per cent under the waterline. The males had scars all over them from fights with other males, often to the death. These were seasoned gladiators. When one moved, a tidal wave hit the shore. Completely oblivious, I wandered back to the lodge to read some more Thomas Hardy by candlelight.

In my room with the windows, the moon danced off the river, silver and grey. I could still hear the hippos, making noises like engines starting. There was also a monster lizard in my room. It was brightly coloured and doing that amazing thing they do of wandering along the ceiling upside down. What a skill. It was eating insects which instantly made it my ally, though it also made some pretty scary noises in the middle of the night. It sounded like Godzilla.

The cool thing about being in a game park where there was only one Land Rover, and that mainly on anti-poacher duty, was that I could go on foot safaris. The problem with looking at animals from a vehicle with a bunch of other tourists, with long camera lenses, and books full of detailed descriptions of antelope, was that it was like watching a movie. Walking in the bush was like being in a movie.

My guide, park ranger Mr Odong, was in a khaki uniform with a bush hat that he wore at a rakish angle. He carried a stout AK-47 with a steel folding stock. I had two pairs of shoes (new basketball boots that chafed, and plastic sandals), as well as my shoulder bag and a water bottle.

The Nairobi park had been great, but the animals there were almost domesticated because of their familiarity with people and vehicles. Here you had to follow proper bush craft to get close to them. So as not to be dangerously close, a tricky compromise was required. There were three main things to get right – namely, understand the wind direction, don't talk, and don't stand on twigs. I was pretty bad at the third one.

We first saw a family of warthogs crossing the road. They looked sort of cute, probably because of the distorted image they'd been given by the *Lion King*. They're actually fierce animals. Even lions don't usually mess with the adults, with their stout, 100kg bodies, and curved tusks that can be up to ten inches long.

Ugandan kob seem to be the sentinels of the bush. They were ever present, never on the horizon, always watching, and skittish. We couldn't get closer to them than 50m.

We turned off the dirt road on to a path toward some swamps, looking for African buffalo. I'd been carrying the AK-47, imagining myself as some kind of cross-breed hunter and freedom fighter – a bastard child of Hemingway and Che Guevara – when the guide took it back. African buffalo look kind of effeminate, with their horns curling away from their heads like 1950s hairdos, but they're deadly serious, vicious, fast, and bloody-minded. Once they decide to charge, only a bullet will stop them (actually several bullets). If a bullet hits the point where the horns meet, it just ricochets off. They're not to be confused with the domesticated Asian buffalo, that drags ploughs though muddy rice paddies, or the European ones that make such nice mozzarella. They're natural born killers.

There were thorn bushes all around, and termite hills, and I was trying to be 100 per cent aware. My eyes were peering through the bushes, and my brain was all high-speed algorithms, burning through the incoming data while trying to work out if that dark blur in the background might actually be a buffalo.

As we got nearer to the swamp, we spotted one about 150m away. Mr Odong had come in from the right direction since we were downwind. This meant it was blowing from the buffalo towards us.

We crept closer very carefully, metre by metre. He couldn't smell us, but if we'd had properly useful noses we could have smelled him. As it was, we had pathetic human noses. We had to rely on our eyes.

Eventually I was standing on a log, crouched low, and just 40m away. Suddenly, another black ball of anger broke cover about 20m away – one we hadn't spotted through the dense bush. Luckily, it bolted in the other direction.

Forty meters was actually too close. Buffaloes charge at over 50kph, which gives you less than three seconds to find cover, aim, and fire. One bullet wasn't likely to be enough, either. I could feel my heart thumping, so we retreated along a creek with steep banks.

Mr Odong was a mischievous fellow and thought I needed another adrenaline rush. He pointed to a big brown shiny lump in the bottom of the creek. It was a male hippo having a snooze in the cooling water to avoid the midday heat.

He picked up a stout stick, as thick as his wrist, and signed that he was going to throw it at the hippo. Then he pointed to my camera and did an impersonation of taking a picture, followed by him pumping his arms and pretending to run.

Hell, why not. It looked like fun.

The stick hit the hippo square on its massive head. It was a monster, and it exploded out of the water like a bomb going off. My camera jerked upwards giving me a great shot of the sky.

Two tonnes of fat, muscle, and herbivorous anger hung in the air before crashing back down into the water. Mr Mischievous Odong was already hoofing it into the distance with me in hot pursuit.

He'd earlier explained, drawing in the dust, that if we were charged, I was not to follow him exactly. I had to run at an angle because if I followed him, and a ferocious animal was following me, he needed a clear line of sight. Without it, he'd have to shoot me before he could shoot the rampaging beast.

I totally disregarded his wise advice and just followed him. I was later reprimanded and told to do better next time.

We stood there out of breath, laughing in the sunshine. Was there anything better? I told him about my picture of the sky. That had him rolling in the dirt. 'He wanted to kill us,' he said. Hilarious.

He decided to go and have another look. So, we went back to the stream and edged closer. This didn't seem very wise, since the hippo was still there. It was maybe 3m from us, glaring back, throwing its head back, and snorting. I took a photo but Mr Odong was skittish, shuffling backwards whenever the animal moved.

The wind shifted and a buffalo four hundred meters away on a ridge had obviously smelled us. We tried to work our way around it. After a lot of walking we came in from the right angle. But buffalo are like the Ugandan kob – super-sensitive and super-alert. We couldn't get close.

When we re-joined the stream, a small crocodile, its tail whipping, slid down the bank and into the water and the thick reeds. Mr Odong wanted to use his stick again, but it wouldn't come out.

A bit later we spotted more buffalo on a plain near a larger river, so we started the bushcraft approach again. Amazingly, we got to within about 15m of two of them, creeping up behind thick bushes. We could see them by peeping over the top. I was sure this was not normal procedure because I heard the click of him putting a bullet into the chamber of his rifle. He was 20m behind me and to one side, so at least he had a clear shot. The metallic sound had travelled through the air, though, and they stampeded off in the opposite direction, followed by another family of warthogs.

The whole day cost me 60 cents, plus a tip that made it an even dollar. It was certainly better than sitting in a minivan painted like a zebra.

Back at Chobe Lodge I splashed out on a beer, and spent the evening with the warden, Mr Bitamagive. He explained to me about the bush and the animals. For example, there was a difference between the Ugandan kob and the impala (they looked the same to me). The former was a grazer. It ate grass. The latter was a browser, and ate trees. I'd also seen a lot of elephant dung on the paths and roads and was rather excited about seeing them in the flesh. He said they moved in a broad circle. As they'd been nearby a few days ago, he thought they'd be a long way away by now.

The warden took a liking to me and offered to let me come along when he drove the anti-poacher unit out to one of their camps. We were scheduled to leave at 3am. We also drank a lot of rum, very little of which I was allowed to put on my bill. We talked about the politicians in their Land Cruiser, and how they were anti-British. He was pretty balanced. 'Yes,' he said, 'you exploited us. You paid us little for our agriculture, and the same for our copper. But you gave us roads, education, and health care. It was a good relationship.' He asked me to tell the world that Ugandans are decent people, and that it's a good country. I've tried to do just that ever since.

I was the only guest in the dining room again. I had chicken, rice, potatoes, and cabbage, which was better than cow's stomach, but hardly *haute cuisine.*

After dinner I sat up on the balcony of my room, watching the moon come through the clouds, and hitting the Nile. Dark spots marked the islands and the hippo backs. Across the horizon, lighting flashes lit up the sky, and fireflies darted around in the trees below the hotel. It started to rain, sheets of water lashing across the river and smashing into my windows.

Instead of going to sleep, I was totally engrossed in reading Thomas Hardy's *Mayor of Casterbridge.* My candle gutted out at 2.30am. I was supposed to get up in half an hour for more African adventures, which is where the expression 'burning the candle at both ends' must come from.

I did my accounts and found I'd burned through quite a lot of cash. Of my original stack of shillings, I only have 9,000 Shillings left. I'd already been in Uganda for six days, and I planned to stay another eight, though this depended on whether I could see gorillas in the south. I resolved to economise and travel more cheaply.

My alarm went off at 3am. I ignored it for half an hour, then threw on some clothes. I went downstairs but there was dead silence. I assumed they'd left without me.

At 5am there was a vigorous knocking on my door. It was the warden. A government minister had checked in after I'd gone to bed, along with a bloke from the World Bank. More rum had been drunk, and he'd also overslept.

The small platoon he was dropping off in the bush would be left to fend for themselves for a week. The rangers/soldiers were dedicated to stopping poachers. They shot to kill. It was war. They had Belgium FN7.62 rifles but their green, army sweaters were comical. Somebody had put them through a hot wash and a tumble dryer. They all sit there with their bellies exposed and their backpacks and tents on the steel floor. Their single Motorola radio was also broken, so they had no way to contact their base.

A hippo lumbered across the road. It was caught in the headlights on its nocturnal forage.

We drove for 20km before the sky started to lighten. We crossed the river on the main road near Kartuma Falls and drove for another 15km down a narrow, rutted track. I was in the back with the rangers getting bounced around. I'd quickly learned to keep my arms in as we passed all the bushes and they thrashed against the side frame. We drove right over a 2m sapling in the middle of the track. The Rover was less than a year old but it looked ten.

The warden told me later than elephants are amazingly destructive and that they had defoliated the place. Amin's crazy culling had gone too far, however. The vegetation was back, and more elephants were needed now. 'But the elephants are smart,' he said. 'Many of them have gone into exile in Zaire. We need to entice them back.' I was thinking to ask if I could go out on patrol with the rangers for a week, but I didn't.

Along the way I was seeing a lot of elephant dung. It was difficult to know how old it was. The rain had made it look fresh and dark.

On the way back there was good news. We stopped and inspected some dung and it was fresh. There were even footprints the size of dinner plates in the wet earth. The trail led towards the lodge. Some prints were on top of our tyre tracks from the journey out. I was getting excited. I then spotted elephants in the distance, though the warder correctly reclassified them as termite hills and bushes. Eventually it was he who spotted some real ones. We backed up and slowly rolled the Land Rover through the bush until we were within 40m of them. There were four, munching on the trees. I was so happy.

Nearer the lodge, we spotted a larger herd, but the others had jobs to do, so we went back for breakfast. I scoffed the food and set out to find a ranger. They were all at the office getting paid (a good sign). Mr Ogong was not around, but another chap called Jason took up the challenge of giving me another near-death experience. I told him where I'd seen the larger herd, and we set off – him with an AK-47, and me with my childlike enthusiasm, and a bounce in my step that belied my lack of sleep.

A mighty trumpeting heralded the elephants' presence before we could see them. Using bushcraft and sign language we moved slowly towards the noise. There were two buffalos up on a ridge, but they were at a safe distance. The thorn trees were not that thick, but it was tough to see more than 50m. We moved stealthily over the marshy ground while I tried to avoid twigs. There were trees smashed to pieces, and mounds of elephant dung. I stuck my finger in one and it was still hot. The wind kept changing direction, which was a problem. We were for ever dropping leaves to see which direction it was taking.

The elephants had a reputation for being aggressive and dangerous in Chobe. They remembered bad humans and they reacted accordingly. If they smelled someone, they sometimes stalked them, before finally charging.

Murchison Falls NP, me trying to look cool with an AK. This is just before we got charged by an elephant. Look at my ridiculous shoes!

We spotted a single grey male, then the wind shifted and we ended up doing a circle to move around him. Elephants spread out when they feed, so we were constantly looking over our shoulders. From 40m I took a photo of it with the standard 50mm lens. No lying zoom. I edged closer, and at about 20m he saw me. We looked at each other for a few seconds until he heard the mechanical click of the shutter. We both then retreated.

We followed a pair that seemed to be the last two of the main group. I was watching for twigs and Jason was monitoring the wind. There was no talking. I was fiddling with my camera when he screamed, 'Run, quickly, run.' I looked up, and right behind us, maybe 20m away, was a big bull with one foot off the ground, sort of dangling. That's the point when they're about to charge. It's when Dr Barnley would have felt unfortunately obliged 'to shoot the blighter'. I didn't have a Dr Barnely, or his great elephant gun. I only had Jason, sprinting ahead of me, carrying his rather under-powered AK-47, with me in my plastic sandals, doing my best to keep up, while remembering to run to one side. The elephant started to lumber towards us. We sprinted and sprinted. My lungs were on fire. I guess we covered about 200m, though I guess the elephant only made a few steps

Murchison Falls NP, just before he charged. Remember, we are on foot and I was wearing flip-flops. One of my many Darwin Award moments.

towards us. The problem was that in the bush, with my heart thumping, and my ears pounding, I couldn't hear. The elephant might well have been still after us, but due to the thick foliage we wouldn't have seen it.

Fortunately we'd made our retreat in the right direction. We came across the larger herd that we'd seen from the Land Rover. They were shifting around, but we counted about 50 elephants spread out over 100m in an open valley. I needed two shots – camera-wise – to get them all in. The younger ones were jousting, the chink of their tusks carrying clearly across to us. We sat there for ages watching them. Some were eating. Some were playing. A couple were watching us, though out in the open like that they were seldom dangerous. It was in the thorn trees and the bush that things could go wrong. That's when they could get a surprise and become aggressive.

Sitting on a termite hill in the sun, smoking a cigarette, and watching a large herd of elephants go about their daily lives, is wonderful. They seemed to me to be soulful beasts. Their small eyes in their big heads had something tragic about them. They plodded along like old men, who know a lot but say little, quietly observing the failures of mankind.

They were gradually getting closer to us. Jason didn't seem to feel like running again, so we moved away from them up to the road. On the way back he explained about all the different tracks to me, as well as their dung. The first group had about 12 animals in it. This one had about 50, making a total of 62.

The warden told me in the evening there were 72 in all, so we'd seen most of them. Jason asked me not to tell the warder about the solitary elephant and our little sprint, or about sneaking up so close to one.

The evening was spent talking with the warder, the manager of the hotel, and the chief internal auditor for Uganda Hotels. The auditor explained a lot about Amin – how he was originally close to the Israelis, and then the Palestinians, and how he'd created a great deal of terror with his informers. He also told a hilarious story about when the Gaddafi sent him troops to help fight the Tanzanians. They were totally useless, and the Tanzanians had cut them to shreds. 'They didn't understand trees,' he said. The other Ugandans fell off their chairs laughing.

I slept in and was woken by a staff member. They were worried I'd gained too much confidence, and had decided to go for a bush walk on my own. Regrettably, though, it was time to move on.

After an omelette and a coffee, I looked for some transport to the road. I'd planned to ask the internal auditor but he'd already gone. Then I found another Land Rover that was leaving. It took me to the park entrance.

There was an army roadblock right outside the park, and a truck was being searched for weapons. The driver was told to take me towards Masindi, close to Lake Albert. Half of Uganda seemed to be on the truck. I was literally hanging on to the steel frame on the side.

There was another roadblock on the other side of the river where a soldier spent a long time looking at my passport. I'd passed it to him the wrong way round and he hadn't turned it back. My little test. Risky, but fun.

My arms were aching from hanging on to the truck. There were two Special Forces guys in their blue camouflage riding with me as well. Bloody hell. I didn't seem to be able to avoid them. They explained they were actually police, not army. The plot thickened.

I got off at the Masindi turn off, and so did they. We then caught a ride on another truck into town. We each paid 150 shillings. I saw them hand over the cash, which I thought was interesting. They even took me to the bus station and helped me sort out a schedule for the next day. It's not that I didn't believe the High Commission, but based on my experience, they were fine. The officer dressed like Stallone was the most sinister. But then again, he was the one who stopped and gave me a ride.

And so I left Northern Uganda for the supposed relative sanity of the southern part of the country, to continue my odyssey in search of the Mountains of the Moon and the elusive Mountain Gorillas hiding in the Virunga range of volcanos.

Chapter 8

Southern Uganda

The cuisine in Uganda wasn't great, further confirmation of its British colonial past. (This, along with their amusing and persistent talk about the weather.) The meat tasted like dog food, and the rice was cold and came in hard clumps. My glasses of water often had dead flies floating in them. And Ugandan tea tasted fishy. All in all, not great meals. (When people say food tastes like dog meat, how do they know? Well, I ate a whole tin of it once, at school, for a bet. Dog food actually smells alright, but it doesn't taste very good, add salt and pepper. The last couple of mouthfuls were a real struggle. I don't remember how much the bet was for, but I did eat a daddy longlegs spider once for 50p.)

Looking for something to clean my mouth out, I went into the slightly upmarket Masindi Hotel where I bumped into the auditor for Uganda Hotels. We had a decent cup of coffee together, and he laughed about my lunch, and hanging on to the side of the truck.

In the evening I was dealt a dose of real life by a schoolboy. He'd just done his O levels and was around 16 years old. He wanted to do A-level economics, but he needed money for books and tuition. I told him that I'd seen Paul Samuelson's germinal text, *Economics*, in Kampala. I guess it had been priced at 1,000 shillings at least. I gave him 100 shillings, which was pathetic. Why didn't I give him the whole amount? It was only about three bucks, for Christ's sake. There are some things I'll always regret, and that was one of them. He was so determined, and keen to learn. He's probably done fine. In the holidays he'd earned 1,000 Ugandan

Shillings a month (next to nothing) working in the fields. I asked about his father helping him pay his way, but he was dismissive. 'He has five wives and 40 children and spends what money he has on wooing 16- and 17-year-old girls,' he said. 'He can only buy love for money now.'

As if to reprimand me for my meanness, a large cockroach woke me up that night by flying into the wall above my head with a crash. I chased it around the room with an old tin, but to no avail. In the morning I bought a new can of insecticide that promised to be fatal, not only to cockroaches, but also to a host of other creepy-crawlies.

I was running low on shillings and needed to try and find the black market. As I said before, it was always difficult to change money in the provinces. The best I was offered was 250 Ugandan Shillings to the dollar, compared to 350 Ugandan Shillings in Kampala. I decided to hang on and try further south.

The bus ride to Hoima was very crowded. I had a little boy on my lap for most of the time. The side of the road was lined with banana plants. It was three hours of banana plants. Near the end of the journey there was an army roadblock. A soldier asked me for 100 shillings. I smiled and ignored him, and got back on the bus. A local couldn't have got away with that.

I wanted to catch another bus to Fort Portal on the same day, but there were no buses until the morrow. I stayed at the Hoima Inn. It was quite clean. I had a bed,

Another happy kid.

a broken chair, a large window with iron bars, and a light that worked. A little girl arrived with two sheets, did a curtsey, made up the bed, and exited doing another curtsey. The sheets were an unexpected bonus. The hot shower wasn't hot, but they did apologise for that.

Lunch was acceptable – much better than dog food – after which I went out in search of the black market. The first shop hadn't even heard of American dollars. The third shop offered me 250 Shillings. I changed a small amount, not by choice. It was obviously a buyer's market. 'How do you like the weather today?' people said. 'It looks like it might rain.' It was like being in Surrey and talking to my parents' tennis friends. Sadly, I'd finished *The Mayor of Casterbridge.* What a *tour de force.* I'd compare it to *King Lear*, which for me is the pinnacle of tragedy.

I must have been a bit cranky that day. It was probably a mixture of not getting a bus to my next destination, and my struggles with the black market. A military policeman (not Special Forces) was sitting at the next table in the restaurant of the hotel and asked me for a cigarette. I turned on him, screaming that he was an arsehole and I didn't know him, and why should I give him anything. Which was rather unwise when I thought about it later. I threw my packet at him and stormed out (there was only one left). Twenty minutes later I went back and he'd gone. The packet of cigarettes was still there with the cigarette in it. The locals were all laughing, and slapping me on the back.

The following day, I got up early for the 7am bus. This decided to leave at midday instead. I spent the time writing letters and diary entries, and drinking tea, and watching the rain fall. The bus was crowded but I got a window seat. I think many people had standing room only tickets, or got bumped by rich people like me. The rain stopped and it started to heat up. I was soon sitting in a pool of sweat. There was an old lady next to me, cradling a heavy package the size of a small shoe box. It was round, tied at both ends, and neatly wrapped in banana skins. When she opened it up, it was full of dead insects. I pointed to my mouth and she nodded. Despite my daddy longlegs heroics at school, I pulled a very long face. Everyone was very happy. Across the aisle there was a little boy who kept looking at me sheepishly. He had lovely eyes, so I took his photo and gave him ten shillings and a banana.

How many bananas do you have to eat before you become a banana? I ate 30 that day. They cost a shilling each, which meant I could've bought 350 Shillings on the Kampala black market for one dollar.

Somehow it took eight hours to go about 200km, though the views were quite good. Luscious vegetation and rollercoaster hills rattled by, with rain forest in the dips, though eight hours next to an old woman holding a kilo of dried insects was definitely enough.

My lodging in Fort Portal had an unwanted ant nest in the corner of the room. Otherwise, it wasn't bad. My killer insecticide finished them off.

Over dinner a chap explained the roadblocks. They were designed, he said, to catch irregular soldiers. Everyone had to show a photo ID and a tax return. This was all very well and good, but as he pointed out, for about 2,000 Shillings (six bucks), anyone could cross the entire country with no documents. He also explained that the senior officers tried to control the number of road-blocks, and keep the troops in the barracks. The problem was that they escaped, and set up illegal and unauthorised ones to make money. It used to be 100 per cent police doing it, but then the army wanted a piece of the action. The code for a bribe was, 'Give me a cigarette.' Everyone paid, or you were kept behind and 'dealt with'. He didn't explain what that meant. The police were better since they only took a bribe if your papers weren't in order. The army took bribes anyway.

The manager put on the hot water, and after dinner I actually had a good soak in a bath. Wonderful. It was a bath by candlelight, out of necessity rather than romantic or spiritual yearnings, because the power was out.

They had an interesting way of serving tea. It came in a huge plastic mug, with a cup and saucer on the side. They transferred the tea from the mug to the cup. This was another take on the British way of life. The mug replaced the teapot, and the tea was pre-mixed with milk and plenty of sugar. At breakfast, it was accompanied by goat's meat and bread.

The Rwenzori Mountains, or Mountains of the Moon, were to the right as we headed south. They reached up to 5km and some of them were permanently covered in snow. I was planning to hike into them from Kilembe, a town in the foothills. Lake George was ahead, and to our left, as the bus descended into Kasese, was the gateway to the Kilembe area.

Kilembe turned out to be a restricted zone. I needed a letter from the relevant ministry back in Kampala for me to enter. After a lot of smiling on my part, and positive profiling on theirs, we finally solved the problem. I noted that one of the officers was toting an Uzi sub-machine gun, a sign that Amin had once been close to the Israelis.

I shared a taxi ride to Kilembe itself in a Peugeot 504 estate, which is a real work horse of a car. It had an official seating capacity of seven, and I know it's going to sound ridiculous, but including the driver there were 20 of us in it. Yes, 20. This was not only incredible but extremely uncomfortable. Peugeot should use this in their ad campaigns. One guy I was wedged next to told me the Ugandan record for a Peugeot 504 was 30 people.

I'd expected a town, but it was actually a mining settlement. Everything was provided by the company. I ate in their canteen, stayed in their guest lodge, and went to their church on Easter Sunday. It was all free, so I donated 1,000 Shillings to their recreation club. They mined copper up there, bashing it into little pieces bits and mixing the pieces with water to create a slurry. This was then piped down the hill, dried it out, and sent by rail to Jinja on Lake Victoria for smelting. If the smelter couldn't get power from the Owens Dam, it just piled up.

They also had a large hospital there where I meet Ernest, an anaesthetist. He was a nice guy. Very open. But he couldn't even afford three meals a day. Understandably, Uganda had a serious brain-drain problem. He explained how a Christian charity, the White Sisters (a reference to the colour of their dresses, I believe), helped people like him get medicines into the country without having to pay for them with foreign exchange. I kept quiet about my nefarious currency dealings.

He asked my opinion about Britain going to war with Argentina over the Falkland Isles. I said I had no idea. So he filled me in by telling me what he'd gleaned listening to the BBC World Service. He said that most of Uganda was on the side of the British.

He also told another amusing story about Idi Amin. In addition to the Israelis, the Palestinians, and the Libyans, Amin had had a dalliance with the Cubans. 'They'd disagreed with his plans to make Uganda square, and they quit,' he said. Apparently, Amin had wanted to turn Uganda into a perfect square, taking territory from its neighbours to do so. Classic Amin. He should have stuck to carrying my biology teacher's gun, or playing rugby.

My next plan was to go for short walk in the Mountains of the Moon, though any chance of an early morning hike was thwarted by a torrential rainstorm. It bashed down on the corrugated iron roof of the guest lodge, so I turned over and slept for another hour. Then I got up and drew some poor-quality maps in the back of my diary of my travels to date. I was very disappointed with how little I'd achieved. I also repaired my jean shorts. I was getting pretty good at sewing on patches. A pity I couldn't make them a little longer.

The weather cleared up by 11am so I set off into the hills. The peaks were covered in clouds the whole time I was there, which rather defeated the point of seeing snowy peaks in the middle of Africa. Ernest had shown me a map of the area, and the contour lines had looked perilously close together. We'd also discussed the rash of roadblocks across the country, and whether he paid. He came up with a very human and philosophical response. 'Yes,' he said. 'In order to avoid a fool, you have to behave like a fool for a moment.' My heart goes out to people like that.

Everyone on the road that day was cheerful and outgoing. 'Good morning, sir,' they said. 'How are you?' 'It has stopped raining. The sun is out.' It was such friendly chit-chat. This was the case especially for the women. I mused on the extraordinary difference between the repressed and closed world of the north, and the bubbly and open world of the south. They were hauling enormous piles of wood or bananas down almost vertical hills, but they always smiled, and they always had time to talk. There was also quite a lot of innocent flirting going on (well, innocent on my side).

The men didn't seem to be doing much, though that said, there were chaps in hard hats walking around, and an extraordinarily steep railway line. There were apparently 3,000 workers at the mine, down from what had been a peak of 6,000. It closed soon after I left as there was no way to process the ore.

A woman was selling food on the side of the path that looked like sausages. Yummy. I bought three. I should have known better. They were cooked bananas. I was deep in banana country. Would I like bananas with my bananas? (Later, back at the canteen, I asked for food, but they only had *matoke*. This was boiled bananas and gravy. It was very heavy going; I decided to wash it down with some African beer, *tonto*. It was sold in opaque, plastic, engine-oil bottles. A look down the spout revealed a grey-brown sludge with lots of bits in it. The taste was terrible. I couldn't manage to finish it and, yes, it was made from bananas.)

I walked upwards and upwards, without a guide or a map. I didn't really have a plan, but I stayed on the larger path at each fork. Sweat was pouring off me. I'd get to the top of a hill only to find another one in front of me. I went on for about three hours, climbing as fast as I could. The contour lines hadn't lied. It was seriously steep.

The amazing thing was that I never got beyond the agricultural belt. No amount of walking got me to the real mountains, which remained shrouded in rainy-season clouds anyway. The fields were not terraced, and were planted with banana, cassava, and other, smaller plants. Bananas were the main crop. They came in all shapes, sizes, and colours. Many were new to me. In posh supermarkets now there's a range of different types, but when I was growing up, they were just bright yellow, and had a Fyffes label on them. They came from somewhere in central America that was also, doubtless, a 'banana republic', and was ruled – indirectly – from Langley, Virginia.

I did climb high enough to have a view of Lake George. The clouds on the peaks sort of separated at one point and some of them floated down into the valleys. I decided enough was enough, and descended to look for Ernest, and to listen to more snippets of wisdom about Uganda and local life.

The Recreation Club had an Easter rock concert planned for the evening and I was invited. They have proper equipment, sang lots of reggae, and the girls danced provocatively. In the best reggae tradition a law student, Moses, from Makarere University in Kampala (he'd been sent up to 'educate' the miners, whatever that meant) offered to get me some grass. I gave him a dollar and he came back with a black bin-liner full of the stuff. Extraordinary. I took a handful and told him to keep the rest. Bananas were obviously not the only cheap cash crop up in the hills.

In the morning I extracted my crumpled tie from the bottom of my backpack, fitted it around my protesting neck, and strode off to the canteen. I got two boiled eggs to heighten the feeling of Easter. I then went to the quaint wooden church, with its corrugated iron roof, tiny steeple, and tinkly piano. A large lizard spent the whole time running from side to side on the wall above the altar. I made the mistake of going to the English-language service, where people mumbled to themselves quietly, and the hymn numbers bore no relation to the book I was given. From outside, later on, I heard the African service, which was held in a local language. It was not dissimilar to the previous night's rock concert.

At the Recreation Club that evening they had pork, which was a big relief, and I said goodbye to Ernest the anaesthetist, and marijuana Moses. In the morning I headed south.

I was being poisoned by bananas. A steady diet of peanuts, boiled eggs, tomatoes, and bananas seemed to have got to me. I had stomach pains for most of the day. I also passed copious amount of wind every five minutes, in a quite spectacular and revolting fashion.

Down on the main road near Kasese, I bumped into a Canadian. I'd seen no *mazungi* (foreigners) since leaving Nairobi, two weeks before. This was quite an achievement for someone not in the deep jungle or the desert. The British High Commission lady had been Ugandan. To tell the truth, I was a bit disappointed to meet another non-local. I thought I'd had the whole country to myself. It was good though. We swapped war stories, and he gave me some information on Tanzania. We laughed about how confusing all the names beginning with K were: Kampala, Kasese, Kabale, Kartuma, Kisoro, Kibale, Kayambura, Kyenjojo, Kagadi, Kigabwa, Kazo, Katanabirwa, Kibooto, Kakoge, Kisumu, Kabalaga, and my likely next destination, Kigali. He then went north and I went south. It was a very brief encounter.

The bus south was ancient. Though it smoked and rattled, the ride was good, and it stuck to the great time-honoured mathematical constant that says in developing countries, no matter how fast the driver goes, you never get beyond 200km from where you started, and you always arrive late in the day. Uganda was not actually developing. It was regressing. But the concept of regressing countries hadn't yet come into common parlance. The concept makes sense, though. The Ancient Greeks did it. The Romans did it. The British did it. The Americans and the Japanese are arguably doing it now. And the Chinese will.

The landscape was stunning. The road cut through the bowls of extinct, exploded volcanoes, and volcanic rocks poked out of the tailored green. There were rolling hills that were a patchwork of terraced fields. There were potatoes, cabbages, cauliflower, and peas, and due to the intensive farming, this was the most densely populated part of Uganda.

I spent the night at Kabale, as there was no transport on to Kisoro until the morning. The New Anita Café not only put me up for the night, but served dinner. The quality of the food was definitely improving. I had fried meat (no idea what type), and chips, with two fried eggs, and a big mug of tea. My room was rather cell-like, and the windows were boarded up, but the cockroach population was manageable.

The taxi service in the morning didn't eventuate, so I spent the whole day waiting for a bus. One left for the south at 2pm, but I only found out about it at half past two. I sold a tin of corned beef and changed $10 at 300 Shillings to the dollar. Not bad. I also offloaded four paperback books. I'm not sure what the locals would make of Herman Hesse or James Michener, but Thomas Hardy was popular in Uganda (as I've said.)

When I was a kid growing up in the genteel Surrey town of Dorking, there was a hotel in the centre that was quite upmarket. It served cream teas and the like and was called the White Horse Inn. Kabale also had a White Horse Inn, which was also the poshest place in town. It was really nice, and had the added advantage of not having anyone from Dorking there. It was another one of the Uganda Hotels properties, and I half expected to bump into the auditor. I sat there with a coffee in a comfortable wicker chair, writing and looking out over the long, English-style lawns. A gardener was trying to scythe off the sub-tropical growth with an old mower that he had to push.

The whole area was a decent distance from the troubled north, and the chaos of Kampala and seemed to be doing relatively well. I noted that there were more things in the shops than in Kampala, and the people seemed to be better organised and better dressed. There were neat little houses with neat little gardens all over the place.

Over dinner, I chatted with three chaps who described themselves as peasants. They each had about two or three acres of productive land. A school teacher had told me earlier that two acres was about the average for a small farmer. I think they were middle-class peasants.

A cash shortage and an expiring visa meant I needed to push on. So, I did.

A shared taxi was leaving at 6.30am the following day, and I paid what seemed to be an outrageous amount for the ride. On reflection, the rough roads, that had to be tackled mostly in low gear, and the modest number of people it carried (under ten!), plus the distance involved, probably meant the charge was reasonable.

It was a pickup truck, and I got to ride in the cabin. Next to me was a school teacher dressed smartly in a black dress. She would have looked quite at home in Oxford Street.

It was cold because of the altitude. We climbed in and out of clouds and there were volcanic hills all around us. Slim lakes snaked off into the distance. When we eventually dropped down, we drove through the thick Echuya bamboo forest.

We finally pulled into Kisoro and I asked around for the cheapest place to stay. It was cheap indeed, and was too poor even to have a name. There was no electricity, no running water, but it did have three super-sweet kids. The youngest one was petrified of me.

I expected to have to fight off the cockroaches in the night, but as it turned out, it was a two-pronged attack. Cockroaches and rats. The price was a rip-off.

More happiness personified ... in rags.

Considerably posher was another Ugandan Hotels property, the Travellers Rest House. Though it had seen better days, the bar was still decorated with blue and pink toilet paper.

Between my hovel and The Travellers Rest House, there was a police checkpoint. I stopped there for a chat and to bone up on some local knowledge. The chaps spoke good English, and were quite friendly. 'What language do you speak in England?' I was asked. That threw me a bit. I guess they thought we were tribal, and English was our unifying tongue. They were right.

They told me that the warden of the park for seeing the gorillas was about 8km from Kisoro. I'd probably have to walk there to find him. It was near the base of Mt. Muhabura. The Travellers Rest House confirmed this information, which was reassuring. The police also told me the rains made climbing difficult. I should have listened. A lot of gorillas had also gone into exile during Amin's time, though some were said to be now coming back.

I shared dinner that night with a pigmy. He was dressed in a long jacket (long on him), a trilby hat, and a curved pipe that had charcoal burning in it at one end. I ate vast quantities of beans and rice, since I expected mountain deprivation to be just around the corner. I'd also bought rice and tomatoes to take with me.

My table-mate kept talking to me, and a little boy explained he was asking for money. I bought him a plate of beans and rice instead, which seemed to make him happy. Quite a crowd collected to watch the pink-faced giant and the pigmy. He wasn't a dwarf, I hasten to add. He was maybe the same height as a ten-year-old boy. The boy told me that the pigmy people from Zaire were even smaller. They were hunter-gatherers who lived on the edge of the Bantu world. I was, after all, very close to the border with both Rwanda and Zaire.

Walking back to the hotel with no name, but with plenty of rats and roaches, it was pitch black. I literally stumbled into the police roadblock, which they found very amusing. They lent me a hurricane lamp to find my way, and asked me to bring it back in the morning.

The morning revealed that my three boiled eggs have turned into two boiled eggs. A rodent had been munching on my backpack. The roaches were small fry compared to the rats, but somehow I found them more scary. How scary would it have been if they'd been bigger. Perhaps the size of a rat.

I was heading, as directed, for Mt. Muhabura, a volcano on the western end of the Virunga mountain range. The range had its peaks just over the border in Rwanda. Virunga was a corruption of a local word, *ibirunga*, which meant 'mountain'. This meant that we call them the 'mountain, mountain range', which is silly. My objective was to find mountain gorillas.

The lower slopes were a neat checkerboard of what turned out to be wheat and peas. Walking along I played Pied Piper to maybe 50 raucous, joyful children. The fields by the side of the road were a market garden of potatoes, carrots, cauliflower, maize, tobacco, sorghum, and, I regret to report, a few bananas. Some of the latter seemed to be permanently stuck inside me, fermenting away. Three women joined the parade, laughing and dancing though there was no music. These women didn't need music to dance. I do, and my sense of rhythm is rubbish. I also need alcohol. Lots of alcohol. They were also kind of flirting. so I started to run away from them. There were squeals of laughter, and their big bodies bustled as they chased me. When we all fell down on the grass by the side of the road, we lay there laughing in the sun. Their white teeth flashed and their bosoms heaved. One of the boys pointed to a volcano to our right saying that it had erupted at Christmas. I willed it to erupt again. My disciples gradually dropped away and went back to Kisoro to go to school, or into the fields, or whatever they were supposed to do. The three women took a side road, waving until they were out of sight. They were happiness incarnate.

You don't get much poorer than this (or broader smiles).

The Virungas, they look nice, just try climbing up the bastards with Seargent Major Zak kicking my sorry arse the whole way in pouring rain. My mountaineering kit consisted of tennis shoes, an M&S sweater, and a corn on the cob!

The Virunga range was in front of me, hopefully hiding a few groups of gorillas, and I was looking for the warden of the park, one Zachariah Ngongo. I'm not sure if anyone had told him I was on my way, but he met me on the road. He looked to be around 30. He was fit as a fiddle, with chiselled calves, no shoes, and a bolt-upright military posture. He had maybe ten words of English, but he had a very big smile, and he was a professional when it came to common-sense sign language. I think he had a couple of rangers working for him, which made only three men responsible for a huge park. Chobe seemed over-resourced by comparison. He also had an enormous old rifle because there were buffalo in the forests too (he made horn shapes on his head with his hands, and snorting noises, and he bugged out his eyes wildly).

Zak's family home was a classic collection of huts made of mud with mainly grass roofs. There was a main building of two rooms with a tin roof. I was given one of those. The floors were made of concrete. There were also four large, round, grain silos made of rushes and bamboo. These were on stilts and had grass roofs, too. The whole compound was enclosed by a 3m-high bamboo-stake palisade. The ground was muddy, there were four or five chickens, and about the same number of kid goats. Smoke poured from the roof of the main room. Both animals and children moved in and out. There seemed no clear distinction where anything lived.

Zak's home with a menagerie of goats, kids and chickens.

Again, I had to share my room with rats, though I was finally getting used to them. The toilet was outside the compound. It was a hole in the ground surrounded by more bamboo stakes. The latter provide crucial assistance since it stopped squatters slipping into the pungent pit. This was especially important in the black of the night.

I'd arrive at lunchtime. Zak let me scoff my two remaining eggs, and some grilled sweetcorn, and change my shoes. Then we were off up the mountain at a blistering pace.

He explained in sign language that we had a 6km climb through the cultivated land before we hit the bamboo forests. In the forests themselves the mud was bad, so I changed into my plastic sandals.

A woman passed us coming down. She was all smiles, with 20, 4m-long bamboo stakes on her head.

In no time I started thinking I'd made a huge mistake. This man was a Marine Corps sergeant, unrelenting and unsympathetic. We crossed a swamp and I tried to jump from grassy hillock to grassy hillock, often falling in. Zak's pace was extraordinary. The black mud was freezing (it was a sort of liquid peat, and about the same temperature as Ireland.) I was in my too-short shorts, and a cape that protected me from the intermittent rain showers but not the cold. My Marks & Spencer sweater did its best.

As we climbed up, the hillocks became more frequent, and I got better at jumping and balancing. In the back of my mind, I was thinking that we had to get down again before it got dark. The swamp was punctuated by some plants that looked like red-hot pokers. I wasn't interested. I was more concerned about my fatigue, and whether I could carry on. Since the peaks were in the 3km–4km range, there also wasn't enough oxygen. This was the highest I'd ever climbed. I probably had altitude sickness, but as I had a few other sicknesses as well, I couldn't tell.

We reached the jungle, which was mainly bamboo, and stopped at a clearing. There was evidence of a fire and poachers. That was one of Zak's ten English words. I shared a tin of sardines with him, and he gave me some more grilled corn. I took a look at his rifle. It was a splendid Holland and Holland 0.375, though the main thing I noticed is how heavy it was. I guess it was over 5kg, and he'd been carrying it without any effort at all.

The clouds came in and we were now sitting in a water-vapour stew with very limited visibility. I was hyperventilating. It was time to move on, but the forest looked impenetrable. Zak disappeared up a narrow path. In addition to his rifle, he also had a *panga* (machete), which he used to cut away the creepers and the bamboo. Wherever we touched the bamboo, it brought down a cascade of icy water. Onwards and upwards we went.

We reached a ridge and looked for movement in the valleys below. Well, Zak looked. I was so exhausted that a silverback could have been right in front of me and I wouldn't have seen him. I must have had the blank stare of a man in deep trouble, exhausted and on the edge. Nothing stirred.

We cut down into the jungle to try another ridge, along a path used by forest elephants, and I spotted my first gorilla droppings. They were about the size of tennis balls. Zak signalled that they were two weeks old. The bamboo had been twisted inwards in places to create rough platforms covered with big leaves. This was how gorillas made their beds. Some of them were 4m up in the air and looked very precarious. There were maybe ten in all, with half-eaten bamboo roots under them, and carpeting the forest floor. They were obviously messy eaters. I got excited, but Zak signalled they were old, too. He pointed to the dead leaves. They were black and rotting.

The ground was a kind of mulch and was infested with vicious ants – large and reddish and big enough to see their pincers. Stooping down to get under branches, it was impossible not to touch the ground. The ants were terrible. I tried to brush them off, but their bites were sharp and real. There were also stinging nettles that flopped across our legs, leaving me with nasty, itchy rashes. Zak didn't even wear shoes. He was hard, and I was soft. While he slashed through the forest with his *panga*, I was constantly trying to avoid the nettles, and brush off the ants.

We eventually got to the next ridge and looked over the abyss into a rain-sodden valley. Nothing. No movement.

We moved forwards and eventually got down into the bamboo again. The good news was that it was easier going, there were fewer nettles, and we could walk upright rather than at a back-breaking stoop or crawl. The bad news was that the bamboo twigs were noisy. Any gorilla would have heard us (me, actually) well before we heard him (or her).

There was a crashing noise in the bamboo. Zak pointed and signalled, 'Fifty metres.' I came alive, fatigue forgotten, exhilarated. We moved quickly through the forest and found the spot where the great beasts had been eating. Bamboos roots had been ripped out of the ground, and there were more tennis balls of dung. I did the finger test and the balls were amazingly hot. They were steaming like big, spinach-based, dim sums. We could still hear the gorillas, but they moved much faster than we did (or I could).

So, did I get to see a gorilla? I did get to stick my finger in some steaming poo. Does that count?

The rain began bucketing down. Zak pointed out a grotesque earth worm. It was like those in a suburban garden, only half a meter long. He poked it with his foot while I took a step back.

It was now late afternoon and beginning to get dark. The clouds were low and heavy. We descended at a blistering pace with no breaks.

I was well and truly exhausted by the time we got back. Mrs Z had prepared a large bowl of hot water, and one of his kids washed my filthy, battered feet. It beat any of those overpriced spas with petals floating in bowls. I was in heaven. I then concocted a soup or stew from boiled rice, potatoes, onion, chilli, garlic, and tomato puree. It would probably have been disgusting to anyone but a person who'd just got down from hell mountain. My body craved calories and warmth. At this point there was a communication breakdown. I thought I was cooking my dinner. Zac thought he was cooking my dinner. So, I had two dinners. Not bad. His dinner was potatoes and beans. We decided the double dinner was a good idea, and decided to repeat it the next night, with lots of thumbs up and smiles. Simple communication. Simple pleasures. I crashed out on a primitive bed made of knotted ropes strung on a crude, wooden frame. It sagged badly in the middle and my bum was nearly on the floor, but I soon slept, or more likely, passed out. Maybe it was something in-between.

Later in the night my bladder told me I needed to get up and go for a pee. At that moment the tin roof was suddenly hit by small-arms fire from the sky, which soon intensified. It became a barrage of machine-gunning rain. It was deafening. I have to admit, I didn't use the toilet that time. I peed out the door.

The rain eased and I fell asleep again, waking before dawn to another storm. It stopped around daybreak, but it made for a dull, dripping, cold start to the day.

Oh my god, it seemed we were going again. My achilles tendons were on fire, the right one in particular. My legs were a criss-cross of scratches and blotches. And my clothes were still damp.

Zak had an enormous smile on his face, happy to greet another morning, with the chance to look for his beloved gorillas, and the challenge of dragging a sorry piece of white flesh around behind him. I found out he was actually 50, not 30. He handed me a bowl of cold potatoes and beans. His white teeth flashed, and children ran around him. The children seemed to be very young. I wondered if they were actually his grandchildren, or the product of wife number X. Before we left, he handed me a new bamboo stake for walking with. It actually helped.

We were aiming for another part of the forest. Great, I thought (sarcasm). I had looked forward to seeing gorillas for weeks, and now all I wanted to do was be somewhere else. A huge, hot bath in England came to mind. Anywhere but the steep sides of a volcano in the rain.

We climbed up a different path. My body warmed and loosened, and my achilles tendons started functioning again. Cheerful people passed us carrying enormous loads.

Before diving into the forest, we stopped for a break. The view was wonderful. The sky had cleared and we could see cultivated land below. In the distance, three volcanoes erupted out of the plains. I was happy to be alive (the feeling didn't last). The sun defined the tightly packed valleys very sharply, as well as the ridges that led upwards. It was spectacular as they were very, very steep. To one side was a smaller volcano, totally covered in a neat mosaic of fields, with a mini volcano that seemed to have burst out of its side.

Volcanoes don't have foothills. They just start out of the plains and go up, up, and up. Which is what we did. We went up and up and up. At least I had long trousers this time to keep the ants and the nettles at bay.

The paths were wet, sometimes muddy, and there was gorilla detritus, torn shoots, twisted bamboo, and more poo. But it was all old. We circled around but we didn't find anything. I was exhausted again. We came out in a grassy clearing and I lay down on my back, my heart pounding. Zak spotted some large monkey's, in the trees on the edge of the clearing. They weren't gorillas, but they were better than nothing.

The next climb defied all reason. We clambered up a narrow gully along a stream as it came down over slippery rocks and creepers. It was very steep, and I found out that the nettles could actually get through my thin, corduroy trousers. They drove me bonkers. The irritation lasted about 20 minutes, which was irrelevant as I was constantly being re-nettled. Rain poured off the bamboo, and it was bitterly cold again.

We ended up in an otherworldly zone of trees coated in moss. It hung off the branches and looked quite strange. There was no sign of any gorillas.

We continued upwards until we came out into an afro-alpine zone. We pushed on, and the sun came out. I was allowed to rest on the sodden mossy ground. I think we were above the gorilla habitat by this stage. Zak just wanted to stretch his legs. I felt annihilated.

After that we hurtled down, the walking stick speeding me up. Zak stopped and pointed at a bent bamboo. He slashed a piece of twine holding the bamboo in place, and it whipped up. He was showing me a snare, set by pigmy hunters and poor farmers. It was designed to catch small antelope. Whenever an animal stepped on the wire hoop, the bamboo lifted it viciously into the air, breaking its leg. It would hang there to die in agony, sometimes taking days to do so. We found five in all. Cheap and simple. Zak brought the wires down with him. It was his day job. I was just a hobby.

Back at base camp it was another foot bath, followed by rice, potatoes, and beans. Zak showed me a gorilla skull, which was pretty much the same as a human one, but huge and with four large, dog-like teeth. Holding it I felt like Hamlet.

Working out what I was supposed to pay him was difficult. He initially refused any money at all. In the end I gave him a paltry sum, though even that was a real struggle to give him. He kept pushing it back. In the end he accepted it and disappeared. He reappeared two hours later with two bottles of Primus beer. He'd walked all the way to the nearest shop, which was quite a distance. Bottles of beer were also not cheap. We sat down on the steps of his hut and drank together. It had been hell, but it had been a great, amazing, exhilarating hell. Maybe even better than seeing gorillas. I'd done it the hard way. I'd got to stick my fingers in their fresh dung. I'd heard them crashing around in the jungle. And I'd cradled a massive gorilla skull. I'd also got to know a big, tough, gentle African.

He had a mildewed guestbook in which someone before me had written, 'One of god's great creatures escaped our eyes. Their home is beautiful. So be it.' Doing things like that – being disappointed, but not disappointed – is how I was learning more about life, and more about myself. How hard it was to do things, and even when I failed, to discover that it was the trying that was the point. Again – the journey, rather than the destination.

The morning was dry. I packed up and said goodbye to Zak's family, but unfortunately he'd decided to walk to Kisoro with me. I was hoping for an amble. It was another route march.

Back in relative civilisation, I had a coffee at the Travellers Rest House Zak reappeared, and explained he was taking another party up Mt. Muhabura in the afternoon, and was spending the night in a hut. I was in bad shape, but I was tempted. It was being organised from a Christian mission that I didn't know about. I speed walked the 6km to meet four Dutch sisters, who spoke good English, but had no idea what I was talking about. So, I trudged back to the Travellers Rest House. (It was quite extraordinary how much I walked. I'd just done a dozen kilometres, and was already exhausted, but I thought nothing of it.) There was a white chap there who turned out to be the one I was looking for. He worked for another charity in the area. Then the rains came in and they decided to call it off. I suggested we try the next day, and we agreed to rendezvous at the Travellers at 7am. The White Sisters showed up, with some Dutch doctors. They were really surprised to hear that I'd been in the north. 'That's impossible,' one of them said. 'You must have been lucky,' the others said. Bill, the white chap, was Scottish and said something about it being 'even worse than Glasgow'. He hadn't met Doddy. The southern area was quite calm and peaceful, compared to the north. They explained about the politics and the rigged elections, and Milton Obote, and how he'd thrown out the Red Cross. Amnesty International was investigating the Ugandan prisons. The governor of the area was Catholic, but the central government was Protestant, so there was a lot of tension. 'You see, Catholics and Protestants, I'm at home. Like Glasgow,' Bill chipped in. He told me the regional Catholic governor was forced to watch some of his followers being murdered as a warning. They'd been buried alive. There were also stories about Obote being present and active at some of the executions. This was the man who forced you to take possession of one of his T-shirts every time you bought some ground coffee.

I went back to my super-cheap hotel for the night, and had trouble sleeping. When I did nod off, I had dreams about living with the gorillas on the mountains. I didn't wake up rested.

Joy of joys. In the morning, one of the White Sisters' drivers took us to Zak's place in an ambulance. The clouds were swirling around the peaks, and Zak wasn't keen, but we set off anyway. Bill seemed to be a teacher, and had a student with him.

It was another manic climb. In an hour we were on the edge of the forest. My lungs were bursting, I was panting like a dog, and my legs felt like jelly. In the larger animal kingdom, I would have been the straggler, picked off by the circling carnivores. As it was, I just slowed everyone else down.

Then we started the real climb. Bill encouraged me the whole way. I rested, took a few steps, and stopped exhausted again. My eyes were locked on the little patch of ground right in front of me. I imagined that I was a grunt in the Vietnam War, and how easy it would have been to have gotten killed while being exhausted. I wouldn't have known I was even dead.

The path was not only steep, but rocky. There was vegetation that appeared to offer something to hold on to, but it was rotten, and came away in our hands. This provided many various opportunities to tumble over backwards. I was told, 'Use your stick!' That was helpful, except I had jelly arms as well as jelly legs. My heart was trying to get blood everywhere at once, and the lack of focus seemed to result in no blood getting anywhere.

We stopped for a rest. To my right was 100m drop. It was almost vertical, so I had to be careful not to wobble that way. Then sun came out. It was very strong in the thinning air.

We moved on and the path became more and more stony. It seemed to consist mainly of pebbles that bit through the thin soles of my basketball boots. The only option was to climb through the long, wet heather.

I was told we were over halfway to the summit, which cheered me up. I was afraid to say it, but I kept on complaining. That day I became the sort of person who really pisses me off. My head was thumping. Both my achilles tendons were screaming. In my whole life, I don't think I'd made so much effort over such an extended period of time.

As we climbed further, the vegetation changed again. By this time we were in the clouds and there were giant, surreal, lobelia plants, with fleshy leaves, like a cross between a cactus and a palm. *Dendrosenecio adnivalis, hagenia abyssinica, hypericum revolutum.* And a luscious, bright-green moss, that hung everywhere from the sparse branches and coated the trees. There were also bizarre shaped plants, the sort kids might draw – all trunk, with just a few leaves on top like a wreath. Some of the trees didn't seem to have any leaves at all. They were just sticks. They had an odd, almost reptilian bark. Volcanic boulders were strewn about, and I half expected a brontosaurus to wander by, munching on some pre-Cambrian foliage.

The Virungas, primordial forest on the slopes of Mt.Muhavura. You sort of expect to meet a dinosaur, we were actually looking for gorillas, which proved just as elusive

The Virungas, summiting Mt. Muhavura with bionic Zak.

The confused miasma that used to be my brain managed to take a photo, but it set the focus on infinity by mistake. Later, an extremely bad drawing found its way into my diary. It was so bad it was funny.

Climbing out of this *Alice in Wonderland* scenery we emerged on to open heather. Bill must have felt right at home. We were on a Scottish moor, with clouds swirling around us. Where were the three witches?

Bill told me again that it wasn't far. My ears were blind, and my eyes were deaf. I was totally losing the plot.

Then, with one more scramble, I was looking over the lip of a ridge. It was actually a crater rim. We were at the top, with a perfectly still, circular lake before us, mirroring the sky. The clouds dropped away, the sun came out, and I was happy. It was just after midday.

We were just over 4km up. I seemed to recover almost immediately. I lay on my back, smiling and laughing, with southern Uganda laid out before me – a vast quilt of neat fields, interspersed with lakes, and picture-perfect volcanoes. Somehow, I'd brought a sandwich along, or someone had, and it was the best sandwich in the world. It was followed by the best cigarette in the world.

Bill took a photo of Zak, his student, and me. Thought the water in the lake was icy cold, Bill and I were thinking of taking a swim, but Zak put us right.

The Virungas, mini volcanos shrouded in cloud, taken from the top of the Virungas, serious mountains. Mt Muhabura is the highest at 4,500m high. I think I (foolishly) summited it twice.

We left at 1pm and hurtled back down, getting to his place at 4pm. I slipped a few times, my knees ached from the constant jarring, but the stick saved me most of the time (as well as Zak's iron grip on my elbow.) At one point, we got hit by a hailstorm. The ice balls came down fast and furious, the size of marbles and peas. We waited it out, the stones pinging off the path.

There'd been no gorillas again, but by now I wasn't expecting any. Bill found a chameleon and put it in his hat. They really do change colour.

Back at Zak's, I had just enough energy to write something in his decaying guest book. Following the tradition of my distant relative, Philip Larkin, my words were short and to the point, 'Fucked, but got to the top. Chris Price 18th April 1982.' The ambulance was waiting, which was more appropriate for me than the driver knew.

Back at the Travellers Rest House, Bill and I had a real beer to celebrate our summiting. We then went to the weekly open-air market to buy some local brew, and settled down to drink that. I bought an enormous cabbage, some tomatoes, and ten eggs. I also bought a huge bag of peanuts which, on reflection, were probably raw, and should have been cooked. They caused havoc with my personal plumbing.

The next day I was still feeling determined, so I set out again on the hike to Zak's. He was out, but Mrs Z gave me a cup of what she described as 'tea'. I think it was hot homebrew. She sat there puffing her pipe, and breast-feeding their youngest.

Zak returned and we set off. My plastic sandals were disintegrating, and since there were no shoe shops for 100 miles, I wore my basketball boots, knowing they'd get soaked in the cold bogs and marshes. It was now or never. 'Come out gorillas, where ever you are.' The joke was over. I'd tried hard enough. They were the ones who hadn't.

We climbed up elephant paths again, traversed ridges, stopped for a smoke, and chewed on grilled corn. There was evidence of gorillas all over the place, but none of it fresh.

I am not sure if Zak made a mistake, but we ended up in a hell of a mess. The foliage became so dense that we had to cut our way through every foot of it. Both of us were bent double, our backs scraping against the creepers and the trees. Our noses and backsides were in the wet humus, being scraped against bamboo stands and tree trunks. It was all solid green. This was *jungle* jungle.

Extraordinary as it may sound, we decided to try and travel on the forest canopy itself. This was painfully slow. We had to crawl along on the thick foliage, and there were holes to slip into and slide through, but it occurred to me that I was then, at that moment, a real primate. Most of the time we'd been 2m off the ground, but here we were on a carpet of green creepers and bamboo, and a whole lot of other photosynthesising stuff.

We stopped for a break where there was a view down to Kisoro. Zak looked across at me with a smile and raised both his hands up, with a slight lift of the shoulders. I think he'd taken a wrong turn. As a result, though I hadn't seen any gorillas, I'd got to live and travel like one.

We spent an exhausting hour trying to get out of this vegetable pit. We finally got to a gully of wild celery, where we were able to cut across to an elephant path. We could stand upright at last, and walk. It was such a relief.

The sun came out again, the rays slanting through the bamboo in long, friendly shafts. I was happy to be alive once more. Getting stuck under the canopy had been claustrophobic. Clambering over it had been profoundly unnerving. The elephant path, by contrast, seemed very hospitable.

We had both had enough. Once we made it down out of the forest, we stopped off at the local bar for some of the local brew. The locals were all armed with enamel bowls and half gourds of the revolting stuff. They were also dressed in old, tweed-style jackets, with long trousers rolled up to the knees. They had bright woolly hats but no shoes. While they chatted away, I looked up to Mt. Muhabura. The clouds were clearing, leaving a belt around its middle. The top was crisp and clear against the late afternoon sky. Somewhere up there were gorillas. I smiled.

Back at Zak's place, I washed my shoes. They were black from the peat-like bogs. My feet were given a gorgeous hot bath again. We had some dark, tender meat for dinner (I think it was goat) that tasted very strong, and I forgot to count how many kids were outside.

It was time to go to Rwanda. Sign language from Zak said I was guaranteed to see gorillas there. The walk to Kisoro was tiring once more, so I stopped for a break, lay on the grass, and become a magnet for kids. There were 11 of them. The smallest one was petrified.

Africa being the biggest small place in the world, I bumped into Michael in town, the chap I'd come over the Sudan border with. He was off to stay with Zak. I told him he'd need some warm clothes. We swapped stories, and we never saw each other again.

I checked into my usual hotel, where I plugged the holes in the walls with mashed paper to try and make it rat-proof. I failed. In the middle of the night, I woke up to find a big, grey one on my bedside table. We eyeballed each other in my torchlight before he made for the door, made himself super-thin, and somehow squeezed under it and away into the night.

The next day I went to the Catholic Mission and thanked the White Sisters for their help. I also met Bill, who gave me a letter of introduction to the white man who ran the gorilla sanctuary in Rwanda. And a Rwandan man gave me the contact details of a brother of his who lived near the park.

It was a long walk to the border. I checked with the chief of police that I didn't need any additional exit stamps. I hid my dollar cash and travellers cheques in a devious place – a secret pocket in my backpack that (almost) nobody ever found – and I set off. A customs official came along in a Land Rover, so I did the automatic thing and stuck out my thumb. He gave me a ride to the border post and disappeared.

Remembering that I had a currency declaration form, I was a bit nervous about the crossing. According to the form, I'd survived in Uganda for a month on $110. That probably wouldn't have stood up in court. I knocked on the door and there was no answer. I walked in to find it empty. There were two desks and two chairs but no Immigration officials. I looked around the back, but there was nobody. I shouted, 'Hello!' Still nothing.

So, I just walked across the no man's land without formally having left Uganda, and half expecting to get a bullet in my back. It felt like one of those Cold War exchanges. I wondered who'd blink first. Well, nobody blinked. In fact, nobody did anything.

And so I bid farewell to one of the most messed up countries of the early 1980s. I'd had the time of my life. As I left, I really wished the Ugandans good luck and much prosperity. They seemed a very decent people, well, except for the child soldiers in the north, and the politicians.

Chapter 9

Rwanda

The Rwandan officials were smartly dressed, with blinding white shirts. My schoolboy French had to be summoned out of my memory banks again as they questioned me about not having a Ugandan exit stamp. Technically, it appeared like I'd arrived from nowhere. After a knowing shrug of their shoulders, I was let in.

It's funny. After 100m of dusty road, a bit of barbed wire and a gate, it's a new country. A lot can change in 100m. French, not English. A little richer, not poor. Smartish, not rags. And a people who are miserable and sour, not some of the most joyful on the planet. As I walked past them they just stared at me. In Uganda they would have smiled, and the women might even have danced. I missed that. Rwanda's horror story was yet to come, but perhaps I saw the seeds.

There may be a bit of wisdom somewhere in here, to do with the poorer the country and the worse their problems the more massive their grins and the louder their laughter. There can be nothing more depressing, for example, than a commuter train in a rich city. And there can be no happier place than the top of a truck, hanging on for dear life, in a poor one. It made me think.

The border crossing was in the middle of nowhere. There was nowhere to change money and I decided not to ask the *Les Immigration* if they could change some dollars. I walked the first 4km to the nearest village. No smiles. I felt like an alien again. No, worse than an alien. I smiled at them and they gave me odd looks back. I felt like an idiot. What had the Belgians done to them?

At the village a pickup truck driver accepted a dollar note instead of 100 francs to take me to Ruhengeri, a muddy town that was the gateway to the Volcanoes National Park, and, hopefully my elusive gorillas. (Another traveller tip, 'Always have a few one dollar bills handy. They're not only useful for New York doormen, but also for Rwandan pickup truck drivers. The US maybe be waning somewhat, but I couldn't have done that with a yuan or a euro.')

I found the family of the Rwandan chap quite quickly. He took me to the Muhavara Hotel to get information about the gorillas. A Belgium lady at the front desk told me where to go to buy a ticket. I then found *le marche noir* and changed a few dollars at only a small premium over the bank rate (a sure sign the country was doing well). After that I had a meal of beans, cabbage, and rice. It was not much different from the gruel over the border. They also sold film openly in the shops that was not past its sell-by date. Wow. I stocked up on some tinned food. Sardines in oil, mainly. These vast shoals of little fish were what sustained me though some pretty rough culinary patches. A few of the small, tough tins were always a good investment. Sardines and rice, sardines and potatoes, even sardines and bananas. Then I'd have a decent meal.

Another pickup-truck took me to Kinigi village (another one of those 'K 'places). From there I could walk into the park.

Buying a ticket to get in proved to be complex though, or rather, it was organised. Unlike Uganda, where I'd just showed up at Zak's place and smiled, here I had to pay $25. And they only took it when I said I was a friend of the white chap who ran the centre. I was supposed to have made a reservation in Kigali, the capital.

It was another 15km to the base camp at Mt. Visoke, so I set off with my backpack. It was 4.30pm (a bit late). The walk was beautiful, but I was tired. Wearing a backpack tilts you forward, so you naturally face down towards the ground just in front of you. As a result, I didn't really notice that the track wound through pine forests and was very Scottish. Mt. Karasimbi, behind Mt. Visoke (the higher of the two at 4.5km) was actually snow-capped.

I played the Pied Piper again, this time to about 50 schoolchildren. The kids were the same as the Ugandan one. Kids are kids everywhere.

I sat down to rest my tormented stomach (peanuts again) and the kids sat down near me, keeping a wary eye out like antelope sharing a waterhole with a predator. If I moved to stand up (just for fun), they immediately scattered into the trees, shrieking and laughing with fear and delight. As the gorilla park was close by, and lots foreigners regularly came through, so the fear thing seemed to me a bit strange. I think the reason was that although plenty of foreigners went past in Land Cruisers or Land Rovers, there were precious few who walked. An adult came out of a hut to look, and they all huddled around me for protection. The fear thing was a game after all. Fun for them and fun for me.

Late-afternoon light is just the best. The sky was blue, and I now had three volcanoes like the ones I'd got to know in Uganda, their steep ridges crisply defined by the light and shade. I sat on a rock thinking how lovely they were to look at, and how bloody exhausting they were to climb.

A dour Yorkshireman in a large, droopy sweater, that his mum had knitted him (or so I guessed), ran the visitor centre. He was certainly not as friendly as Zak. Sullen would be how I'd describe him. Considering we came from the same country, it felt a bit strange. I'd actually been able to communicate better with Zak.

I had to pay to stay the night, though there were no rats. That was nice. It was cold, and my rubbish sleeping bag, with its pseudo baking foil lining, did me no good at all. It was close to zero and white plumes of water vapour arose from my nose. I found a grubby blanket to supplement my bag and tried to sleep again.

My white lie about being a friend of the white man who ran the centre began to unravel, as only a six people were allowed to visit a gorilla group at any one time. There were now five visitors, plus two guides, to see what was called Group Eleven. This was made up of the gorillas that were used to people. The problem was solved by splitting up the visitors into two groups. I went off with a Dutchman, who was also alone, to see Group Nine. Apparently Group Nine was the least used to human contact.

I bought a cute poster of a baby mountain gorilla, a map that explained some of the weird vegetation I'd seen in Uganda, and looked around at other information. Apparently, there were only 200 *Gorilla gorilla beringei* left in the Virunga area, though a recent check had reported an increased to over 1,000 now. Great news.

We got a ride in a Peugeot 504 up to the departure point. Luxury! Our two guides were armed with *pangas*, but they had no guns.

Thirty metres into the bush we came across some gorilla beds from the night before. Astonishing. Another 100m in we spotted movement in the foliage down below. Then a dog started to bark. The noise it made meant that when we got to the right spot, the gorillas were gone. The soft, olive-green poo that they'd left behind also showed that they were nervous. It seems pigmy hunters had been about, since they were the ones who used dogs.

Because the gorillas seemed scared, the guides decided to hunt the dog down first. After a lot of scrambling, hacking, and climbing, we found it. The guides only spoke French. *Enrage* seemed to be rabies. They cut long bamboo poles, with the tips at an angle, and cornered the howling, yelping hound with them. I can't say I saw it frothing at the mouth, but it was certainly going bonkers. It had wild eyes, and was thrashing about. This was dangerous stuff, so I moved back. After many unsuccessful jabs they managed to spear it. There was a long, final yelp and a moan, followed by silence.

The gorillas were still nervous. The wet shit index was very high, and after all, this group was the most wild. The guides weren't hopeful, but we pressed on anyway. Then the guides started to make low grunting noises. I immediately changed from being fed up and tired, to being lively and excited. We were close.

Then we spotted one at the end of a long corridor of vegetation. Was it really a gorilla or just a shadow? It moved. And then there it was. It was a female, about 8m from us. We crept slowly on through a thick wall of green. Then there was another female, sitting down, with a young one on her back. She stretched out a long arm to tear off some food. They both seemed somewhat nervous, perhaps because of the dog, and kept moving on. This was not one of those moments when people sit around with the gorillas like they're having a picnic in a park. They kept doing whatever they wanted to do. And we kept crawling after them.

We eventually saw seven females, and one silverback. I think the guides said they'd never seen them all together.

A silverback – a male – weighs about 200kg. Its job is to defend the whole group. Everything was very peaceful and domestic until the group's silverback turned. Then he hurtled through the bush towards us. His massive head, and long, muscular arms were swinging, and he was screaming and shrieking. He stopped 2m from us, shaking a clump of bamboo, and jumping up and down. He was clearly incensed. It was awesome, and it was fearsome, too. I was the nearest to him on the path. The guide pulled me down to the ground so that I'd look small and useless (easy). The silverback then sprang on to the path to confront us, face to face. We were a metre apart. At that point the silverback was resting on his knuckles. His arms were vast. His back was arched. And his head was held high.

The Silverback gorilla just before he charged and scared the bejesus out of me

He was breathing noisily through his big, black nostrils, pungent vegetable aromas poured out – silage breath. I was trying to shrink into the earth. He stared at the guide for a few seconds, and he stared at me as well. I don't speak gorilla, but I was pretty sure he was saying 'FUCK OFF'. Then he turned and sped off back to his family. They moved away again.

Wow. From that sudden display I could see why gorillas have a reputation for being ferocious. He moved so fast, and he was so incredibly strong. He didn't hurt us, though. He just wanted to scare us. It worked. He had.

I asked the guide if we could follow the gorillas a bit further. It seemed that one adrenaline rush hadn't been enough.

What happened next is still engraved in my mind.

There was a female to our right in a clearing. The sun was out. It was quite bright. Everything seemed very calm. I took a photo from about 8m of a silverback that was also sitting there.

Suddenly, there was explosion of energy. Foliage flew left and right as he hurtled towards me at extraordinary speed, his eyes glaring, his right arm swinging through the air parallel to the ground in a huge reaping motion that cut through the undergrowth like a scythe. He could literally have taken my head off. I could see my own death.

Again, the guide yanked me to the ground. The silverback screamed and kept closing fast, its mouth open, its teeth exposed. Everything happened very, very fast, and yet, seemed to take place in slow motion. It was all over in less time than it takes to read this sentence. At the last possible moment he swerved off to the right, crashed through the bushes. He sat down, invisible but present, grunting, and thumping his chest. The sound was hollow, like knocking on wood.

The whole thing was a blur. One second we were looking at domestic bliss in the sunshine. The next a massive lump of black-silver, hairy muscle was hurtling towards us. I didn't think he'd stop. Technically, he didn't stop. His movement had been precise, engineered, and perfect. He'd swerved at the absolute last moment, before he had to deal out death and destruction. At top speed, he'd sliced through the vegetation just a hand's breadth from me. It was surgical in its precision.

I was shaking like a leaf. The guides didn't look too happy either. And the Dutchman's face was as white as a sheet. Needlessly to say, we retreated. I wanted a cigarette, badly, but it wasn't possible. I just couldn't light it. The guide lit one for me but I just couldn't hold it. Even my lips felt out of control. As we moved off, we could still hear the silverback ripping the jungle to shreds.

On reflection, the entire episode was exceptional. The gorillas had been on edge because of the rabid dog. They were also not used to humans. The silverback had felt extraordinarily responsible for his family. He'd appeared to us to be in a fury, but his actual response, and his subsequent actions, had all been immaculately controlled. And they'd done their job. We had stopped disturbing the whole group.

What an outrageously powerful, beautiful, decent creature. At the time I'd been petrified, stunned, shaken. Only later did the magnificence of the beast, and the meaning of what had happened, sink in. I ultimately came to see that charge as a wonderful thing. Not only did the locals not shoot *khawajas*, but the gorillas were prepared to let us live as well.

I wrote a poem that night. Not exactly Phillip Larkin (a distant relative), but from my heart:

Obscured by thick foliage and tangled creepers, she sits,
Stretching out around the forest floor for food.
Her great form shrouds the small face of her child
Clinging to the soft warm hair of her broad back.
She turns her face slowly to the disturbing movement,
Leaves her food and disappears into the blackness.
The enormous old man sits.
Sunlight glistening on his silver back, he slowly turns.
The strong proud head of the protector looks on.
'Please leave us alone, please go, this is ours.'
In a flash he bursts through the bush, fast and unstoppable,
Screaming and shaking the bamboo close to the intrusion.
Bounding on to the jungle path, his torso resting on his knuckles,
Glaring into the small weak faces.
Bounding off, his beautiful form disappears.
But they cannot leave him to his peaceful life.
He tries again, hurtling through the bush closer and closer,
His great arm scything through the foliage,
So close to the stunned little faces, yet so controlled,
Swerving at the penultimate moment,
To avoid the simple carnage.
For his heart is bigger than that, so big.
A show of force without parallel, but he does not touch.
That beautiful gentle giant, that honourable beast.
Protecting his kin, yet refusing to harm another creature.
The power to destroy all, but with a blessed mind.
Pay no heed to us. Sit on the wet humus reaching for food.
Live well in your home. Prosper please.

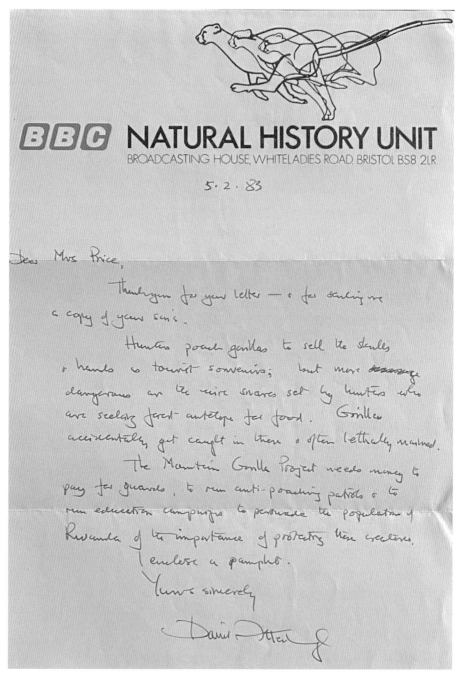

BBC NATURAL HISTORY UNIT

BROADCASTING HOUSE, WHITELADIES ROAD, BRISTOL BS8 2LR

5 · 2 · 83

Dear Mrs Price,

Thank you for your letter — & for sending me a copy of your son's.

Hunters poach gorillas to sell the skulls & hands as tourist souvenirs; but more dangerous are the wire snares set by hunters who are seeking forest antelope for food. Gorillas accidentally get caught in these & often lethally maimed.

The Mountain Gorilla Project needs money to pay for guards, to run anti-poaching patrols & to run education campaigns to persuade the population of Rwanda of the importance of protecting these creatures. I enclose a pamphlet.

Yours sincerely

David Attenborough

Look who took the trouble to write a proper letter to my Mum after my gorilla encounter.

We climbed down out of the jungle. The place was eerily quiet. No dog. No chest-thumping or screaming. My heart had calmed down. The sun was out on a meadow of wild celery. My head was light. I felt like I was walking on air.

We met up with the other visitors and they told us that they'd sat with their group of gorillas as if it was a scene with John Lennon and Yoko Ono. It had all been crossed-legged love and peace.

Then it started to rain, so the Dutchman and I decided to have a celebratory beer at the Muhabura Hotel. Once the rain stopped, it was back to reality. I left to find a cheap place to stay. As it turned out, there were rooms attached to the Catholic Mission that fitted the bill.

My insides were giving me real trouble again. I blamed the raw peanuts and the gluey bananas, but I suspect there were bacteria at work there as well. I woke up and rushed to the toilet, but I didn't make it. Pretty humiliating.

The base camp, Ruhengeri, was muddy, and the people were sullen, but I spent a couple more days there. My body and mind needed to take it easy for a bit. A 70-year-old Frenchman who used to be a merchant seaman showed up at the hostel. The last time I'd seen him was in Aswan, in southern Egypt. It seems it's never too late to be on the road.

Everything was damp, so I did a major wash. No matter how many times I rinsed my stuff, the water was never clean. I guess the dirt was ingrained. The air was very chilly and my clothes didn't really dry out until Tanzania.

When I say the Rwandans were sour compared to the Ugandans, I wonder if I wasn't somehow experiencing the growing tensions that resulted in the unimaginable genocide in 1994, when a large proportion of the Rwandan population was murdered. The killing was totally premeditated, and the world stood by and watched. It still makes me shudder.

When I moved on to Kigali, the rain came down in buckets, and the distinction between what was a road and what was a river became very blurred. The Chinese were trying to build a better one there, keeping one eye out for primary resources, but it was a quagmire Rwandans wandered around with arm-loads of dynamite, while giant, yellow, Caterpillar earth-movers shoved mud from one place to another and back again. We drove through the mess at a crawl.

In Kigali I tried to find the Anglican Mission on Avenue Paul VI, but I ended up at the Presbyterian one instead. It was cheap, and there were more travellers in my dorm than I'd seen in the whole of Uganda.

The best thing about the Belgium colonisers was that they'd left behind decent *boulangeries*. A *croissant au chocolat* sure beat boiled bananas with gristle and gravy.

The other great thing about Kigali was the postcards. There were plenty of shots of gorillas, and even ones of the strange, high-altitude vegetation. I bought lots and plastered them all over my diaries.

The European beer was expensive, so I resorted to the banana beer. I had to be back at the Catholic Mission by 7.30pm. Getting blotto on banana beer was also prohibited. So I didn't.

The problem with dormitories is that there are other people in them. In this case there was a guy who snored incredibly loudly. It reminded me of my gorilla, snorting away at the bottom of the hill. I still had my ear plugs from the Brent Delta oil rig. They came in very useful that night. One American guy was driven so crazy that he ended up sleeping out on the grass in the rain.

It was a two-day bus journey to Mwanza, on Lake Victoria, so I began to prep myself. I stocked up on Lomotil, and I bought some stuff called Diarsed. There's nothing worse than an involuntary bowel movement on a 48-hour bus trip. It's no way to make friends with others, or yourself.

The American guy who'd slept on the grass was called Steve. I travelled with for some time after that. He significantly broadened my literary universe by lending me *Hamlet* to supplement my battered copy of *King Lear*. A man carrying *Hamlet* though Africa was a man I could like.

We overdid it on the banana beer on the last evening, and had to scale the wall to get back into the Catholic Mission. The Belgium father caught us and gave us a good dressing-down. It was like being back at boarding school. We were trying not to laugh, but he was fuming.

The next day I walked to the British Embassy. This turned out to be way out of town in an industrial estate. I'd gone to find out what was happening in the Falklands War, but they didn't have any newspapers, and they only had one Brit on the staff. I suppose it was the ambassador, and he was away.

Chapter 10

Tanzania

The bus left at 9.30am, which was nearly on time, but we got to Mwanza a day late. As usual, the bus was full, and had loads of stuff on the roof.

The border between Rwanda and Tanzania was at the Rusomo Falls. The water cascaded down like thick, brown chocolate. The crossing itself was uneventful. As we approached it, though, almost all of the locals got off. We drove on, stopped for the night, and slept in the bus. At dawn we started up again, and by 9.30am we disappeared down a dirt track that looped back in the wrong direction. After an hour of bumping along, standing there in the middle of the road were our fellow passengers from the other side of the border. They clambered back on to the bus with their big bags and boxes. They'd clearly been through the bush. They were covered in scratches. They were muddy, dishevelled, and tired. They must have walked all night. What was going on? A Tanzanian called Mohamed explained. 'We didn't have passports. You did,' he said. And, 'We were smuggling. You weren't.' The latter was not entirely true if you included my secret stash of dollars, but it was simple really. I asked him what he was smuggling, and he showed me a shoulder bag full of Kodak film – those neat little yellow boxes that have now become extinct. He had more on the roof. This explained why the Tanzanian shops were better provisioned than I'd expected. Human ingenuity.

We came to a bridge that had partially collapsed. Its wooden legs were rotted and twisted. Everyone got everything off the bus so the driver could rev it up.

He then launched it into a flying leap in a bid to get it across. He actually made it. We all piled back on once more. It was this detour that caused the extra day of travel.

After that, the road turned to red clay. It was like a long, thin, French Open tennis court, snaking away into the distance. The driver rejoined the main road at a different point and headed towards Lake Victoria. The land was flatter and sparser than Rwanda. It was more like savannah, though we saw no wildlife. The air was also dryer, which was good, given how dank and musty my clothes were. After various crossings by ferries across the fingers of Lake Victoria, and various mechanical problems, we finally pulled in to Mwanza.

Steve and I end up at the Farahah Guest House, which was an Iqbal-like place with a big roof terrace. This was the main communal spot. Quite a bit of dope was smoked up there.

I needed to do some business. The discrepancy between the government rate of and the black-market rate made it inevitable. The government was having a crackdown, though, so nobody was offering. I could usually walk into a town and find what I wanted in ten minutes. Not in Tanzania. I changed $50 at the Mwanza Hotel at the official rate in order to satisfy the currency declaration form, and as the clerk wasn't paying attention, I put on a rubber stamp that let me fill in the details later.

I could not find the black market, so tracked down Mohamed. I gave him $100 and he said he would do his best. Never, ever just give someone money like that! It was madness.

Steve and I went for a leisurely stroll. The town was on a lake, but we couldn't see it.

We walked up a small hill to a shack at the top. As we got near it, we could see bits of cloth waving around an artillery barrel. The bits of cloth were camouflage.

Then all hell broke loose as a platoon of soldiers arrived, shouting, jabbing at us with their rifles, and generally being rather nasty. They didn't speak much English, but the words 'spy' and 'Uganda' were easy enough to understand. Our bags were emptied, and there was more rifle-jabbing. It felt even more threatening than northern Uganda.

To put this in context, they'd only stopped fighting the Amin regime three years before. The place was still in turmoil, and the army was still on the alert. An artillery round wouldn't have reached Uganda, which meant it was probably aimed at the lake. (I couldn't imagine the Ugandan navy being much of a threat.) Now was not the time for logic, though. Now was the time for, 'Yes sir, no sir, very sorry sir, tourist, tourist, tourist.'

We didn't seem to be getting very far with the humble approach, so Steve pulled out his trump card. He showed them his American passport. The soldiers could see he hadn't even been to Uganda.

This worked work for him, but not for me. I was sure they couldn't read very well, but flicking through the pages of my passport they found I'd been to Uganda twice in the last few weeks. And according to the stamps, I'd never left. 'SPY, SPY, SPY,' they cried. There was more poking about with their AK-47s. They were in a circle with us in the middle, pushing us around, not too seriously, but we did feel pretty helpless, and at the same time, angry. US dollars and Tanzanian shillings from my backpack were mingled in the dust. My Swiss Army knife also attracted a lot of attention. They must have thought it was part of my James Bond kit. My Pentax was in the dust as well, along with its guilty-looking accomplice, my crap, bloody heavy zoom lens. They spent some time fingering my small electric alarm clock. What, they obviously thought, did I plan to do with that? Then their thespian skills came to the fore. Two of them acted out a firing squad. One stood with his eyes closed and his hands behind his back. The other lined up the sights of his rifle and said 'bang'. It sounds silly, but it felt pretty real. Another one took up a karate stance as if to imply they might execute us using martial arts. This had Steve and I rolling about on the roof of the hotel later on (helped by some dope).

We were strip-searched, and they actually found the inside pocket of my trousers. This revealed a small, smelly, plastic bag, containing another roll of greenbacks. This seemed to be more evidence that I was a spy. One of them spent much longer than necessary searching my genitals. I put this down later to local curiosity about the foreigner's dick. I was wearing a hat, and they knocked this off. The situation was becoming very volatile, though Steve remained super-mellow. He was never one to pick a fight. All the time I was running through various scenarios in my mind. The minimum, I thought, was that we'd lose our stuff. Though I was quite battle-hardened by this stage of my trip, I was shaking, and my heart was thumping. These soldiers didn't seem to have the hardwired good nature of the silverback.

One of them seemed to be slightly more senior than the rest. He finally told us to put everything back into our bags, and we were led off down the hill to their

The only photo I have of my essential piece of kit, my Berghaus backpack (about 12kg) and my Pentax camera case.

camp. We then had to explain everything again to a guy who turned out to be a sergeant. He asked if we'd taken any photos. The honest answer was no. The sergeant then wanted to take the film out of the cameras. He wasn't stupid. So, we asked him to ask if the soldiers had seen us with our cameras out. They said no, too.

The sergeant led us back up the hill and pointed to a sign which, in our defence, was facing away from us. He twisted it towards the road to make it more visible.

We kept apologising, but it seemed that the crisis was over. We told him we needed to meet someone at 5.30pm, and asked to leave. We finally walked off briskly having learned that even *khawajas* accused of espionage don't get shot. They did rough us up a bit, and they did make us feel scared. But that was fair enough.

Looking over our shoulders we saw that one of the soldiers was following us. We took him on an extended tour of Mwanza before getting back to the Farahah. On the roof, a few other travellers were smoking. We told them to chuck the stuff over the side.

Then all of the other soldiers showed up. It was the sergeant. He asked us for our home addresses, and our next destination, and why we'd tried to lose the man tailing us. 'We were lost,' we said. 'We couldn't find our hotel.' Which sounded rather lame, even to us.

Then Mohamed, the film-smuggler from the bus, showed up. That was all we needed. He cottoned on pretty quickly, though, and started talking in rapid Swahili. We could see the sergeant was becoming deferential. He eventually apologised for our trouble, and left.

I was totally confused. Who was Mohamed? 'Ah,' he said. 'I used to be a senior officer in the Mwanza police force. Unless you take bribes, your salary is almost zero. That's why I prefer smuggling. I still have a lot of friends there, though.' Jesus Christ.

Steve and I went out for a drink and I had a large gin and tonic. The interrogation and the aggressiveness had gotten to me. I'd been totally drained by the combination of the gorillas, the long bus trip, and the spy saga.

Back in my room I read *Hamlet* by candlelight to put things into perspective. There was electricity, but the Tanzanian socialists had forgotten to put in any bulbs. I set the fan at its highest setting to try and pin the mosquitoes to the walls, which made it rattle wildly. I fell into a deep sleep and woke up to a cockroach invasion in the pitch-black night. The little bastards were scampering all over the bed. There was not much I could do but turn over, close my eyes, and not sleep with my mouth open.

What with all the hassles, Steve and I decided to leave town, and to change our plans from taking the train to going on a safari. We negotiated a deal with a driver to take us through to the Serengeti for four days. Sylvester showed up at 5.45am, which was 15 minutes late, but massively early by local standards. We then thundered down the dirt roads, dust flying out the side of his long wheelbase Land Rover. Steve and I were in the back. There were nine of us, so it was cramped. There was also a big drum of extra fuel on the roof that leaked. The smell was nauseating.

We came to the Serengeti via the Ikoma Fort entrance. Serengeti means 'endless plains', which is about right. It was much more than that, though. It was a massive ecosystem. A vast world of diversified nature. There were rolling hills that led on to a flatness that extended as far as we could see.

This was big sky country. The clouds raced around in their blue home, white and fluffy and sometimes ominous. Some were cotton wool, and some were black with rain. They create a mottled pattern on the land that seemed to shift it and stretch it all the time.

The land itself was packed with wildlife. There were zebra, wildebeest, warthog, impala, Grants gazelles, Thompsons gazelles, giraffe, ostrich, water buck, absurd-looking ostriches, tiny dik-dik, mongoose, baboons, vervet monkeys, and my old adversary, the dark buffalo. Vultures perched in dead trees. There were no lions, elephants, or rhinos, but there was an extraordinary profusion of every other

Serengeti entrance, thanks Steve.

animal. I didn't see any migrating, but there were such a vast number of them that it looked like a migration. Sylvester was pretty clear that this was normal. Apparently, migration is a recent phenomenon caused by a massive increase in the number of wildebeest. They'd dropped to about a quarter of a million due to disease, but they were now up to over 1.25 million. They had to move to find food.

We arrived at Lobo Lodge to the north. It recently got a poor review on TripAdvisor because a hairdryer didn't work. Who needs a hair dryer on safari, in one of the most magical places on earth? Did Hemingway use a hairdryer? Sylvester said the Masai wash their hair in cows` urine to bleach it, and to ward off the flies. They don't use a hairdryer.

The Lobo Lodge setting was amazing. It was built into a rock formation, and had huge, plate-glass windows that looked out over the plains. It was luxury for me. No cockroaches. No vile rats.

We set off for a pre-dinner safari with my head poking out of the top of the Land Rover, looking for wildlife. In Uganda I got excited when we saw five buffalo. Here we saw a herd of 100. The others hadn't seen elephants before, so there was an uproar when we spotted a herd of about 40 or 50. They had cute, baby jumbos with them as well. The biggest thrill for me, though, was seeing a pride of lions in the long, green and khaki grass, their faces covered in blood, and with flies all over them.

The clouds were changing from grey to ink black so we raced back to the lodge to beat the watery onslaught. The lodge dinner was excellent. Thankfully, there were NO BANANAS.

The next day we saw herds of wildebeest again, mixed with zebra. They surged around the vehicle like a river in flood, kicking up the dust, with their heads held low. Some stopped and stared, looking very stupid.

The whole vista was once more enormous. There was a lioness under an acacia tree; jackals that walked confidently among the black buffalo; a family of bat-eared foxes; secretary birds that ran and ran before finally taking off; and hyenas that stalked the plains close to the Thompson gazelles. Impala floated through the air in slow motion as they leapt across the dry water courses. Small birds, red, blue, and yellow, flashed through the trees. Hippos snorted, submerging and rising, submerging and rising, in the dirty brown pools. Sharp-nosed baboons bounded off into the undergrowth. Vultures circled always on the lookout. And giraffes munched on acacia thorns, some oblivious, others with their legs split wide, in ungainly yoga poses, as they stretched for the grass far below.

Olduvai gorge was just outside the park. Preserved there were layers of human history, right back to before we were even human. There wasn't much to see, but I closed my eyes, and thought about the ancient humanoids who'd made the decision to chance it on the plains by standing upright, learning to use fire and flint stones, surviving, thriving, and spreading out until they'd covered the whole world. Unfortunately, we only spent a few minutes looking down at millions of years of the pre-history of our species. What could compete with lions and elephants?

It's the Masai and their cattle that share the place with the wildlife these days. The Masai are proud and tall, dress in simple red and brown cloaks, and carry spears (not threatening). They also wear brilliant tribal jewellery that consists of intricately woven blue beads, an example of which I wore around my ankle until I got to South Africa. I still have it.

The Land Rover climbed up, its diesel engine straining under the weight of nine adults. At 2km the grass was greener, and the air was cooler. It was perfect. There were meadows of yellow flowers, and lots of zebra, but the wildebeest seemed to have been left behind.

Olduvai Gorge, our ancestors, Homo habilis lived here 1,500,000 years ago. It`s a special place, not necessarily portrayed in my over exposed photo.

Sylvester stopped the vehicle at the lip of Ngorongoro. It used to be a massive volcano. Imagine an explosion big enough to leave a caldera 15km wide and 600m deep. It was packed with wildlife. The lake had a milky way of flamingos on it, though we couldn't see anything in detail. We only had one cranky old pair of binoculars between the nine of us. Clouds drifted across the crater, the sunny parts catching the lake, the plains, and the dark green forests on the other side.

We checked into the Ngorongoro Crater Lodge for the night. It was an amazing mish-mash of different styles. Imagine a posh African hut meeting Louis XIV of France, with zebra skins, and ornate gilt edging.

In the morning we found ourselves in swirling clouds. Our safari became an impersonation of misty Scotland again.

As we descended the steep track to the crater bottom there was light rain on the windshield. We were slipping and sliding, but Sylvester seemed to know what he was doing. We passed rainforest vegetation, and a micro stratum of huge, cactus-like plants. One moment we were in clouds, and the next the crater would open up before us. Despite all the slithering, we managed to get to the bottom in one piece.

The lake was a soft, pink haze of bird biomass. The flamingos were elegance incarnate on their slender legs – both the males one and the female ones. Sylvester pulled up by a dead wildebeest. They're quite large, cow-like creatures, but all that was left of this one was a dark-red ribcage and a horned head with the juicy, middle bits sucked out. Three female lions and a big male were lolling about, with the rest of the wildebeest making its way through their digestive systems. Their faces were caked in wildebeest blood. Another male appeared out of the grass and snarled at us. (It's sometimes good to be in a Land Rover, and not wandering around the bush in a pair of plastic sandals.) Its eyes were deep yellow, and they had penetrating black slits in them. We were close enough to really see him. The

Ngorongoro lion feast.

Gorgeous flamingos.

place was swarming with flies, which was disgusting. It also seemed to annoy the lion, though post-snarl he flopped down on to the mud and fell asleep.

As the morning passed, the clouds lifted, and we could see up the rim to the other side. There were patches of rain that looked like pencils lines coming out of the heavy, low clouds, peppering parts of the crater plain at random.

Another pride of lions occupied a kind of raised mud platform. A jumble of

Ngorongoro crater by Steve - just after the worst fart ever.

cubs rolled around them, flapping at each other with their cuddly toy paws. The reality of their future lives was caked around the adults' mouths, though. Dried blood.

As we approached the lake itself, the mass of pink became actual individual flamingos. They looked like cherry blossoms and candy floss on black sticks. It all seemed so at odds with the bloody remains of the wildebeest carcass.

I destroyed the atmosphere (literally) by passing some highly noxious wind. The Swiss passengers in particular were not amused. Apparently, the Swiss don't fart. My guess is they do, but they store them in numbered bank accounts.

We moved on in search of a black rhino, passing beautiful, grey-crowned cranes, which I personally liked better than the flamingos. The black rhino is a very odd animal. It has a weird, hooked lip, a gigantic head, and tiny eyes. It looks all wrong, and it doesn't have knees. It's a solitary animal that seems rather sad, like an armour-plated Eeyore. We found one grazing under an acacia tree. Biology books say they're mammals, but they look like dinosaurs. I think that's why they look lonely. All their mates died out 50 million years ago. Through the long grass we saw a couple with their baby. The young one started to charge us, but thought better of it, and hid behind its parents. The black rhino is much more aggressive than its white cousin. Even this little one, which was about the size of a German shepherd, wanted to attack a long wheelbase Land Rover.

As silly as it sounds, we only spent a few hours in the crater, as we had to get to Lake Manyara Park to be there for the whole of the next day. After that, it was on to Arusha, where we were to become poor travellers again.

Ngorongoro - a majestic rhino, you can see the crater rim, the crater is about 18km wide and covers about 260km².

The Land Rover roared and slid as we climbed up out of the crater. We passed through Masai villages after that, where the women wore their amazing necklaces, and the immaculate men stood aloof with their spears. The rain in the distance produced a spectacular double rainbow across the massive, grey, water-laden skies. Everyone was smiling and laughing, even the Swiss.

In the evening I managed to defend myself against the aggressive and amorous advances of the voluptuous lady who owned and ran the hotel. Apart from a few scientists, nobody had heard of AIDS. Perhaps my bashfulness was fortuitous.

I'd never heard of Lake Manyara Park. It turned out to be excellent. On one side was one wall of the Rift Valley, and on the other was the lake itself. It was cherry-blossom pink.

There were lots of pelicans, yellow-billed storks, cormorants, egrets, Malabu storks, Egyptian geese, Ruppell's griffin vultures, and more that had names I didn't know. It was like watching competing aircraft manufacturers buzz the lake at an all-natural air-show.

The highlight was being vertically separated two meters from a lioness, as she lay drooped directly above us across the branches of a tree. Monitor lizards about

Generally not wise to park directly under a lioness. A bit of a Darwin prize moment.

the size of small crocodiles scuttled ahead, running sideways through a swamp. A family of mongooses shot off up a dry river bed as we approached. We saw

"I'm a bit deaf, what did that skinny white guy just say".

hundreds and hundreds of baboons. And there were baby elephants, with their tiny horns, playing with each other.

Everything was intermingled. Behind us was an acacia tree where a couple of graceful giraffes looked over at us with their Elizabeth Taylor eyelashes. It was a bit of a leap, but it made me think of the Star Wars bar, where the creatures were all different, and humanly quarrelsome, but they were all there together. Lake Manyara was about harmony – unless one of the predators happened to be genuinely hungry. There was no gratuitous violence, unlike our species.

Out on the vast plain there was a single wildebeest. It was looking around bewildered. Wildebeest are not very good at being solitary. I imagined a cartoon with a lone wildebeest saying 'Why me?' just before he enters the digestive tract.

That day I had my first introduction to the baobab tree, with its strange, stubby branches, poking out like a bad drawing. They became more and more prevalent as I got deeper into Zambia and Malawi.

The Masai did impress me. They wore lots of cool earnings that hung from loops of flesh below their ears, and the women's tunics came down to below their knees (the men's ones ended above them). The weapon of choice was a spear, but some had sticks with hefty knobs on the end for whacking things with. Perhaps their cattle. They all carried a long, thin staff. The women made the guys look dull, with their shaved heads, and their beaded jewellery. Their necklaces in particular were superb. They were made of rings of bright beads – blue, red, green, white, and orange – and there were even white shells. This was odd, as we were hundreds of kilometres from the sea.

I attempted a few more lines of poetry:

The Plains of Africa
...but what do our Olduvai ancestors think?
Or our children? Ashamed and let down.
The fate of man is also interred within these spaces.
Do not try to share this place.
They do not need us. We are fatal.
When that dust has long settled,
Pictures and stories are no inheritance.

I just love African bus stations.

Steve and I took the bus from the appropriately named MtoWaMbu (Mosquito) Creek, at the top of Lake Manyara, to Arusha. A boy and girl Masai, both in their teens, were riding on the bus as well. We couldn't understand a word they said, but they chatted and laughed a lot. They got off at different stops, which suggested they were just friends.

The New Continental Hotel in Arusha was not very new, though Arusha itself had good food. The curries were getting better as we got closer to the coast. It was muddy and raining, so I concentrated on buying postcards of wildlife.

Steve and I had been talking about climbing Kilimanjaro. At nearly 6km it jumps straight out of the plains. Imagine a ladder that goes nearly vertical for nearly 6km. There are a few theories about the name. The local Chagga expression, *kile-lema-irho*, apparently means 'We failed to climb it', which just about sums it up for me. I really needed the Chagga for, 'I didn't even try'. I'd seen it hitchhiking in Kenya, standing on the road side and waiting to be recognised by a trucker I'd last seen in Juba. I couldn't even see the peak, and I was tired, sick and weak. Steve was keen, but I pulled out. There aren't many things on my travels I didn't do, and I still wonder if this time I made the right call, but clambering over the Virungas with the bionic Zak had made me wary of volcanoes. The Virungas were also pimples by comparison.

Before I stop talking about the Serengeti, I should mention the documentary *Serengeti Shall Not Die* by Bernhard and Michael Grzimek. As they say, 'Neither today, nor tomorrow, but in three or four generations' time, when Bolshevism and capitalism have long been forgotten … many people may be glad that during our era, someone gave a thought to the wild animals of Africa. Most national and political; ambitions for which people suffer, are transient. But nature is of an abiding importance to us all … Political anxieties and hates will only have an existence in history books, but men will still consider it important that wildebeest should roam across the plains and leopards growl at night. It will matter all the more if human beings are increasingly condemned to live in soulless concrete cities … When 50 years from now, a lion walks into the red dawn and roars resoundingly, it will mean something to people and quicken their hearts. They will stand in awe as, for the first time in their lives they watch 20,000 zebras wandering across the endless plains.'

As to the relative merits of having the Masai share the park with the animals, their book quotes a Masai elder, 'If we move out, the other tribes will move in, with their poisoned arrows and snares. They dare not enter our lands now for they know we would chase them off like dogs. We let the wild animals live in peace.' The Masai abhor the meat of any animal other than their own cattle. Apparently the Masai came originally from Egypt. They believe in a rain god, and that there's no afterlife. Sounds sensible to me.

Despite the delights of Arusha, It was time to move on. The rains had abated, and everything was beginning to get dusty again. I was on the night bus to Dar es Salaam, and not looking forward to arriving. I'd heard lots of bad stories about the robberies and muggings there. I'd also just bumped into Donna and Ian (last seen in Wau in the southern Sudan) and they'd had almost everything stolen there. They were on their way back to the UK.

On the upside, I was looking forward to getting for mail from home at the Dar Post Office, as well as getting some hard currency out of the banks, and posting some trinkets home to lighten my load.

I have to admit I was getting a bit tired of travelling. It was the constant looking for hotels, and buses, and trains, and edible calories, that was starting to bug me. I'd been going for eight months, and pressure from the lack of stability, the discomfort, and all the other problems, was beginning to build. Everyone has a limit to their endurance.

The proud Masai

Mt. Kilimanjaro put in an appearance from the bus as we bounced along. When the sun finally dipped below the horizon, the purple dark sky took its place, but the mountain continued to stand out to the west as a great black silhouette, with streaks of deep orange, red, yellow, and indigo on its sides. The stars came out, and the road degenerated into a series of potholes, which made sleep difficult. Classic understatement. Sleep became impossible.

We pulled in for a break and two British Leyland buses did likewise. They were splattered with dried mud that was different shades of brown, like a Jackson Pollock painting. Naked lightbulbs hung from the stalls (so that's where they all went). We were near the sea now, the humidity was high, and sweat glistened off the black faces (mine was the only white one). Capitalism was represented by the Shell and Caltex petrol signs, glowing with electricity. Insects zipped around the bare lights before diving in and burning up. Large moths flapped after them. The sky above was crammed with stars. Crude wheelbarrows were piled high with oranges that were still green, and boys with sharp knives peeled them expertly in a few seconds, the peel cascading down. There was a disproportionate number of people selling toothpaste and toothbrushes, too. Either oral hygiene had suddenly become popular, or the socialist production process had stuffed up (again?). A small, rickety wooden table was piled with packets of Sportsman cigarettes, and bars of Cussons Imperial Leather and Lux soap. Grey smoke poured from the kebabs sizzling on oil drums cut in half. Men stood around eating the rich-smelling meat, wrapped in old newspaper, the grease splattering on the dusty ground. A boy walked around selling single cigarettes. (Now, that's a way to control smoking. Allow the sale of only one at a time.) A Muslim man sat cross legged on a mat in a white shirt and a skull cap, selling small bundles of green shoots. The purchaser was supposed to strip away the outer leaves, and chew on the rest. It was a mild amphetamine, though it didn't work for me. It completely dried my mouth out.

A couple of young Masai wandered through the throng. They looked like young Greek gods, with their perfect posture, their tunics, and their spears held like an extension of their long, lithe bodies. Next to the cheap, western clothes, with their overly large collars, and bellbottom trousers, they really did look like emissaries from Olympus. I wandered around on high alert, very aware of my pockets, and mind-sizing the nefarious motives of everyone around me. Reggae thumped out from one of the restaurants, where the customers were shouting and laughing. Its breeze-block walls were covered in bright paintings of wildlife from the savannah – zebra, lion, giraffe, impala. Oh, and kangaroos.

Then the diesel engines roared back into life, and the place emptied in a few seconds. The stopover was left to the night and the stars, until the next bus arrived, its twin beams promising another 20 minutes of frenetic commerce.

I had trouble finding a room in Dar so I ended up splashing out on a single room at the Y. This was a luxury for me. The post office produced a treasure trove from home, as well as letters from Cookie and Betsy. Mum spent a lot of time explaining the new, one way traffic system in Dorking. It must be difficult to know what to say to a son who's just written to you about being charged by an elephant in Uganda. Dad's letter was mainly a furious diatribe against the Argentinians. I went to all the banks, but I couldn't get any hard currency. Damn. I hoped it'd be easier in Zambia, which was the next country along.

I didn't get robbed in Dar. In fact, the only thing I could think to say about it was that it had more air-conditioning that I'd expected. It was a sort of dulled-down version of Mombasa, on the coast of Kenya.

Chapter 11

Malawi, Zambia and Zimbabwe

I was looking for a change, but I wasn't quite ready to jump on a plane and go home. The solution came in the form of two Germans – Frank (known as Maggie, though I called him Zappa), who had very long hair and a moustache, and his rather more shorn travelling companion, Martin. They'd come overland from Europe. The third and most critical member of their team was a 14-year-old long-wheelbase Land Rover. This magnificent vehicle, decked out with several appropriately named jerry cans along its sides and on the roof (20 in all), plus spare tyres, aluminium sand ladders, water containers, and tents, was no African virgin, since this was their fourth trip together. It did look great. It had a special air filter coming out of the bonnet, and its lights were protected by heavy-duty wire mesh. It was the real, transcontinental McCoy. What's more, though I've always had trouble myself telling the difference between a camshaft and a carburettor, Frank was a magic mechanic. There was just room for three in the front. It was crowded, so I crafted myself a space on the roof. It felt like being atop one of those machines in *Mad Max*.

We agree that I could ride along with them if I shared the petrol costs and other expenses. For me, it was perfect. I got a break from overnight bus rides, cockroach-infested hotels, dodgy food, and the constant change and uncertainty. And I got the chance to spend more time in the bush. Part of the deal was that I be a mediator, though. Frank and Martin had been on the road for months, and were crawling up the walls.

The deal was open ended in that we talked about seeing just Zambia together, but we actually carried on until South Africa. We traversed the Kalahari and the Namib deserts along the way, and we visited the Okavango swamps, all of which would have been pretty impossible by bus or hitchhiking.

We set off, hurtling down the dirt road with plumes of dust flying out behind us, the occasional vulture in the air, and the wide blue sky above. We were on the Trans African Highway. This was supposed to be a paved road, that extended all the way from Nairobi to Cape Town, but my reference to 'plumes of dust' was more like the reality.

In the late afternoon we found a place to camp. Night came fast and we had to prepare quickly. I was mainly in charge of the fire. I also did some cooking. The air was pungent with the sweet-smoke smell of dope, and there was real coffee brewing on the coals. As the sun set, the Rolling Stones blasted out of the cassette player, powered by the Land Rover battery. The stars were so bright I felt like reaching up and grabbing them. The fire licked up between three well-positioned rocks that I'd found, and I thought to myself, 'What more could a chap ask for?' It felt perfect.

At night I slept like a log, sometimes in the tent and sometimes under the stars. I had trouble waking up in the morning. I was desperately tired, and that very much needed addressing. The only other concern was my stomach, which was still in a rather dire state. It was another reason why Frank and Martin were not against me riding on the roof.

We drove through the Mikumi National Park in southern Tanzania, where we saw elephant, wildebeest, impala, zebra, and buffalo. Michelin maps mark the scenic roads in green. We were driving along one of these. It was a long, thin valley, perhaps part of the Rift Valley. We only stopped in Iringa, in the southern highlands, where there were lots of Land Rovers, and we could get original spare parts, copies of parts, and cannibalised ones. Frank was an expert in buying what we needed. We also loaded up on fuel, which meant buying more than 500 litres. This was a lot, given that a regular tank only held about 80.

I dispensed with my shoes for most of the rest of the trip. I was determined to indigenise my feet. This resulted, as I said earlier, in me getting a large, black thorn stuck in my instep. It was about a centimetre long, and it didn't exit until Johannesburg. Somehow it found its way through to my heel, and passed out beside my achilles tendon. Very strange.

As chief fire-builder, I was responsible for making the hearth. Lifting up a suitable rock, I found a small white scorpion clinging to the back of it. I should have thrown it away, or at least put it down, but the scorpion just sat there. I gently shifted it off with a stick. My dad had told me that in the Second World War, when he was posted to West Africa, they'd had vicious black ones as big as my hand. They used to douse them with petrol. I let my little fellow go.

The Stones tape had finished, so we switched to the Doors. It was night-time again. The fire was roaring, and we piled on even more wood. Sparks flew up into the blackness like fireworks.

My first border was coming up in the Land Rover. We were going to pass through Zambia and into Malawi. Border crossings were more complicated when there was a vehicle involved. There were official documents to complete, and all sorts of inspections. This meant more opportunities for graft, and more money. There were the currency declaration forms, too, with their smudges, and all the creative mathematics that was meant to balance the books. If it went wrong, and we were searched carefully, we all had a lot to lose. My substantial amount of under-declared dollars was only part of it.

The Tanzanians let us out easily. The Zambians letting us in were more difficult. The first issue was something about paying four *kwachas* in car insurance. We didn't have any *kwacha*. In the end we paid with two-dollar bills. They then asked why we had dollar bills when we'd said in our currency declaration forms that we had no cash, only travellers cheques. This cost us another 20 deutschmarks to resolve (paid – you guessed it – in cash!) They then came out to inspect the vehicle which, as described, was piled high. The senior guy said if we were smuggling something it would take them all today, and all tomorrow, to check it. So, they sent us on our way.

This had all taken longer than we'd expected. It meant we weren't about to get to Malawi before nightfall. So, we stopped for the night just off the road on an expanse of dry mud in the middle of nowhere. We were at a relatively high altitude, and it was cold. The wood was damp, and I had trouble discharging my duties as chief fire-builder. A splash of petrol did the trick.

As darkness came there was the slight cracking noise of a twig breaking. Something was stealthily stalking us. Our eyes were accustomed to the fire, so we stared into the blackness of the African night and waited for them to adjust. Gradually, the whites of about ten other pairs of eyes came out of the

Not so shy kids.

gloom. The silhouettes of ten bodies appeared as well. We were surrounded, and we were outnumbered, three to one. Finally, ten scrawny, smiling kids edged closer as they built up confidence. It was cold, and they were all in ragged T-shirts and shorts, with their bellies sticking out. Big smiles erupted as we beckoned them to come closer, and gave them some of our food. The eldest kid was 12. Though he lived in a village in the middle of nowhere, he somehow spoke better English than Frank and Martin – a point I made to them at the time. The kids saw that our fire was a bit miserable, so they went and brought more combustible wood than I'd been able to find. Then the chief of the village showed up, but he only wanted to cadge a cigarette before going away. We talked to the kids until the 12-year-old said it was time for them to go to bed. In the morning they returned with a few of their well-endowed mums. I took a photo of them silhouetted against the sky, standing on a mound of red earth. It was a top shot.

The Zambian exit point into Malawi was a mud-hut affair. They asked us for magazines. At first, we thought this was the Zambian code word for a bribe, but it turned out they really wanted magazines – on reflection, probably of a pornographic nature, but they got *Der Spiegel* instead, with a long interview with politician Willi Brandt – in German.

The Malawi entry point was at Chipata, and was predictably bizarre. We knew it would be, so we were getting quite excited. They were very friendly, but they asked Frank, 'Why do you have your hair like a woman?' They had pierced ears, but we didn't say anything about them; long-haired hippies weren't allowed into Malawi so I sat Frank down, with a smile and a laugh, and set to work removing his Frank Zappa locks. My first attempt wasn't sufficient for Malawi's Anti-Hippy police. I was forced me to lop off even more.

Back in the Land Rover, our German Samson was laughing. We wondered how they thought that cutting someone's hair would stop them being a hippy. I should mention that by then we'd started calling Martin 'Sporty', probably because he wasn't. When it came to joke time, it was usually Chris and 'Maggie' baiting 'Sporty'.

Many had told us that Malawi was a conservative country, but we found it to be full of friendly people who'd drop whatever they were carrying to wave wildly at us as we drove passed. They'd jump up and down, and smile broadly, at the slightest provocation. And the women would dance, whether there was music there or not.

Local people with small budgets to build with usually went beyond making mud huts, to using concrete breeze blocks. And so did the Malawians. In line with their happy dispositions, though, they didn't leave them a miserable grey. They painted them with extremely exuberant images that were very, very cheerful.

We were aiming for Lake Malawi – the third largest in Africa. It was part of the Rift Valley. Some of the roads were amazing. They had the hairpins and zigzags there are in Switzerland.

In the town of Karanga (the 'K' sounded to me like I was back in Uganda) I had the odd experience of going to a bank and cashing a traveller's cheque. They didn't have a black market, which suggested they were doing reasonably well too. It was strange, but also good, not to have to muck about with currency declaration forms.

The shops also had things in them. This was both positive and negative. The upside was that Frank could buy white flour. He claimed to be able to make the best *chapatis* in the world. The downside was that we ended up buying stuff. The cool thing about much of Africa was that we hardly spent any money, not just because their stuff was cheap, but because there was nothing to buy – unless we wanted more bananas, or a sachet of washing powder, or a toy bicycle made out of a coat hanger. I later found another downside in that German hippies don't make good *chapatis*. They also burn lot of them.

We tried to find a place to hang out for a few days that was by the lake, free of bilharzia, relatively free of mosquitos, and peaceful. Bilharzia are evil little snail-like things that climb inside you and give you schistosomiasis, which Wikipedia says is the second most devastating parasitic disease after malaria. They live in muddy, freshwater areas, so we looked for a sandy shore.

We found Nykuta Bay, about a kilometre from a village, down an outrageously bad road (Frank's vehicle was one the few that could make it). The cove beach was rough and sandy. The water was crystal-clear and warm, and free of salt and chlorine. This was not an easy combination to find. There was a stiff onshore breeze most of the time, that helped keep the mosquitoes at bay, and the temperature was perfect. It seemed to be free from crocodiles, and since it shelved quickly, there were no hippos.

The kids from the village collected firewood for us for a few cents. We'd wander over there from time to time for a beer. We'd sit in the sun with the locals and laugh, and admire their murals. A partial list of some of them would read lions, elephants, people dancing, huge malaria tablets, Coca-Cola bottles, Carlsberg beer bottles, toothpaste, de-worming tablets, and sunset over the lake.

My Land Rover companions, Martin (L) and Frank (R), at a cheerful café, some R&R from travelling.

We shared our camp with a majestic fish eagle that sat in a bare-branched tree about 80m from us. He'd soar out over the lake, occasionally swooping down into the blue waters, the air rushing over his jagged wing tips. Small monkeys came out on to the beach from time to time, and he delighted in diving towards them at high speed, causing them to flee left and right.

One evening there was a lot of activity. The locals were out on the lake in their dug-out canoes. One of them had an outboard. They were casting a net in a broad circle. (Later that night we saw the most astonishing shooting star, 50 times bigger than I'd ever seen before.) In the morning the fishermen pulled in the net but it was a very meagre catch. A marine biologist we met later said there wasn't much nutrition in the water for fish. The eagle was a lot better at finding those that were there than the Malawians. He never seemed to miss.

When we finally left our camp and headed south again, a waving, smiling menagerie of kids saw us off. In the side mirror I could see them jumping up and down. On the road, we slowed down as we passed people so we could shout, 'Hello.' 'Thank you, sir,' was the usual reply. What a buzz.

We spent hours on a really rough road. So much for the good ones. We were being shaken to pieces at only 20kph. Frank drove very carefully. He knew what the Land Rover could take. He didn't want to have to lie on his back in the dust, changing one of the leaves on the suspension.

That night, the sunset was perfect, and the moon was a thin crescent against the inky sky. My *Africa on the Cheap* guide had told me that the people were really repressed, and there were a lot of informers. Our very simplistic analysis, based on a week in the country, suggested that they were one of the happiest people on earth. One man in a bar did say that it wasn't wise to talk about politics, though.

Though Lilongwe was Malawi's capital, it made a town like Guildford in Surrey feel big. The population at that time was only 60,000. The good news was that I could walk into a bank with my Barclays pound sterling cheque book, write one out one for £50, and be given pounds. We'd ended up with too many Malawian kwacha and had to go on a binge at the market. We mostly bought food, but my blue-cotton airline pilot shirt, which I'd worn to the bank, was worn out. At the market I found an excellent replacement for two dollars that was all-wool, American, and only slightly stained.

We passed back into Zambia and stopped for breakfast. It was one of those fun occasions where we had 27 spectators. Ah, the children of Africa – dressed in rags,

African kids are such fun. No money, ragged clothes, but they are full of sunshine. We shared some breakfast with them.

with no shoes, but the most gigantic smiles. Their eyes couldn't avoid our food, which must have seemed lavish to them. It would have been nice to feed them properly, but where do you start with so many? We sliced up a pineapple into 27 bits, and some oranges.

At one point in the proceedings, the local policeman showed up. He was worried that we might be attacked by the kids, and asked for our passports. We'd heard that Zambia had recently had some 'internal problems'. He was probably just checking us out, and using the children as a polite pretext.

After packing up, we firmly shook 27 eager little hands, and drove off. Frank gave the horn a few long, powerful toots as we picked up speed. Lots of skinny bits of joy chased us down the road. I sat in the Land Rover recalling one of my favourite lines from *King Lear*, 'Allow not nature more than nature needs/Man's life's as cheap as beast's.'

We had an easy drive through green hills with the occasional mud-hut village, and in the distance some incongruous-looking radar installations. My Tanzanian experience had taught me to stay well clear of such places, and to keep my camera in my bag. Who the hell wants a photo of a hill with a white disc on the top of it, anyway?

Martin managed to muck the day up regardless. As we approached a bridge over the Luangwa River, there was a large truck coming the other way. Martin jumped out to take a photo. 'Don't!' I yelled, but he had his German ears on. A soldier leapt out of the bush with his AK-47 aimed squarely at Martin's scrawny chest. Because Martin's English was a bit stilted and domineering, I got out to try and calm the chap down with a few words, with lots of smiles, and some cigarettes. Ironically, he asked for some dope as well. I feigned not to understand him. Now that we were good mates, he disappeared into the bush and came out to show us his pet monkey.

Sometimes the moon seemed lazy and arrived late. Sometimes it was just raring to go, and couldn't wait until the sun had gone down. This was one of those days. We were down a narrow track off the main road. The sun was dipping, and the moon was already high – bright and big. There was plenty of firewood, and no recent rain meant that it burned very well. We spent hours watching red-hot lumps of log slowly disappear into the night, making perfect embers. There was a canopy of bright stars above us (when the moon arrives early, it disappears early) and the air was cool. We lounged on our cushions smoking cigarettes, and the occasional pipe. Perfect.

The Zambian capital, Lusaka, was much more developed than I'd expected. It was more of a wannabe Nairobi than a Dar es Salaam. The people were quite sophisticated. There were lots of hair dressers, which meant there were lots of smartly dressed black women in heels with abnormally straight hair.

I needed to do some bank business. A white guy I met there told me the city was not safe. Guns, he said, rather than knives. We decided not to go out at night. We were staying at a campsite behind a petrol station out of town, where we met an old Scot who said he'd been in Zambia for 30 years. We sought clarification. It seems he'd been staying at the campsite for 30 years.

The vehicle next to ours was a caravan, wildly painted with animals and buxom women. 'Exclusive private hospital' was stencilled, rather badly, across the back door. We peered into the gloom to see a man dressed in a lion skin, sitting on the floor, with a load of old animal bits hanging around his neck. It smelt weird very musty. He had various roots and powders, and seemed to think he was the local medicine man. He offered to sell us stuff that would enhance our sexual prowess.

That evening we ended up at the home of some West German foreign aid workers, and I met my first citizen from the (then) Soviet Union, 'Sasha from Minsk. He spoke English, but he used the words 'of course' too much. This made him sound somewhat pre-programmed. He then made the mistake of calling

One of my favourite photos with gradations from yellow through shades of purple to black. The moon crescent tops it off.

the USSR 'communist'. I nailed him for that, pointing out how it was still in the pre-communist stage of revolutionary socialism, and the state had certainly not yet withered away. This made him rather glum, so we discussed the weather instead. He blamed the crop failures in the Soviet Union on the CIA, which he said had been seeding the clouds. As alcohol began to lubricate our conversation, he did admit that everyone wanted western clothes, beer, and cigarettes. Later in the evening I introduced him to the joys of dope, and he eventually fell asleep singing *The Internationale*.

Understandably, most of the conversation was in German, though Frank and Martin came in for a lot of stick for not being 'proper' Germans. It seems they were Schlesians. They had to contend with an avalanche of jokes that were translated for them into German since, apparently, they couldn't speak the language. Maybe that's why Frank gave away *Der Spiegel*.

The morning was bright and chilly as we set off in the direction of the great Zambezi River. We came to the Kariba dam, which was truly huge. Martin was under strict instructions not to take any photos. We stood on the top and tried to work out how high it was by dropping pebbles, but nobody could remember the formula.

We camped at a place called Eagles Rest. The Zambezi shore was sandy, so we went for a swim. The water was warm, but not as clear as Lake Malawi.

The following day we headed for the town of Livingstone at the Victoria Falls. We spent the night next to a railway line, which proved to be a bit of a mistake. Our experience of railway lines was of one train passing every blue moon, or at best three times a week. This one had a train roaring passed, and shaking the earth, three times an hour.

The Land Rover had a cracked windscreen. It'd been hit by a stone flicked up by a truck that was passing in the opposite direction. The next morning, we stopped at a garage run by a white chap who had stock and could replace it. 'No charge,' he said. 'You've come so far.' He was half Greek, half English, but he'd been educated in South Africa. His big, oily arms were covered in dark hair. He and Frank conversed in the international Land Rover mechanic language for over half an hour.

Mosi-oa-Tunya translates as 'the smoke that thunders'. What a wonderful way to describe a wall of water that falls off a ledge and drops 100m before it explodes in white spray and rainbows. Its name in English – Victoria Falls – is simply dreadful. Please try and remember the local one.

The amazing Mosi-oa-Tunya (the Smoke That Thunders), sadly known to many as Victoria Falls.

We parked upstream from the main falls. I guarded the Land Rover while the others went to the InterContinental Hotel for a drink. A Zambian girl with plaited hair and wearing a short skirt showed up and sat on the bonnet. I had Bob Dylan playing. The sun was disappearing, leaving an orange and purple horizon that rose upwards like blotting paper dipped in ink. The girl on the bonnet sang along with Bob (doing a much better job, to be honest). It turned out she was the singer at the InterContinental, and had a contract with CBS.

The water was quite placid, so I had a wash. It didn't know that in a couple of hundred metres all hell would break loose. It would become 'the smoke that thunders'.

The moon appeared like a second sun, and I wondered if its brightness wasn't somehow magnified by the water vapour thrown up by the waterfall. It started off a warm orange colour, with all of its craters well defined, but as it rose higher, it turned cold and grey-white.

Frank and I went down to the falls at night to see the rainbow created by the moon, and to go on a hippo hunt. Had I learned nothing? A large black lump, maybe 20m away, materialised into a big male, his back scarred from ferocious encounters. He started lumbering towards us, picking up speed like a freight train. We sprinted off through the trees, laughing. He must have stopped, or that would have been that.

The Smoke that Thunders at sunset, just before being chased by a hippo, another of those Darwin Award moments. They weigh up to four tonnes, with a top speed of 30kmh!

The next morning, we went to see the falls again. They were magnificent. Mesmerising. There was nothing to stop us clambering over the rocks close to the edge. I could have looked for ever.

The spray had created a profusion of vegetation that clung to the sides of the ravine at improbable angles. The water burst upwards so loudly that it was deafening. You couldn't possibly talk to other people. It reminded me of an avalanche of snow on a perpetual loop, albeit one with a rainbow halo.

Our next hurdle was crossing into Zimbabwe. The Zambian side of the border turned out to be easy. They didn't ask for our currency declaration forms, and one of them even gave me his newspaper. The Zimbabwe customs and immigration took more time.

Once through we passed a train station that had a real steam engine in it. Talk about black power. Frank, the mechanic, was very excited, especially when the chap who shovelled the coal to the stocker let us clamber all over it. He said it was a good job. I guess that if you shovel coal for a living, the best place to do it is in the open air, chugging through bits of African bush. Frank asked lots of questions about power ratios and revolutions per minute. The driver was white, and seemed to treat the blacks as equals, laughing and joking with them all the time. Not that that did much to alleviate the dominant structure of systemic discrimination.

At least remember the English version of the African name: The Smoke that Thunders.

The Victoria Falls Hotel was a colonial pile, glaringly white, with high backed wicker chairs and long lawns. The scene was rather spoilt by three scruffy travellers (us), lounging about sipping colas.

We slept by the railway line again (cheaper than the official camp site as it was free), but we returned to the posh hotel for breakfast. We got dressed up as smartly as we could, but we still looked like over-landers in our crumpled shirts, with our unshaven faces, and mops of wild hair. The breakfast was great – a buffet of sausages, bacon, omelettes, fruit juice, and toast. A post-breakfast Coke on the terrace made us feel almost civilised.

The plan was to drive in a big loop around Zimbabwe. After we left the hotel, we immediately found a massive baobab tree that looked like it was the biggest in the world. We followed a road that ran roughly in the same direction as the railway lines. The whole place looked very developed, even compared to Kenya. We made camp that night near the train tracks because Frank was fascinated by machinery, and they made him feel more secure (an illusion). We were also able to find lumps of coal for the fire. This was a bonus for the chief firewood-forager (me).

In the early morning, a steam engine went passed. It looked like a matte-black torpedo. It looked timeless. It was much quieter than a diesel train. In the darkness we could also see the glowing red firebox. In Lusaka we'd discussed Magritte, the Belgium surrealist painter, with the German aid workers and Sasha. He'd once done a painting of a steam engine coming out of a fire-place. Even he'd painted it black.

We were heading for Wankie in north Matabeleland. It's now called Hwange (thankfully). A white man running a petrol station warned us not to go to Bulawayo, the regional capital, as there'd been a lot of guerrilla activity which hadn't, he said, been reported in the newspapers. We went anyway. Another white person in khaki trousers and a safari jacket with a broad-brimmed hat chipped in to say the whole of Matabeleland was unstable and dangerous.

The road wasn't sealed, but it was well maintained, so it was a relatively smooth ride once we got the speed right. In the early afternoon Martin made a mistake with the map and we didn't know where we were. Frank got mad at him, and tensions ran high. We stopped at around 2pm and Frank got under the vehicle to work on the suspension for an hour or two. That was his idea of meditation and stress release. He emerged much refreshed, and more tolerant of Martin.

I was on cooking duty that night. I fried three enormous steaks, and put fried eggs on the top. There was so much meat that we had some for breakfast. That night there were no little African faces smiling out of the bush. We really were in the real middle of nowhere. When I went to the toilet in the morning, though, I found I had 20 pairs of eyes glued on me. They belonged to the baboons.

The bush in Zimbabwe didn't seem any different from the bush in Zambia, Malawi, and Tanzania. Most of the people we passed also had the wonderful, Malawian habit of dropping everything they were carrying, and waving wildly, when we passed by

We were heading towards Zimbabwe's capital, Harare. My mum had been very resourceful about getting me the addresses of people to visit there, and Frank also had a German diplomatic contact in the city. We thought his was the better choice, so we drove to the embassy. Suddenly, Frank slammed on the brakes. We came to a squealing halt and reversed. It was a Wimpy hamburger bar! We parked the vehicle where we could see it, locked it up, and rushed inside. Everything being relative, it was a dream come true. Once hamburger-ed up, we drove on until we came to another sharp halt. A supermarket! Wow. It was as well stocked as a Sainsbury's. We were in danger of spending lots of money on 'stuff'. In an amazing show of German-style willpower we continued on. I wasn't even allowed to buy a bar of chocolate. I think Frank was hoping his diplomat-friend would have a fridge full of it.

Zimbabwe was no longer under white rule, but apart from the staff, the German Embassy had almost no black people in it. It had white women instead. Really white. Like pale. Their billowing, flowery, cotton dresses seemed to have come straight out of the 1950s.

Naturally, the German diplomat was in a starched white shirt and had blond hair that looked like it had been cut three minutes ago. He'd never heard of Frank. This didn't seem to matter, since we were taken off the street and welcomed in regardless. A junior aide took us to the diplomat's house. It had an industrial-sized WASHING MACHINE! Fantastic. We washed everything we owned, except for our underwear. We sat around waiting for it to finish. When the wash cycle was complete, we put everything back in and washed it again. It came out almost clean.

Frank wanted to sell the Land Rover, since he didn't think it would make it back through Africa. He also needed to get to Germany to complete his degree.

We went to a garage run by a white man, who kept making useful comments like, 'All Africans are stupid.' Nobody had any hard currency, though, so it looked like Frank was going to have to try further south.

We had dinner with Wolfgang, the diplomat, and he tried to explain the war, and the problems between ZANU (the Zimbabwe African National Union), and ZAPU (the Zimbabwe African People's Union). I got very confused, but I did enjoy the copious beer. After independence, he said, something like 40,000 whites had stayed, out of a total of 240,000. The rest had left to become *whenwes* ('when I was in Rhodesia …'). Many of the whites who left were working people – artisans, electricians, plumbers, and mechanics. They were not fat-cats or farmers. The brain drain had affected all the practical stuff. Now the phones didn't work properly.

Wolfgang took us next day to the national stadium to see a colourful dance festival by all the local tribes. The sky was blue. The sun was warm. The grass was soft. And the black women gyrated enthusiastically in front of us. We were having pork knuckle and sauerkraut for dinner, our clothes didn't stink, and we didn't stink. Life was sweet. The Zimbabwe army put on a show, incongruously dressed

Locals get their chance to perform for Mugabe (and us).

194

in kilts and sporrans, and playing the bagpipes. The whole performance came to a close when some slender Indian women danced about, swaying their hips in saris.

At that point we were getting around Harare without the Land Rover. This meant hitching. A white policeman in a squad car stopped and gave us a lift to our front door. He spent the whole time telling us, 'I hate bloody *kaffirs.*' He told us how he was planning to go to the US. I told him that there were rather a lot of *kaffirs* there (one of whom was ultimately to become president. Ironically, he also had some Kenyan heritage). This shut him up. He brooded on what was clearly a travesty for the last five minutes of the ride.

Since we were leaving soon, Frank and I bought a bottle of wine for Wolfgang and his wife, Chantelle. Considering our budget, and our complete lack of taste and refinement, I sometimes wonder what they did with it, but being diplomats they accepted it graciously. On the same shopping trip I bought a new zip for my shoulder bag, though I then had the challenge of sewing it in. I also bought a second-hand copy of *The Odyssey* by Homer.

Wolfgang had guests coming for dinner, and we were invited. We tried to look presentable, and speak intelligently about our experiences in Africa. Some of my stories from Uganda made them laugh, as did my chance encounter with English Mr Smith in the wilds of the Sudan. The strawberries and cream were excellent. So was the slightly murky German beer, that had come in via the diplomatic pouch. A freelance journalist was the centre of attention. He was banned from South Africa because he'd written positively about the outlawed ANC (the African National Congress). There were heated discussions about ZAPU, ZANU, SWAPO, ANC, the USSR, and something called the Lancaster House Agreement. They were all Germans, and they all spoke in English for my benefit. I was a bit lost, and likely a bit drunk, as we didn't imbibe all much on the road. It was either too expensive, or too unpalatable, or just unavailable. Once on the road again to Umtali, on the Mozambique border, I felt much better.

Around this time, we became quite fanatical about Bushman art, searching out cave paintings around the country. We might even have 'discovered' some, though we were pretty random in our approach. I'll never know if what we found was already known, seriously old, or relatively recent.

We learned from Wolfgang that there were some great examples about 30km out of town. We got hopelessly lost, and were about to give up when three school girls in smart, spotless, blue and white uniforms came to our rescue. After much clambering over large boulders, and wading through cold streams, we found them. They might or might not have been the intended ones. The main paintings were under a large rock overhang rather than in an actual cave. Some of them looked like a three-year-old had done them. Perhaps a three-year-old *had* done them. Others were fluid stick figures that had all the motility and vitality of the Bushmen themselves, as they surged across the landscape with their spears and their bows and arrows. The figures chased equally fluid animals. The art seemed to capture the absolute essence of movement. It was wonderful. Buffalo, rhino, antelope, giraffe – all done in black and red. I imagined these people, scraping a living, killing when they could, picking nuts, fruits, and leaves when they couldn't, and taking the time to paint the pertinent parts of their lives on cave walls. On reflection, perhaps life wasn't so tough.

One man against an antelope seemed pretty hopeless. But a stealthy, coordinated group, approaching from different angles, must have upped the chances of a kill significantly. There was, after all, plenty of game. it was just a matter of getting close enough to catch it. Then it could be chopped up, carried back to the communal cave, and roasted over an open fire. Perhaps it wasn't such a bad life, unless people got injured or fell ill. There probably wasn't much 'old age'. I was so used to the

Cave art, such fluidity of motion.

196

relaxed nature of the locals that I didn't think it at all unusual that three teenage girls should decide to walk into the back of beyond with three scruffy travellers in their early 20s. Neither did they. Wherever they were originally going – school or home – we'd made them an hour late, but it didn't seem to matter.

Frank had bought a new tyre In Tanzania before I'd joined him. He might have looked like a scruffy, unkempt hippy, but underneath he was German. He numbered all the tyres, and he kept a record of each one's lifespan. 'This forking shit tyre from forking Tanzania,' he said. 'It's only done 4,140 forking kilometres!' It had burst and disintegrated. 'I like this word forking,' he said. 'You can use it any time. It means many zings.' He paired it most often with 'Martin', 'road', 'map', or a combination of all three. We only had a sand tyre to replace the burst one with, and so we went in search of a garage where we could buy a proper one. I wound him up by saying that Tanzania had been colonised by the Germans, and this wouldn't have happened in Kenya. Frank sat grimly, hunched over the steering wheel, driving carefully on a tyre that was only supposed to be used in dunes.

We didn't find a garage. We were in farmland, so we pulled up to a farm. Two crazy-eyed Alsatian dogs went wild, barking and jumping up at the doors of the Land Rover. The house itself was behind a 3m barbed wire fence. An old white

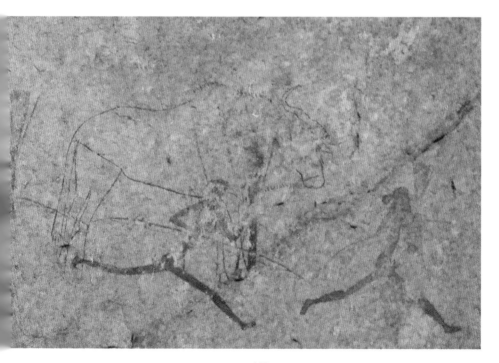

fellow, with a 12-bore shotgun, came out and pulled off the dogs. 'My dogs don't like *kaffirs*,' he said. 'They thought you were *kaffirs*.' Being dishevelled travellers, but nonetheless white, he let us inside the barbed wire and showed us where to get water, go to the toilet, and put up our tent. The next morning, he invited us for breakfast. Being a farmer, this was at 6am, and we didn't make it.

When we reached Umtali, Frank delved deep into the recesses of his storage area in the Land Rover and emerged with a pile of second-hand clothes. We set up an impromptu stall in the market, next to the ladies selling vegetables and fruit, to raise some cash. His original idea was to give the clothes away, but our cash was running low, and some of the stuff, like the jeans, was quite valuable. At one point we were led to the back of the market and into a dark shack. An old hag, sitting on a plastic bucket, held out a bottle full of white powder. Frank, Martin, and I were known to smoke a few joints, but we weren't into the hard stuff. She said, 'You need medicine for men?' There seemed to be quite a lot of insecurity around the penis in Africa. What happened is that we'd been heard to whisper the word 'drug', and the old lady thought we were too embarrassed to speak loudly. She thought we had sexual problems. It was a simple enough misunderstanding. She sent her son out to buy us a small bag of sop and refused any money. Frank gave her a shirt.

The Germans brought old clothes some were give away, some were sold.

There was a big Shell garage on the edge of town where we finally got a proper tyre. I was shocked by the toilets. They had a hot shower with soap in them. We drove on from Umtali towards Bulawayo in Matabeleland, and the countryside was very beautiful and very varied. There were even high passes through Scotch pines that opened out into valleys strewn with monster boulders.

The first night out from Umtali we camped high up on a flat slab of rock. It was surprisingly warm for the altitude. We wondered whether this was because we were only a couple of hundred kilometres from the Indian Ocean. We also wondered if the massive slab of rock might not have worked as a sort of heat store, absorbing the sun's rays during the day, and letting them out at night.

The next morning we broke camp and drove through Moodies Pass. There were high, bare mountains on either side, then valleys, and a series of large villages. Even the huts seemed larger than usual. There was short, cropped grass, sparkling streams that meandered about, piglets that squealed, and kids that smiled.

We took a detour to visit the Chamawara caves but we couldn't find them. We stopped for water at a small stream, and people began to accumulate, but nobody spoke English. A shy little boy hid behind a white pillar, peeking out at us. I took his photo. With hindsight, I should have taken more photos of people, and a lot less of the countryside.

We camped on another big, flat rock. Frank and I went looking for cave paintings, and we met a little boy who spoke no English. Frank drew a stick man on a rock. The kid got it immediately and showed us some caves. For his trouble we gave him some bread and honey, and three German lollypops that Frank extracted from one of his secret compartments. I spent the last two hours of daylight sewing the zip into my blue shoulder bag. After that it was steak and salad for dinner, and a good lie-down on the warm rock, looking up at the stars.

In the morning we set off in search of the Great Zimbabwe ruins. This was a civilisation that lasted from around AD1200 to 1450. It was built on gold and ivory, and had traded extensively with Arabia, India, and China.

The buildings were unusual. They were solidly built, of relatively small bricks, carved from granite. There were no corners. We discussed whether this was because they hadn't invented corners yet, or whether corners were against their religion. The main building was a conical structure, and vaguely phallic in shape (at least, for those with an active imagination). The white Rhodesians of the late 19th century had tried to get the government to proclaim that 'the blacks hadn't built it'.

It's the largest historical structure in sub-Saharan Africa. Not bad, but not much compared to the pyramids of Giza, the Forbidden City in Beijing, or the Colosseum in Rome. The lack of corners meant there were interesting narrow, curved passageways to play silly games in, though. They didn't seem to have invented roofs either, though these were probably made of perishable stuff. At least, we thought so.

We drove on to Fort Victoria. Famous for its association with Cecil Rhodes and his white settlers, it was now just a clutch of gas stations, and had two impressive supermarkets. We dragged ourselves past these seductive sirens of commercialism, lashed to our Land Rover. Having escaped their clutches, we drove on to the huge reservoir at Lake Kyle. (This analogy obviously appears here because I was reading at the time Homer's *Odyssey*.)

On the way we saw a white rhino. They're not white, just as the black rhino isn't black. They have a broad, lower lip which the Dutch described as *wijd* (wide). Being rubbish linguists, the Brits thought they were saying 'white'. They can grow to about three tonnes, and four metres long. Textbooks describe them as the 'most social' and the 'least aggressive' of their sub-species, which is why I took to stalking them in the long grass on foot. I got to within 20-five meters of the one we saw. Again, I was doing something completely stupid, because though they're less aggressive than the black rhinos, or the buffalo, but they're still massive, powerful, wild beasts. Anyway, I survived. Their horns, by the way, are really long. In the tall grass, this was the only bit of them I could see. Frank was up on the roof as my intrepid spotter. Even he was worried I was getting too close.

There were some other animals around, but the giraffes seemed to be somewhat bleached. Their patchwork colours were far less clear than they'd been further north. There were also impala, eland, Grants gazelles, and some warthogs.

We drove on and came to the lake. Bare tree trunks stuck out of its mirror-like surface, which meant that the flooding must have been relatively recent. It was strangely beautiful. There wasn't a breath of wind. Close to the shore, the grass reeds were perfectly mirrored in its surface.

Frank spotted another long horn poking up above the tall, dry grass. I was out of the cabin in a flash to try and stalk it. As it seemed to be a solitary bull, I was more nervous, but this didn't seem to affect my idiotic behaviour. After I hopped back on the roof, we moved on, and spotted four more in the open in the short grass. This time I convinced the Germans to join me. I hadn't been charged yet, so

Sheer madness, stalking rhino on foot. Frank called out instructions from the roof of the Land Rover. In a panic he sometimes shouted "LAUF, LAUF", I got the gist of it. Another Darwin Awards moment.

I figured it would be OK. Flawed logic, but it worked. There was a certain amount of rivalry between the Germans and the Englishman, but most of the time it was Frank and Chris baiting Martin. We sat on the short, sharp grass as the rhinos munched along.

Leaving the rhino behind, we drove the 280km to Bulawayo in search of the black market. We had two addresses for change places. The first guy said it was too dangerous, though. We never found the second.

Frank drove to the campsite to look for other travellers who might have a lead, but we were the only travellers there. The campsite itself was splendid. It had 24-hour hot water, baths, and coin-laundry machines. The works. The baths actually came in useful for keeping us warm, rather than for washing ourselves. It was bitterly cold at night, and we didn't have our vast fires to keep us warm. The camp had rules against that sort of thing.

A small Indian supermarket proved to be the place to change money. They gave us a good rate for a decent amount of pound sterling, but they refused to change any dollars or deutschmarks. 'Too many forgeries around,' they said.

The next afternoon we strolled around the National Museum. There were lots of references to Cecil Rhodes and his pioneer column. They still made up only 50 per cent of the total, though. Whatever that meant. A kind of balanced unbalance?

Back at the campsite, I jumped in the tub to get warm, and to read *Odyssey*, and a book on rock paintings I'd bought from the museum shop. In the following days we actually managed to find some of them. (We did find, not far from Bulawayo, the spectacular and slightly spiritual Matopos Hills. They're strange-shaped rock outcrops, made of enormous boulders perched at precarious angles, that have spectacular views.)

Despite our best endeavours, we didn't get going the next day until 11.30am. It was another beautiful morning, with antelope leaping across the road. We went to see the grave of Cecil Rhodes. He said, 'Remember that you are an Englishman, and have consequently won first prize in the lottery of life.' How times have changed! He was also a megalomaniac. 'To think of these stars that you see overhead at night', he said. 'These vast worlds that we can never reach. I would annex the planets if I could.' He died when he was 48. His instructions were to bury him on the top of the Matopos Hills, at a place called World's View. The local name is *Malindidzimu* – 'hill of the spirits'. Not a bad choice for a resting place. We sat in the sun there on the warm rocks, our knees up to our chests.

Later we drove around spotting cave art from my book. In the white rhino shelter there was a line, in deep red, of men running fast and holding bows and arrows. The paintings were very simple, but they portrayed such grace and

Cecil Rhodes grave plate at Motopos. Not a bad final resting place.

movement. There were also drawings of white and black rhinos. The detail was sufficient for us to differentiate them.

A guide took us around the Silozwane cavern. Here a profusion of paintings covered all the walls of a vast cave. It was a mixture of Bushman and Bantu art (we were told). The guide was Bantu but he freely acknowledged that the 'black' or Bantu stuff was of inferior quality. The view from the cavern was down a long, flat valley. I imagined sitting there, one or two thousand years ago, when most of the animals had been copied from real life. There were mythical creatures there, too. They were a mixture between giraffes and snakes. There were even men with massive ears. I was fascinated by the tiny paintings of flying termites. They were perfect, like the work of draughtsman, not artists. One of the oldest drawings was of a line of Bushmen holding hands. Was it a community, or a big family? Our guide explained that the paintings lower on the wall were between two and three thousand years old. The newest ones, near the top, were about 500 years old. The cave we'd been siting had been inhabited for 2,500 years or so. I thought about how these people were so much part of nature, and how we, the current masters of the planet, were busily destroying it, with our amazing technological achievements. Our guide also told us that the last known Bushman in the area didn't die. He was killed, in the late 19th century. He said the Nswatugi cave had wonderful pictures of giraffe, in motion across the plains. He was right. A video couldn't have depicted them better. Michelangelo and Leonardo would have been absolutely enchanted.

We spent the night in the Land Rover, huddled in the lee of one of the enormous boulders. In the morning, the sun made the ones higher up glow a golden yellow. After a breakfast of omelette, friend onion, and tomato, followed by bread and honey, and polished off with coffee brewed over the open fire, I went for a wander. Under an overhang I found some more Bushman art. I was not good enough to date it, but out there in the bush, it did feel like a discovery. Of course, it wasn't. The Bantu had been there for hundreds of years. They wouldn't have missed it. But it seemed no more strange than Livingstone 'discovering' Victoria Falls. (David Livingstone actually found 'the smoke that thunders'. He was simply the first European to report back on it. He happened to be British, and named it Victoria Falls. Bah.) With an omelette in my stomach, the sun on my back, and a pseudo-Bushman art discovery dancing through my mind, life felt like it couldn't get any better. I felt supremely happy and free. I ran back through the bush calling out to Frank to come and see, like a kid wanting to show everyone the huge green beetle he'd just found. I pointed out a buffalo, a mythical animal with a long neck, and a third one I now forget. Scrambling around, we found even more. They looked quite abstract – a bit like some Australian aboriginal art.

This was supposed to be a dangerous area, so we decided to take a short cut to Plumtree via the back roads on the border with Botswana, rather than go via Bulawayo on the main road. How can a border crossing be called Plumtree? It sounds like a town in Essex or New Jersey. (I give my permission to change the name from Plumtree to something more local at any time.)

The town itself was actually a few kilometres inside Zimbabwe. Since Botswana was vast and largely empty, we went to the petrol station to buy fuel. The legal limit in Zimbabwe was five litres in excess of the regular tank, which wouldn't have got us far. We persuaded the white owner the rule was purely to stop black terrorists, and he agreed to fill up our jerry cans to the top.

The crossing out of Zimbabwe was very professional and smooth. No AK-47s. No whispers for bribes. The Botswana border was still 10km away, so we barrelled down the straight dirt road, plumes of grey dust blasting out from the sides of our intrepid Land Rover. There was a dead vulture on the road, which somehow seemed odd. Other vultures flocked down to eat one their own.

Chapter 12

Botswana and South West Africa

Botswana had a free-floating currency and therefore no black market. It turned out there were plenty of petrol stations, too, and the price was the same as we'd paid in Zimbabwe using black-market money. There were also no currency declaration forms, which felt a bit strange. It was almost too easy. It left no room for improvisation.

Botswana was a democracy – the first one I'd been to since Spain (this was the early 1980s. General Franco had only died in 1975, so even Spain was a newcomer.) It made its money from gold, diamonds, cattle, and tourism. It was huge and empty (about half a million square kilometres, and about two million people. The UK is a quarter of a million square kilometres, and at that time had about 60 million people. This made it 120 times more densely populated.)

A map of that part of the world shows South West Africa (now Namibia) to the west, and South Africa is to the south. South West Africa was nominally independent by then, but it was actually part of South Africa. One incongruous piece of South West Africa stuck out to the east as far as the Zambezi River. It was called the Caprivi Strip. This odd segment had come about when South West Africa was a German colony. Germany had been desperate to get physical access to the east African coast, and the Indian Ocean, as well as to its colony in Tanganyika (now Tanzania). The British offered them a four-hundred-and-50-kilometre strip of land connecting South West Africa to the Zambezi, in exchange for Zanzibar and the North Sea island of Heligoland (a few miles from the German coast, and strategically rather interesting.) The deal was done. The Germans got some jungle and elephants and their corridor. And the Brits got Zanzibar and an island in Germany's own backyard.

Francistown was the first proper town we got to in Botswana. Frank made directly for a garage to ask about selling the Land Rover. The man said that Maun, up near the Okavango swamps, would be our best bet. He thought Frank could get three to four thousand US dollars for it, which in those days was not bad for a 14-year-old vehicle on its a fourth transcontinental odyssey. Land Rover should have put it in a museum. To this day I've never seen a cooler, more completely kitted-out, overland vehicle. Another garage explained something about the South African Customs Union, and how it slapped a duty of 110 per cent on any vehicle imported into South Africa, Lesotho, Swaziland, South West Africa, and Botswana. The last was supposed to be a front-line state in the battle against apartheid in South Africa, but they all seemed pretty chummy to me. As an Indian trader said, 'Botswana would have starved if the South Africans had closed the border.' Money talks.

We'd planned to go to Maun anyway, as it was the gateway to Okavango. We wanted to take a trip from there into the delta. We were arriving during the wet season, which was perfect. In the wet season a large river flows into the desert and doesn't have anywhere to go, so it spreads out, creating a myriad of waterways where life proliferates. Eventually it dries up, and everything waits for the next flood.

Back on the dusty road we encountered a large black squabble of vultures, bouncing up and down. They were focused on something, and didn't notice us until we were about 25m away. There must have been 30 of them. Most thrashed their wings and took flight, but ten of the more intrepid ones stood their ground. The young zebra they were feeding on was still pretty much intact. As there was no sign of the usual 'kill', we assumed it had been hit by a vehicle. The vultures first on the scene didn't seem to have broken through the hide. For that they needed the cats, the hyenas, the jackals, and the wild dogs. They'd only taken the eyes so far. They were also attacking the anus. They were revolting. They looked ugly and satanic, like Victorian school masters. As they squawked, and fought among themselves, a couple of jackals circled around, though they didn't approach because we were there.

The days at Maun were hot, and the late nights were numbingly cold – though not cold enough to stop huge swarms of mosquitoes from draining our blood. It

Zebra roadkill (not by us) and a bunch of evil vultures.

was a miracle we didn't get malaria. Their buzz was deafening. Whenever there was a change in tone, I knew one had landed and was spiking me. I'd thrash about, but it was hopeless. I'd swat at their fat, brown bodies, and yelp at the self-administered pain. The *tsetse* flies also hit us hard. They're the nemesis of both livestock and people, since they result in sleeping sickness. Their bite is vicious, though they usually die in the process, unlike the *ninja* mosquitoes.

Our Okavango safari involved traversing the deep bush in a canoe with Willie, our 18-year-old guide. He did most of the work. He paddled and polled us deeper and deeper into the swamps, heading for Chief's Island (no Cessna, fly-in-and-fly-out, for us.)

As we approached the river bank we saw vultures (again), and some vile-looking storks. The latter had gross, bloody beaks, bulbous eyes, and were even more revolting than the vultures. They edged away in hops, flapping heavily into the air as we approached. They also left three leopards munching on a kill. It's rare to see leopards. It's a privilege. They usually hunt at night. Their deep, yellow eyes glared at us, and they bared their teeth. Willie scared them off (this was easier than I'd expected) by shouting at them, and waving his crude paddle. In the daylight, away

Sorry about the Speedos! [Note to Krish Gupta, my photo editor, if there is a 2nd Edition, replace the Speedos with something more modest]. But they are very space and weight efficient.

Our resourceful young guide scared leopards off his kill and hacked off a hind leg for our dinner.
He probably did the leopard a favour by skinning it.

from the jungle, the leopards seemed to be shrinking violets. They backed off and turned, and with a single bound, they disappeared into the undergrowth.

We leapt from the canoe, Willie with his *panga* to the ready. The small antelope they'd been feeding on was pretty much mangled. One of its haunches was gone but the eyeballs were still there. Willie hacked off the other rather-less-mangled leg, skinned the whole carcass in a few seconds, then sliced off some other bits of choice flesh. We kept an eye on the undergrowth but he didn't seem concerned. We smoked a celebratory cigarette, since we now had good food for the rest of the time. Leaving the remains to the circling the vultures, and the lurking leopards, we pushed off up stream.

The sun was hot and the water was slightly murky. It not only hid crocodiles, but we were on the watch for hippos as well. Crocs never attack boats but hippos do. We sought to avoid them at all costs. I was beginning to learn (at last).

Pieces of broken reed bobbed up and down in the current like fishing floats, jerking like there was something on the line. It was very peaceful now we'd left the vultures behind. A fish eagle soared above us, the banks were crowded with reeds, and there were palm trees that grew a few metres back from them. The waters were calm and smooth, and there were wonderful reflections. There was no doubt

Beautiful reflections, but crocs and hippos lurk below.

game, but it was well hidden. No matter. Okavango was more about the serenity than game.

The fish eagle seemed to be following us, his wing tips clearly defined against the sky, his head and tail white. Swallows and house martins flashed across the surface, hoovering up insects. Dragonflies skimmed by, which the birds thankfully seemed to leave alone. Then a blue bird with iridescent wings zipped across right in front of us. Turquoise and orange kingfishers sat on sticks, looking pompous. I now know there are 440 bird species in the Okavango delta. No wonder I noticed lots of them, though it's a pity they have such little impact on the insects. (These were driving us mad every evening.) Orange termite hills dotted the landscape beyond the water, and I remembered how, in Uganda, I thought one was my first elephant. We lay back in the canoe lulled by the rhythmic swish of the paddles, and the distant call of the birds.

Willie pointed out some crocs on the shore. Crocs are usually pretty nervous. They'd slide into the water before we came close. One big one didn't move. We got to within about 5m of it, and it still hadn't retreated. Then I spotted flies on it. It was dead. Shot. Willie laughed and laughed. He'd known it was dead all along. Seeing us getting all excited had made his day.

We made more detours around hippos. Further upstream the water became clearer, and in some places we could see the sandy bottom. There was no wind, and there were white and mauve lilies, perfectly reflected, and perfect. It was then that Willie got excited, pointing at the shore. We could see nothing. After much face-pulling and finger-drawing, we realised he'd seen another leopard. I suppose it was my poor vision but I just couldn't see it.

We camped on the shore, which is probably impossible now. The fire roared as the temperature dipped, helping to keep the insects away. Three fish hung from the branch of a tree. (Willie had found time to catch them earlier.) Dinner tasted great. Afterwards we sat thrashing around at the mosquitoes, waiting for the cold of the evening to set in and send them to sleep, or whatever they did when they were too cold to come and drive us crazy. They could bite through two layers of clothing. Sometimes I'd sit in my sleeping bag, with only my head protruding, sweating profusely. It was better than being bitten. The *tsetse* flies only hit us in the late afternoon. (Baboons were the other problem. They were the 'hoodies' of the bush. They made gangs of marauding thieves, so we tried to keep the fire going all night to keep them away – and anything more hazardous. The baboons

Sorry a sunset shot, which totally fails to capture the horror of the insect attacks.

also made eerie screaming noises that they kept up most of the night.) What with the mosquitoes, the heat, the cold, the rough ground (inevitably there was a sharp stone jabbing me in the back), the screeching baboons, and the sundry other jungle noises, I got very little sleeping done.

We stumbled up off the ground at sunrise, the mosquitoes soon returning with the warmth. They drove me bonkers. I did have a mosquito net, and I spent ages trying to erect it, but it always collapsed, which made me furious. They seemed to find ways through it regardless, so what was the point?

At one point Willie pointed, and managed to get us 3m from a big (live) croc. It must have been sleeping. One eye finally opened, and it hurtled into the water, swishing its tail from side to side. It was surprisingly skittish for a predator. Apart from the enormous feet (and anger) of the hippos, I wasn't sure what crocs had to worry about. They hadn't bothered to evolve beyond how they were for 50 million years, so they have been doing something right.

After five days on our water safari, we arrived back in Maun. I gave Willie my mosquito net and a decent tip, which was probably embarrassingly small. Our Land Rover was still there, and we had the best hot shower in the world. I was brown from all the sunny days, but I had souvenirs from the insects, and scratches from rummaging around in the bush for firewood.

We sat up until 2am in the camp drinking with some South African visitors. I remember one of them stressing that while South Africa's politicians might seem reactionary to people from Europe, the real resistance to change was among the government officials. They were terrified of being replaced. It took another 12 years for Nelson Mandela to be released from Robben Island (the local version of Alcatraz), and for there to be free elections so the ANC could take over.

After five days in a swamp, we were back on the dusty dirt roads that skirted the Kalahari. We didn't see any sand dunes, just scrub, scree, and more scrub. There was the occasional oryx. It's such a beautiful, imperial antelope. It has black and white markings, and perfectly straight horns. We were to see many more in the Namib.

As we headed for the South West African frontier the road deteriorated. We really were in the middle of nowhere again. Even Michelin couldn't think of anything to put on their map. There was just an expanse of yellow, with a thin red line marking the way. On we rattled, bashed, and ploughed, for another 500km.

The majestic desert Oryx. Their body has adapted to the environment and can heat to 46.5ºc (apparently we max out at 44ºc, flop over and die).

Though the small town of Ghanzi did get a mention on the Michelin map, it only had one shop. Mind you, this sold everything – horse saddles, spices, footballs, batteries, and bad-taste shirts. Botswana had a large ranching industry, hence the saddles for the cowboys. There were even Stetsons, though no guns. There were also a few Bushmen sitting in the shade wearing woolly, colourful hats. It was winter. Some of the women did seem to me to have big behinds, which I assumed functioned in the desert something like camel's humps do.

The upcoming border with South West (and hence South) Africa was the most important one for me in all of my travels. I needed to get a long visa so I could work, replenish my coffers, and take a break from the nomadic life. I put on my new Okavangan T-shirt and long trousers.

An Afrikaans-speaking official was the one who dealt with me. I'd heard conflicting stories. Sometimes the official demanded onward airline tickets (I didn't have any), or wanted to see proof of substantial amounts of money (difficult). I asked this one how long I could stay for. 'As long as you want,' came the guttural reply. So I asked him for a year and I got a year. Yippee. Amazing. There were stories of people being turned back at the border, or getting a month, or getting only two weeks. I could now stay for a whole year if I wanted. This is one reason why land-border crossings can be so much better than those at airports. At Johannesburg International this would never have happened. By putting an entry stamp to South West Africa into my passport, the same official had given me access to South Africa too, since there were no border controls between South West Africa and South Africa. (Since a South African stamp could be a hassle in those days, a South West African stamp was even better. I also noted that it was only stuck in, and could be peeled off after leaving, like one of my mum's jam pot labels.)

Windhoek, the capital of South West Africa (now Namibia), was then like a small German town in the sunshine. It was very *lederhosen*. There were sausage shops, bierkellers, and lots of tall, blond Aryan-looking chaps marching around in farmers' clothing. The general post office had four letters for me from mum and dad, from Rwanda-and-Tanzania Steve, from Aswan Betsy, and from Irish Cookie (the last telling me to call her, and telling me that I had a bed waiting for me in Johannesburg). Mum had included a balance sheet, which showed a stronger financial position than I'd expected (a first – never to be repeated).

Frank had a contact in Windhoek, whose wife was blonde and friendly and told us where to go around the country. Her husband arrived home blind drunk and was sent to bed. The following day he was sober, and as he was in the military reserves, he told us where not to go. He got out his army maps and marked the areas he thought we should avoid. There were lots of *ja, ja* and nodding of heads by Frank and Martin. I even got the gist of it. It seemed there were lots of no-go areas up around Etosha, which was our next destination.

Windhoek was a sign painter's paradise. Everything was in German, English, and Afrikaans. It was also freezing. At our campsite there was light snow. Windhoek is on a plateau more than 1km above sea level. The light snow was due more to a lack of humidity than a lack of cold. We spent the night praying for the morning, and the sun.

One thing Windhoek did have was bookshops. They'd been pretty rare in my travels. I dived into one, all anticipation. The selection of magazines was amazing. Or, to be more precise, the selection of magazines about guns, ammo, mercenaries, how to mount a machine gun on the back of a jeep, and other such useful stuff, was amazing. I went out to check that it wasn't a survivalist bookstore. It wasn't.

I bought a copy of the *Windhoek Chronicle*, which turned out to be surprisingly permissive. It had three pages of what in Britain are called 'page threes', but no news on the local troubles. This said, there were a lot of soldiers on the streets. I

Etosha Pan around lunchtime. Searingly hot and siesta time for hunter and hunted.

also met a man in the showers at the campsite who was naked except for a bar of soap, a beard like Moses, a German beer belly, and a large revolver.

We set off north to towards the Etosha Pan. It was a fabled game reserve, and not far from where the freedom fighters made raids from their camps in Angola. We were putting ourselves, in effect, on the Cold War's front line.

We stopped between Otjiwarongo and Outjo, not far from the reserve. It seemed better to arrive in the morning and get a full day there, thus saving on the park's expensive accommodation. Frank drove up to a farm. The windows were covered in heavy steel mesh. We knocked on the door but there was nobody home. There were also empty rifle cartridges in the dust. We drove on and found another ranch. There were no whites around, but the black staff, all smiles and white teeth, told us it was fine to stay. The house was surrounded by a double fence inside which were four Dobermans. We stayed outside. Needless to say, it was also cold.

Etosha Pan was a blindingly white salt flat that stretched as far as the eye could see. The word means 'great white place', which says it all. Images shimmered in the distance. We saw a few zebras, a giraffe munching on thorns, and a springbok. (The latter is a cute, medium-sized gazelle, and the South African national animal. They're spectacularly athletic, capable of jumping four meters in the air – which seems ridiculous – and of running at 100kph.)

Packing up in the morning took time. The saloon cars from Windhoek just had to put their camping gas away, wipe their kids' noses, and drive off, but it was a quasi-military operation for us. It had to be done in the right order to get everything to fit, and ready to be unpacked in the evening.

Out on the pan, I squinted into the distance, the blue sky overhead gradually whitening as my eyes moved towards the horizon, to finally merge with the salt of the earth. Lines of game moved across it in the distance, quivering in the heat. Beyond them, and only just distinguishable, was a convoy of army lorries, driving very slowly, and shimmering and bending in the hot air.

Springboks bouncing up and down are always a joy to watch. It's difficult to see how a predator could ever catch one. It would have to be well off its game. (Humans keep people alive on all sorts of expensive medical contraptions long after they would otherwise have died. In nature, for springboks that can't bounce, it's curtains.) I continued to be entertained by the ostriches as well, with their chunky pink thighs. They churned up the dust as they rushed hither and thither for no apparent reason, their heads held high.

At Salvadoa waterhole, a herd of nervous zebra were sloshing around in the mud. A few proud oryx strutted passed, their vicious long horns looking the match for any predator. Their black and white faces were magnificent, and their bodies rippled with muscles. For me, they looked like the ultimate antelope. More springboks bounded around in the background, and there were ostriches, too, courting each other. Beyond there was nothing but white. As we moved on we spotted a herd of elephants, grey from rolling in the dust.

Some herbivores, just before I saw my only "kill" … sadly only a duck!

They were making distance, and were maybe nervous, as they had calves with them.

The Aus waterhole looked deserted. We sat in the Land Rover, with me on the roof scanning for movement. Then lions appeared. This explained why there were no other animals. First came two lionesses, their heads bloodied from a kill. They were camouflaged perfectly in the long, yellow grass. Then two more materialised out of the dry undergrowth. I thought that if all the other animals had just knocked down the grass around the waterhole by walking and rolling on it, the lions' cover would have been blown. Not likely. We got out from the Land Rover because the lions had obviously just eaten. When one of them moved quickly, we jumped back. This made them nervous and they loped away.

Everyone wants to see a kill in Africa. This is when I did. The lions were returning slowly to the waterhole, but one lioness crept along on her belly, inching towards something, slowly and methodically and with her eyes focused forwards. It took five minutes. Then she exploded out of the grass, hitting the still brown water in huge rush of raw power, cunning, and death. The kill was a duck. Not very spectacular. I suppose that technically this counts, but it's more embarrassing than dramatic. We wondered why the lioness had bothered. Maybe it was just practicing. Or doing it for fun. The other lions wallowed in the muddy waters instead, getting rid of some of the blood from their heads and legs.

After a midday break, we moved up the west side of the pan. Most of the waterholes were dry there, which we didn't know until we arrived. Neither, it seems, did the animals. The idealists among us discussed how nice it would be to try and tell them not to plod on through the heat and dust to the next hole, since there'd nothing there to drink. A line of giraffe moved lethargically across the flatness, and four silver-backed jackals were making antelope five or ten times their size very nervous. That was it until evening.

We camped that night at Okaukeujo waterhole. The discomfort of Okavango, and the bitter cold nights in South West Africa after that, meant I'd hardly slept for days. I had a sort of jet lag. But the hole was lit up, so I sat huddled in my sleeping bag watching the comings and goings. I thought I saw all sorts of exciting animals, though they turned out to be rocks, trees, and shadows. It reminded me once again of the elephants in Uganda that were really termite mounds. Then an oryx came for a drink. Oryx only have to do this once every two weeks. They have a special radiator system which consists of a network of veins in their noses that cools their blood before it gets sent to the brain to keep it cool. Normal mammals sweat to keep their body temperature steady at 39°C or so. Oryx consider this a waste, and so they let their bodies go over 45°C while still keeping their brains cool. Smart. A couple of elephants showed up and pushed the oryx out of the way. They drank for a seriously long time. After they'd finished and left, two younger ones showed up, though the older ones returned when they realised the smaller ones were still drinking. The four of them left together in slow motion. A few springboks flitted about. I wondered if they ever slept. The night must be terrifying for animals that predators want to munch on. At dawn, I returned to the camp, exhausted.

After that, we left the tourists behind and headed off into the barren wilderness (this describes most of South West Africa) towards the town of Khorixas. It was a dusty place, but it had a petrol station. On the map the national parks are coloured green. The truth is that it's literally the least green place I'd ever been. The desert was unrelenting.

The roads weren't sealed, but they well graded, which meant we could travel at 100kph. I was on the roof, holding on for dear life. It was great. When the road dipped down through dry river beds, Frank slowed up a bit, and I got bumped around even more. It was all part of the fun. At one point we stopped at a petrified forest, so it hadn't always been this dry. The huge logs had been frozen by the arid climate, and then, over millennia, had literally turned to stone. The detail was amazing – knots, bark, and even rings. There was also more Bushman art work, engraved on some rocks. It was mainly of elephants, lions, antelope, rhino, and flamingos. There were no people, or mythical creatures.

The scenery was stark and harsh and the rocks were different colours – black, orange, and a deep yellow. They were best in the morning and late afternoon. In the middle of the day all their colours got washed away.

Mt. Brandberg was a big black rock and rather boring, but nearby was a famous cave painting called the White Lady. We hiked for an hour or so over rough terrain to see it. We found a human figure with white trousers or legs. I preferred the ones of animals in motion, flowing across the savannah, though the figure did have the same bearing as those on the murals I'd seen in Egypt.

We left the official road and set out across country, Frank driving skilfully to avoid the holes and sharp rocks. We were aiming for the Ugab river, which was

The coolest Land Rover out there ... occasionally got stuck, I loved riding on the roof, sorry about the Speedos [Note to photo editor].

actually a river bed. We planned to go down it to the coast. It was desolate and desperately inhospitable. If the Land Rover had broken down, and if it had been beyond Frank's ability to fix, we'd probably have died there. We were well off the grid, and nobody knew we were there.

I was still on the roof and whenever Frank hit the occasional hole I was bounced up into the air. At I one hole I nearly broke my jaw on one of the jerry cans. That was enough. I came down into the cabin.

We saw the river when we saw green bushes. They lived on the water below the ground. We turned right for the sea to discover that the water was just below the surface. We sank into the river bed, and driving became more and more difficult. We had to retrace our steps until we found a little, rough track to follow, going bump, bump, bump, passed some deserted mines. We came across a dead zebra that was as stiff as a board. The skin was still intact, but the carcass was completely empty except for the bones. I yanked out one of its unexpectedly large teeth.

We were all tired after hours and hours on the rough track. We were also on edge as we didn't want to admit it, but we were probably lost. Martin and I clambered up a mountain to get our bearings. Considering how good a mechanic Frank was, I found it difficult to believe that we'd been heading north west, when we should have been going west, and then south west. We decided to retrace our steps and take the proper road.

Once back on course we sped towards the Atlantic through the Namib desert. I stayed on top again as there was a strong tail wind. We were able to do about 110kph. It was beautifully warm under the scorching sun. The land was flat and dry, and mirages shimmered in the distance. Suddenly the air was chilled by cold air streaming in from the Atlantic. I climbed back into the cabin, musing on the paradox presented by the Namib and the Atlantic. There was the sand, and then there was the sea. There was the heat, and then there was the cold. It was dry, and then it was wet.

Waves crashed on the shore and pelicans swoop around us. We couldn't see it, but somewhere below the sea's surface was life in profusion. A few metres away was the desert, with almost no life in I at all. It was the same dichotomy again.

The coastal road took us down to Swakopmund. It clung to South West Africa's littoral, surviving on fishing, mining, and tourism. It was very German. We had coffee and Black Forest gateau, which was an amazing change from the being out in the desert, essentially lost, eating baked beans, and Frank's endless pasta without sauce. There were palm trees, and Bavarian-style buildings, and it all felt rather odd. A flock of flamingos flew overhead in a perfect line, pink, with black under their wings. Standing in ponds they're beautiful. In the air, they're like a squadron of science fiction fighter planes, streamlined, extraordinarily long and straight, elegant, and fast. They were off in search of richer feedings grounds.

'Ve must find ze bierkeller!' the Germans cried. So we did.

At Kuckis we got to meet half of Swakopmund, and I got into an argument with an Austrian about politics and apartheid. There were also men from the nearby Rossing uranium mine, and even one who used to work on the Brent Delta rig in the North Sea. Others just caught fish. It was like the Wild West and, even then, it seemed to be of an era that was long gone. The women looked like Janis Joplin, with headbands and kaftan shirts. Many of the men were in Alpine kit, their solid legs showing between long shorts and their long socks. They had round beer bellies under their shirts, and long sideburns. It was more German than Germany. We'd already eaten dinner at our campsite, but we ate pork knuckle and sauerkraut anyway, and downed large jugs of beer, and got drunk. The place closed officially at 10.30pm, which was when the tourists were booted out, but we were invited to stay on with the locals. We left at 2am, completely blotto. It was quite a struggle to find the campsite and the Land Rover.

The next day, through the haze of my hangover, I tried to remember the conversations I'd had. Only one stuck in my mind. One older man, a German farmer, said he was past talking. When the time came he was going to pick up his gun and fight for his land. We freshened up by swimming in the icy Atlantic and had fried eggs. It was a winning combination, as it seems to cure our hangovers.

The three of us had been living in close proximity for about six weeks, mainly in the bush, so we spent the rest of the morning on the beach, ogling the girls. Not surprisingly, given how skinny, weird, and bedraggled we looked, they didn't ogle us back. I thought it was Maggie's fault, as he was beginning to look like Frank Zappa again.

We went to the museum in the afternoon, which had a number of white-supremacist explanations of the White Woman cave painting. It was a shipwrecked white woman, they said. It was the Queen of Sheba looking for Zimbabwe (off course). It was an Egyptian looking for gold and diamonds (an artistic resemblance I'd noticed myself.) This was all bollocks, of course. It was most likely the image of a witch doctor woman dating back 2,000 years, who happened to have her lower half painted white.

Walvis Bay, just down the South West African coast, had the most amazing dunes – deep red, massive, and curvaceously sculpted by the wind. The play of light increased as the sun slid lower, the shadows adding more contrast to the macro-curves and micro-ripples. It was beautiful, but bloody tiring to climb up and down.

We camped at the base of a dune on some hard sand. The moon rose early and was very yellow. It must have been the moisture from the ocean. We were too tired to cook properly, so we had soup. Though the lack of sleep and the hangovers were getting to us, we couldn't resist climbing the dunes in the moonlight. It was absolutely silent. I was used to noisy nights, buzzing insects, baboons having sex, and the fire crackling, but up there, apart from the soft crunch of my feet on the cool sand, it was completely quiet. I left a line of lonely prints behind me. The wind died down, and didn't obliterate them the way it did in the daytime. It was all black and silver, and peaceful and serene. We slept after that for ten hours.

We headed on in the morning into Walvis Bay itself. It was an ugly little port, mostly dedicated to shipping out minerals. It was nothing like Bavarian

The magnificent Namib desert, sometimes it's red sometimes it's yellow.

Swakopmund. I spent a lot of time on the Land Rover's roof, with people coming in the opposite direction gawking at my hair being ripped about, and my skin being shrivelled – as well as at our crazy vehicle, festooned with jerry cans and sand ladders.

We noticed a vast, pink haze out on the flats, so we parked and set off on foot to try and get closer. We started sinking deeper and deeper into stinking black mud and had to turn back. We found out later that it was part of the Walvis Bay sewage system. That explained the stink, and the profusion of life forms that were food for the elegant, but none too picky, flamingos.

Driving further, the road sort of disappeared, though the tracks of previous vehicles continued. There are, in fact, all sorts of sand, and they all have very different characteristics when it comes to driving on them. This was one of the worst types. It was energy draining. The engine was roaring as we ploughed on through it, and whenever Frank put his foot down to try and escape. Despite being an expert driver, who really knew his machine, he couldn't balance the need for power against the engine overheating. Steam was pouring out from under the bonnet, so we stopped to let it cool down. When we moved on, the sand changed from one of the worst types to an even worse type. We came to a grinding halt with sand up to the wheel arches, and the number plate hidden. Out came the sand ladders, which had been carried thousands of miles for just this eventuality. They were basically stiff, aluminium tracks for the wheels to climb over, thereby getting us out of whatever we were stuck in. We also fetched spades to dig under the wheels at the back and wedge the ladders there. Frank jumped in, the engine roared to life. It screamed non-stop as he reversed. The vehicle lurched and bounced up on to harder sand, leaving a hole like a bomb crater. Any regular vehicle would have been doomed.

We were trying to get to the point where the dunes met the sea, but the going was too tough, so we turned back. First, though, we decided to go for a swim. Digging in the sand had been hot work. There were flocks of cormorants migrating above is as we flopped about in the freezing ocean. They streaked over the surf, skimming the breakers just above our heads.

We turned inland at the Kuiseb River, which was sometimes a river, and sometimes a river bed. It ended abruptly at massive dunes. We stopped at a campsite – at least, there was a sign that said 'campsite'. There were no facilities. It was already dark, but the morning revealed a beautiful scene. We climbed up out of the canyon that the riverbed had snaked through, and before us were massive dunes that marched off to the south – red, orange, and ochre.

When we drove on next day the heat caused mirages, distorting the horizon. Ranges of mountains floated on silver lakes. There were ridiculous ostriches, rushing across the horizon with their heads held high. Unlike the zebra and the wildebeest, I never saw a dead one, though. They must have been doing something right. Then some zebra raced against us for a few minutes, their muscles rippling, and their hooves churning up the dust. A lone oryx strode passed, proud and strong, and a couple of jackals eyed us nervously. There were also some stunning yet strange desert plants, with brilliant yellow flowers, that stood out against the dull desert and the deep blue sky.

Some 100m to our right an ostrich panicked, ran in our direction, abruptly stopped, ran in the opposite direction, stopped again, then ran in the same direction as we were going. It was clearly confused, and seemingly incapable of working out where we were headed. (The mood in the Land Rover cabin was correspondingly mixed as the radio was on, and West Germany were losing to Italy in football's World Cup Final.)

Windhoek, the capital of South West Africa, was a terrible, cold place. Sitting there in the late-afternoon sun, we watched as the shadows brought with them even deeper cold. To make matters worse, I'd washed nearly everything I owned. We spent the evening with a German farmer and his family, and inevitably, the conversation turned to politics. There were elections coming up, and the farmer was pretty sure that the Marxist-oriented parties would win and take over. He wasn't bitter, but he did describe it as a failure of the West. The parties he was referring to I didn't think were really Marxist. They just wanted equality for the blacks. The West had refused to support them, however. It's continued to prop up South Africa's apartheid regime, instead. The liberation movements had been obliged to seek support from somewhere, and the USSR had been only too happy to help. The farmer described the sanctions against South Africa by the West as a charade. He was also very critical of the failure by the whites to give the blacks any political education. The blacks have not been able to hold any positions in government, which meant if they did win, they'd be coming to power with zero experience. They'd be expected to run the country, and the whites would point at their failings and say, 'We told you so.' He seemed a reasonable man.

We didn't stay in the capital for long. We headed off south again to see the famous Sossusvrei dunes. There was an annoying system of bookings to enter the park, but chaps in cool Land Rovers don't book to see sand dunes. When we did roll up, the campsite was full, so we parked outside. Everyone came to look at us. There was a delightful mixture of pity for our bedraggled condition, and admiration for our adventurous spirit. We were given large quantities of wine and beer, and asked about the lawlessness in the north. Basically, we said, all the black Africans had been nice to us. A discussion then ensued that turned into an argument between the liberal German speakers and the conservative Germans and Afrikaners. They forgot we were there. We sat quietly and drank their wine.

Maybe at home I'd mixed in the wrong company, but I could go a year there without being involved in a political discussion. In Africa there'd be one every day. Even in the boondocks of Uganda, they knew more about the world than I did. And they had very definite opinions. (I remember having an amazing discussion about socialism with a man in a mud hut in the Sudan.)

Despite overdosing on wine, we managed to get up really early to see the dunes. The light was best in the early morning, and we didn't want our view spoiled by a bunch of tourists. The others there had had the same idea, but our Land Rover could go further over the rough tracks, so we won. The red dunes, with

Such incredible colours.

their perfectly sculpted curves, were both beautiful and surreal. We parked and climbed. The wind increased until at the top the grains of sand hit our legs like needles. Away in the distance, over miles of dunes, was the Atlantic. Below us, the Land Rover was a tiny, brown dot. We raced down, causing liquid landslides, to cook a distinctly gritty breakfast.

An Afrikaner family invited us over for coffee. They owned a tobacco farm and were fascinated by our stories. They were trying to map the future, and decide what best to do for themselves and their children. They knew big changes were on the way.

We drove south through high-walled canyons that were the less famous cousins of the Grand Canyon in Arizona. Different rock strata were defined by their different colours. We saw three bat-eared foxes. These usually only come out at night. I'd last seen them in the Serengeti. The air was getting colder, which meant I had to resign myself to another freezing night. Before dawn, I lit two candles to try and get warm. Ridiculous.

The drive down to the South West African town of Luderitz meant cutting through the prohibited lands of the Consolidated Diamond Mines company (part of De Beers). They gave us a tour around the deserted mining settlement of Kolmanskop. Some of the buildings were in the process of being destroyed by the sand and the wind. Whole corners had gone, and whole rooms had already been filled with mini-dunes. The staff were paranoid about us wandering off. Where could we go? We hid in the deserted buildings to worry them. Infantile.

Another tyre burst but Frank managed to keep control. We never had slow punctures, only big bangs. There'd been no rain for two or three years, so while Frank was fixing the tyre, I got out a spade and tried digging to see what I might find. Only a foot below the surface there was water.

The Portuguese had done some of their proselytising here. They'd even planted a cross at Diaz Point, where the Atlantic still crashed around it. Assuming the pace was a desert in 1488, there must have been nobody there to convert. Which didn't seem very practical. What I did notice was that the seals and the flamingos occupied the same ecosystem. This was not something I would have expected. It seemed surreal. It was explained by the fact they were both after edible stuff from the sea.

Luderitz was another little bit of Bavaria lost on the Atlantic coast of southern Africa. How about this for the name of a road: Zeppelin Street. Being down at sea level was good, though, since we were less likely to freeze.

Seals were playing on the shore, leaping off the black rocks and reappearing with decent-sized fish with flapping tails. We camped on Shark Island with a view of not only the Atlantic, but also the dunes, and of the picturesque little town with its German architecture and fishing boats. Down on the agate beach we saw a stunning sunset reflected on the wet sands. The sky turned orange, mauve, and dark-blue, and finally fell back over the dunes.

We splashed out for dinner at the Blue House Restaurant where we had lobster for the main course, and cherry ice-cream with schnapps for dessert. I thought back to my Ugandan banana-mush and gravy. The owner noticed that we'd tried to dress smartly, and took a liking to us. He plied us after our dessert with liqueur coffees.

Luderitz is a quiet place. We failed to find a bar after leaving the restaurant, so we went back to the campsite, where we found three black women and a man dancing together. We sort of joined in. When they left, we went to bed, but 20 minutes later they were back with a crate of beer. They were fun people. From the Herero tribe, they said.

Luderiz may be quiet but it has a dark history. The Germans made their first attempt at genocide there, and it was the Herero that they'd tried to eliminate. They built a concentration camp, and they even carried out 'medical experiments', injecting the locals with smallpox, typhus, and TB. Around 3,000 skulls were sent to Germany, where experimenters tried to prove that those they'd belonged to were racially inferior. Some 85,000 people were reduced to 15,000. At the time I didn't knew about this history. We were just young people drinking beer and dancing. But the racial views of the whites quickly became apparent when one of them said, 'Please don't ignore us, if we meet you in the town.'

The Fish River Canyon in South West Africa is the second-largest in the world after the Grand Canyon. It was as spectacular as it sounds.

We drove on to the Ai-Ai hot springs, and considering how often we'd been cold at nights, they ranked higher for us than the Fish River canyon. They were also a jolly good way to get some of the embedded grime off us. The waters were very salty, though, and made our eyes sting. Frank had trouble driving for a while after that.

When we crossed into South Africa, there was just a sign by the road. Our water was running low so we stopped off at a farm to fill the containers. Frank and I generally got along. We didn't experience much friction in our travels. But

Sort of artistic by my standards

this time he accused me of not being aggressive enough, and not getting us an invitation to dinner. Maybe he was right, but it was awkward. When I'd knocked on the door, they were already sitting down to dine.

Chapter 13

South Africa

Cape Town is one of South Africa's main cities. It's picturesque, and relatively liberal, but at that time there were amazing signs all over the place. There was 'White Toilets', and 'Black and Coloured Toilets' (the latter included all Asians, except for the Japanese, who were categorised as honorary whites). The law wasn't always followed, and I've got an amusing photo of a whole bunch of blacks sitting on a beach under a 'Whites Only' sign. My later experiences in Johannesburg were of a national melting plot. Some areas of society, it seems, were well ahead of the law, and some even ignored it.

I was back in the industrialised world and I didn't much like it. The footloose traveller, waltzing around, stalking wild game, and eating meat grilled on a campfire, was gone. The king with his backpack had been replaced by a miserable specimen of a human being, looking for a job in a place with no real friends, and no real prospects. I'd gone from peak to trough in a few days.

Frank and Martin had left to drive up the coast. This was a big psychological blow, too, as I'd been with them for ten weeks. They were like family. That was just as big a mental shock as flailing around in the job market with no work permit. We'd done everything together. There'd been an amazing intensity about it. The comforts of the Land Rover, the road, the freedom, the fun – it was all gone.

We'd spent the first few nights in South Africa with some Germans we'd met in the supermarket in Swakopmund. They'd foolishly given us their address while choosing which cut of beef to have for dinner from the display cabinet, not

The irony! a Whites Only beach, but only Non-Whites on it. Sometimes apartheid was taken with a pinch of salt.

really expecting three scruffy travellers and their Land Rover to show up on their doorstep a few weeks later claiming a bed. It was probably fine. We did get the free bed, as well as laundry privileges, and food. They, meanwhile, got bragging rights for having the coolest overland vehicle on the continent parked in their driveway. They also got to have us telling them hairy stories from the continent to their north. (The whites in South Africa never tired of hearing about the 'other' Africa. They had oodles of government propaganda, but they craved real stories. They all knew what was coming, even if the white government in Pretoria continued to impersonate the stereotype of the ostrich.)

When we got to the Cape of Good Hope, I'd felt quite proud of myself. With almost no travelling experience I'd taken on a tough continent, and I'd survived. Actually, I'd done more than survived. I'd thrived. I think my basic plan had been to 'make a man' of myself, or at least, a more well-rounded version of what I was. And I had. I'd become fearless with people (and foolishly fearless with wildlife). I was all skin and bone, but I was well tanned. I should have been happy but here I was, now preoccupied with the immediate future – having to find a job, with no contacts, and the wrong visa.

Poste restante was a bonanza. There was one from Cookie giving me the address of a kind soul called Graham, a school teacher who lived in a suburb of Cape Town called Sea Point. Cookie had written to him, and he was expecting me. He gave me a key and a room, which was a huge step in the right direction. Through him, I also met a load of other school teachers. Gareth, in particular, became a good friend, I was already deep into the liberal English community. I told them about the Afrikaners and Germans I'd met. I knew more of the 'other side' than they did. Gareth was always goes off *piste* in his classes, teaching the kids what he thought was really happening, and getting into trouble for doing so. He was also gay. The kids loved him. At my school we had interhouse debating competitions. I'd always been a backbencher. Gareth put me in front of 300 kids to talk about my experiences, and I had a ball. Chris Price had made some progress in life. He'd got well beyond the schoolboy phase. This didn't get me get a job, though. I went from office to office of the oil service firms, but I made zero progress. I needed to think again.

I went to the newspapers and talked to them about writing stories on Africa. This worked a bit. I managed to get one or two published in *The Cape Argus*, and one in *Scope*, a liberal men's magazine that combined pictures of breasts (sometimes even black) with interesting articles. It was constantly being censored. I don't think I ever got paid.

My social life was a lot better than my professional life. I went to the Space Theatre with my liberal friends, and watched a play about Soweto, the infamous

Gareth and other friends and some Lion lager - what else.

black township near Johannesburg. Then a letter arrived from my parents with one enclosed from the plucky Afrikaner girl, Gerda Visser, I'd travelled with in Spain. It invited me to her parents' place in the wine-producing area of Stellenbosch. This proved to be very picturesque, though Gerda herself had become more Afrikaans again. Her boyfriend was also not too impressed with having an Englishman talking to his girlfriend all night. (The Afrikaners didn't like the English South Africans much. There were lots of reasons, like the Boer War, when the English put them in concentration camps. The English also sided with the blacks a lot of the time, and often had better jobs than the Afrikaners. They knew that when the day came, the English would continue on as bankers, lawyers, and accountants, but many average Afrikaners would be competing for their jobs with the blacks.) Gerda was at the Universiteit Stellenbosch. It had lovely buildings, but the girls were dressed up like secretaries, with high heels and smart, dark dresses. The boys only talked about rugby.

Gerda's boyfriend, Ekhart, was actually quite interesting. He'd been an officer for three years in the military. He showed me photos of himself and his colleagues dressed up in Rhodesian Army uniforms, that were taken in what was then Rhodesia, just before it became Zimbabwe. He had other photos of himself with various military forces in Zambia and Angola. He was no toy soldier, stamping around a parade ground, and learning how to clean a rifle. He'd made real incursions into other people's territory, performed black ops, and dealing death.

South Africa at that time was being torn apart. The people were radically at odds with each other about their rights, and the direction in which they thought the country should go. As a consequence, it could be extraordinarily vibrant. There was a lot of raw emotion. Everyone seemed to feel they were arguing for, and fighting for, their very lives, and those of their children. This produced a lot of good literature. I fell in love, for example, with the novels of Andre Brink. I thought *Rumours of Rain* was amazing. I also loved the poetry of Breyton Breytenbach.

Also on the social side, I fell into a relationship with a rather paranoid school teacher called Caroline (another Gareth introduction), who took way too many drugs, and drank way too much vodka. There was a whole subculture of druggies in Cape Town. They were a million miles from the prim, Afrikaner students of Stellenbosch. They all read the *New Musical Express*, and acted like they lived in London. I just wanted to go to bed, or to keep Caroline away from her cronies. She was nice on her own.

After a month in Cape Town, I'd made a lot of friends. They even organised a going-away party for me. It was very touching. Everyone gave me something – sea shells, a Band-Aid, a T-shirt, a pen, toothpaste, two colourful condoms, a roll of toilet paper, a joint. I felt bad about leaving. Caroline looked very cute in a fluffy pink sweater, a blue-and-pink-striped miniskirt, and white tights. The party ended at 1.30am, mainly because there was a problem out on the street, where a white guy was waving around a chunky automatic pistol. He'd found a black guy asleep in the back seat of his car.

My lift north to Johannesburg came to pick me up at 3am. The drive was through the Karoo desert. It was low scrub and boring and I fell in and out of sleep. When we got to Bloemfontein, the capital of the Orange Free State, and one of the Afrikaner strong holds, I was told that no coloureds or Indians were allowed to live there. I was also told that just letting on I was English was a bad idea. We crossed the Vaal River into the Transvaal and got to Johannesburg at about 9pm.

Cookie welcomed me enthusiastically, and we took up where we'd left off. I seemed to forget about Caroline rather quickly. I started looking for work, and I finally found a job in a pub. It was called the Prince of Wales, and it was in the Park Lane Hotel in Hillbrow. Cookie and I started fighting (again), and I had to find another place to stay. As it happened, Frank and Martin had fallen in with an interesting bunch while trying to sell the Land Rover. Lance was an editor on *The Sowetan*, a newspaper from the infamous black township just outside of Johannesburg. He shared a house, and they had a spare room. Perfect, except that under my bed was a pile of banned books, and large stacks of ANC pamphlets. The other people in the house were Sharon, Johnny, and Bonnie.

When Saturday morning came around, I was asked, 'Want to go and watch a football match?' In South Africa at that time the whites played rugby, and the blacks played soccer. Four of us set off in the car. 'Where's the game?' I asked. 'Soweto,' I was told. 'I can't go to Soweto,' I said. *'I don't have a pass!'* The other three were all journalists, and had special passes that allowed them to enter. They told me not to worry. We'd take a back road. Which we did, though it meant we arrived a bit late for the game. There were 36,000 blacks and six whites (we seemed to have met two more there).

The game had already started, and the stadium was packed. The others already had places to sit, so I moved up the stands to find a space. 'Can I sit here?' I said when I found one, deploying my best 'please don't hurt me' smile. 'Please do,' came the roaring response from the enormous guy in the seat next to it. He then explained that game was the Kaiser Chiefs against Durban Football Club, and that he was a Zulu who supported the Durban team. When he found out I was from England, he became animated. The conversation went something like this, 'I work in the mines. Life is really tough. I'm away from my wife and kid who live in Natal. We work really hard for not enough money, and live in a dormitory with maybe 30 of us to a room. The best part of our week is when English football is on the TV in the evenings. I love your football, but there's one thing that worries me.' I asked him what that was. 'It's your crowds. They terrify me,' he replied. This was when football hooliganism was endemic. 'What about me here then?' I said. 'I'm on my own in a stadium of 36,000 blacks.' He looked at me incredulous. 'You don't have anything to worry about,' he said. 'You're with me.' The honest-to-god truth is that I didn't have anything to worry about, and I somehow knew that. I'd only said it for effect.

After that, we sometimes went to Soweto in the evenings to visit the huge, illegal drinking halls called *shebeens* (which, not surprisingly, is originally an Irish word). There was local beer, lager in bottles, raunchy black women swinging their hips, guys in outrageously colourful shirts, laughter, dance, sweat, and music pumping out from speakers. A thousand happy people. A thousand people who were politically oppressed, but managed somehow to have a better time than the liberal English or the fearful Afrikaners.

The Prince of Wales clientele was mainly English tradesmen, plumbers, electricians, carpenters, and skilled artisans – exactly the sort of men who might be football hooligans back in the UK. On my first night a tall, fat chap came stumbling in with blood seeping out of his dirty white shirt from a knife wound. Bloody hell. I'd never seen someone who'd been stabbed before. He made it to the bar, where I assumed he'd want me to call an ambulance. I couldn't understand his accent. The black guy who washed the glasses translated for me. 'He wants a beer and a whisky. His name's Panga Pete,' he said. Pete drank a few more pints and disappeared into the night.

People threw glasses all over the floor. I was expected to break up fights (though I didn't really have a clue what to do). Luckily, some of the locals got to like me and helped me throw out the real trouble makers. Panga Pete actually turned out to be one of them.

The people in the pub made stalking game in Uganda on foot seem tame. For example, it was frequented by mercenaries on rest and recreation. They were not very discrete. 'Mad' Mike Hoare, a famous mercenary leader, was in a South African jail after a botched coup in the Seychelles. His son frequented the bar and told me about his dad's cryptic messages from the inside. He'd got ten years, not for organising the failed coup, but for hijacking a plane to escape when it didn't work. I was offered a job as a mercenary in Chad earning 3,000 rand a month. I declined. It seemed that a *coup d'etat* there was being orchestrated there by the South African intelligence service. This fitted in with Ekhart's escapades in Zimbabwe, Zambia, and Angola.

Mike Hoare's son turned out to be a bit different from the other soldiers of fortune. He was a journalist working for the *Mercury*, a Durban newspaper. One of the cryptic messages from his dad was from *Hamlet*, Act IV, Scene V. On inspection this proved to be a very long scene involving ghosts and the like. William Shakespeare knew what he was talking about when it came to mercenaries. It was Mark Antony, after all, who'd said in *Julius Caesar*, 'Cry "Havoc", let slip the dogs of war.' The mercenary world proudly took this up as a way to speak for the whole industry. Just as he finished telling me about his dad's cryptic message (I assume he'd worked out I was the only person in the bar who actually knew anything about *Hamlet*) there was a clatter of small arms fire from 100m down the road. People looked up from their beers for a moment, then went back to their conversations. Hillbrow was an edgy place, even then.

A white professional hunter from Botswana showed up in his khaki safari jacket, shorts, long socks, and bush hat. He did look funny. I was deferential because I wanted to ask him for a job. Anything had to be better than the Prince of Wales. I served him a beer, and tried to get him to tell some interesting stories, but unfortunately, he turned out to be a crashing bore. The plumbers and fitters started taking the piss out of him. They eventually they ran him out of the pub. They didn't take the piss out of the mercenaries, though. Those blokes were professional hunters, too, but hunters of people.

It was a 20-minute walk back from the pub to my home in Yeoville. Nothing had happened yet, but it was pretty scary. I tried to get Mr Smith, the manager of the Park Lane, to organise transport for myself and the other staff (mainly blacks), but I failed. Back in my store room for ANC literature, I devoured my own,

Opposite top: Our multiracial street; Opposite bottom: The (Jewish) Yeoville tennis club; Top: My annoying Pentax; Above: My bed, under it was loads of illegal ANC literature, more on the balcony.

chosen works. I read Freud, Alan Paton's *Cry, the Beloved Country*, a school text on economics by Richard Lipsey, and Christopher Hill's *The World Turned Upside Down*, about the radical movements at the time of the English Civil War.

So, at one end of my life I had mercenaries and reactionary plumbers, and at the other I had radical journalists. I went between black mine workers and Irish nurses. Like the ANC literature on the balcony, it seemed wise to keep things in separate boxes.

Cookie made the mistake of coming to the Prince of Wales and was amazed that such uncivilised creatures could even speak (albeit with an accent). She carefully disguised her Irish one. Almost immediately, she managed to get into an argument with one of the customers. Thank goodness she was who she was, or there would have been a fight.

There are bar scenes in movies when someone gets thrown through a window and out on to the street. Well, I saw the real thing, and what's more, I got blamed for it. There was a big fight one night, and I was tardy in making my way from the relative safety of the bar to try and sort it out. By the time I got there, Panga Pete had lifted up the troublemaker and thrown him through the front window. The guy was sprawled out on the street, groaning. There was lots and lots of blood, real glass all over the place, and broken chairs. Mr Smith was upset with me for not stopping the fight earlier. I gave Pete a free beer, and he winked at me. His stabbing seemed to have been a mere 'flesh wound', to quote *Monty Python*. As I said, he was a nice guy really. He reminded me of my criminal mates on the Brent Delta. When the shit went down, he was someone you really wanted on your side.

Yeoville was officially a 'whites only' area, but it seemed to be about 50-50. Out the back of our place, there were three rooms that housed three black families. Not only were they not supposed to be in Johannesburg, but they weren't supposed to be sleeping in a white neighbourhood. Nobody seemed to care, though they might have moved out if they'd known I was sleeping on ANC pamphlets.

We had a part-time helper called Esther, who had a sweet daughter who played with the white kids in the street. The place was actually pretty integrated. There were even some Afrikaner families in the street, which were pretty cool.

Next to the local pool was the Yeoville Tennis Club. I wanted to get back into the game so I explained my poverty to them, and my lack of equipment, and asked if they could do me a three-month membership. I was 'played in' by the club captain, which meant I had a game with him, and a couple of others, to assess my standard. I was very rusty, but I had managed to qualify as a tennis instructor in the UK. I started playing there quite regularly, which meant I got to meet a lot of the members. They had names like Mike and Pete and Louis, and of course, they were all white. There was one of those boards with the winners of the various club tournaments on it. There seemed to be a large

Two kids having multiracial fun.

number of Goldbergs, Bernsteins, Markowitzes, and the like. After a game I asked Mike, 'Why are there a lot of Jewish names on the board?' He said, 'Well, it's pretty much a Jewish club.' 'Oh,' I said. 'But I'm not Jewish.' 'We know that,' he replied. 'So why did you let me in?' I asked. 'Because you asked us to,' he replied. Simple, really.

My liberal friends were amazed at the stories I told about the clientele at the Prince of Wales. They'd sometimes come down to do a spot of research. Sharon and John from the flat came down and had fun acting like reactionary whites, and agreeing with the locals about the mental inferiority of the *kaffirs*. Sharon even brought her dad.

I couldn't really socialise with the black guys who worked with me. They stocked the place, cleaned the glasses, and mopped up the blood. They also earned a quarter of my already-paltry salary. It shocked me to think of how little the management paid these happy, hard-working men. No wonder they stole the occasional packet of cigarettes.

I worked for a short while with an Aussie who added some sanity to what was a pretty mad place. Sadly, he and his wife left for Zimbabwe. They showed up a few weeks later, fed up with Africa, having decided to leave for good. It was a mad place, but because of my friends, the pub started to gain a sort of liberal corner. I was on edge, always aware of the possibility of war breaking out. The guys were much better at controlling their feelings than Cookie, though, so there weren't really any problems.

One day Philip, one of the black guys who worked in the bar, pointed at the window, his eyes wide. There was a big, white police van outside. The others stared at it, too. Their shift finished at 4.30pm. Would it still be there? 'Mister Chris, please ask Mister Steve to get us registered quickly,' Philip said. The black workers lived in constant fear of the police, as well as of the local robbers, and the whites in the bar.

The place continued to be a riot. One man was giving me a lot of shit so I ignored him. Later on, all hell broke loose in a far corner. He was being attacked by a wild-looking woman who was going berserk, hitting him with bottles and chairs and anything else she could lay her hands on. I jumped over the bar (I was young once) with Ryan, one of the managers, and we waded in to separate them. There was broken furniture, broken glass, and beer all over the floor. The woman's eyes were burning with drunken rage. She would have killed him. It turned out that she lived

My cool colleague at The Prince of Wales.

opposite me in Yeo Street. Ryan called up her home and a man came to fetch her. Since it was closing time, they offered me a lift home. It turned out they were from Brighton in England. They were also a criminal gang family with loads of convictions – a very heavy mob. They were even rumoured to have been involved in a murder in Yeoville a few weeks before. They invited me in for a drink. The woman couldn't remember what the fight in the bar had been about, but the family got animated over the murder thing. 'The floppy was sut before my brother was there!' I was told. 'It was Steve,' they said. Steve was a British guy who was living locally under a false name, because he was wanted for murder in the UK. My street in Yeoville, in other words, was home to tennis-playing Jews, radical journalists, unregistered blacks, and white criminal gangs. And, of course, me. It was quite a mix.

I continued to read Andre Brink's books, though I stopped reading Doris Lessing's *The Grass is Singing*. It was too depressing. Cookie and I broke up (again). We were like one of those Persian carpet closing down sales. A never-ending saga.

Bandana Duncan showed up one afternoon at the pub, purely by chance. His arrival reminded me of the Africa beyond the urban squalor I'd got stuck in. He got drunk and fell asleep in the corner. After chucking-out time, I managed to get him back to my place. Before passing out again, he told me he was flying on to India. He showed me a gold Krugerrand he was smuggling in to sell when he got there. The Indians, he said, loved gold.

By late November the social injustice was beginning to get to me. I've already mentioned the miserable salaries of my fellow black workers in the pub. Daniel was one of the bottle washers. Another barman, a Brit called Billy, took a dislike to him, and kept pushing the management to sack him, saying he was lazy. This was nonsense, so I spoke to them myself, explaining that Billy was a racist arsehole. Thankfully, they re-employed Daniel in the restaurant. It was a small victory amid a sea of defeat. Then Sharon decided to put up some radical posters on the walls at home. We now had wallpaper supporting the Marxist government in Mozambique, just in case the police were unsure of our sympathies. This also helped a bit, but it was symbolic at best.

Christmas was approaching, and I was working double shifts. Around midnight, a black man came running into the bar followed by two policemen. In thick Afrikaner English the police asked me if the man had a pass. Why they expected me to know, I had no idea. The irony was that I was working illegally myself. The black man, by contrast, was supposedly in his own country. He got hauled off in the white van.

After closing the pub, I ended up going to a place called the Summit Club with Panga Pete. After the initial shock of his stabbing, he turned out to be the customer I got on best with. He came in a bit bloodied on another night, so I'd asked him, 'What happened Pete?' He said he'd been on his own and he'd been set upon. He'd obviously held his own. 'There were only four of them,' came his somewhat understated reply. We drank until 5am. I actually ended up there with him on Christmas Day.

To stretch my traveller's legs, in mid-January I left for Cape Town. It was the middle of summer. I hitchhiked south, getting a couple of rides from blacks (they gave me far more lifts than the whites), but I was still struggling to escape the urban and industrial sprawl. Standing by the road, I could see in the distance the huge, flat-topped, slag-heaps of the gold-mine workings. What massive piles of discarded and smashed rock! Gold was the life blood of Johannesburg.

An old Israeli stopped and said, 'Can you drive?' I nodded. I'd not driven for over a year, but I figured that it couldn't be that difficult. It was a good, straight road, after all. I drove him for over 500km. The Karoo was burning hot, and he slept most of the way. I put a Bob Dylan tape into the cassette machine on the dashboard, and listened to him sing something like, 'How does it feel, to be without a home ... Like a rolling stone ... To be on your own ... A complete unknown.' How appropriate. I could feel the wind in my sails once more. I was starting to feel free and powerful again – like I could do anything.

He dropped me off in a terrible place called Colesberg. It was in the middle of nowhere. A hot wind at blew at me for 18 hours by the side of the road. Eighteen hours, and no lift. My Dylan-induced euphoria quickly dissipated, so I resorted to a small bottle of cheap brandy.

In the middle of the following morning, a removal van with three coloureds finally stopped for me. The back of the van had foam cushions in it, and seemed to be air-conditioned. Dylan was back in favour. They were like good Samaritans. They picked up a soldier on leave, an old man who'd written off his car in Zimbabwe, and an Afrikaner plumber from Cape Town. We clattered on through the Karoo with the white heat outside, and the semi-desert, and the sheep.

In Cape Town the big news was about cricket. The South Africans had brought in some West Indians for a tour. They were paying them a huge amount of money to be honorary whites. The liberals, like my old friends Gareth and the teachers, called it hypocrisy.

We went to see a movie about the beat generation in America in the 1950s, and how they'd travelled around having a ball for no particular reason. 'That's you, that's you!' they all screamed afterwards, when we were having a postmortem about 'what it all meant' in a trendy cafe. Perhaps. But it did inspire me to read Jack Kerouac's book *The Dharma Bums*. It also suggested that I might just have a purpose in life, though what exactly that purpose might be was rather difficult to pin down.

After a few days in Cape Town, I hitched out along the coast road to the east. I ended up getting to know an Afrikaner family there quite well. Benny had a small delivery business. He'd picked me up just outside the city, and invited me to stay with his family in George, which was 400km away. He was scared of the blacks, and he was scared of the future. This all came out when he was drunk. He called the blacks *karos*, though most of the Afrikaners, and many of the English, called them *kaffirs*. He told me the English equivalent was 'mate', though I never heard 'mate' used as a racial slur before, except ironically.

He employed me to drive his crappy little truck up to Sedunda near Johannesburg. Secunda was the home of a petrochemical firm that specialised in converting coal into liquid carbon products like petrol. This was critical in the apartheid era, when there were official boycotts on selling South Africa crude. They'd gotten the technology from Germany, another place rich in coal and poor in oil.

We set off at 3am. He was driving a lorry, and I was trying to get his ancient Ford Cortina *bakkie* (a dilapidated pickup) to pull a heavy trailer. This was definitely not the same as roaring across Uganda in a massive 16-wheeler with cannabis-smoking, Swahili-speaking, Kenyan lorry drivers. This said, it was good to be on the road again, though it was a long haul back up through the burning Karoo in a vehicle that has to be put in first gear to get up even a modest incline. Downhill was just scary, since I was basically pushed all the way by the trailer.

We crossed the Groot River and hit the Karoo proper. This was not a pretty/dry place, like the Namib. It was ugly/scruffy dry. I squinted against the low, bright sun, while the pickup swayed from side to side. I struggled to keep awake. We stopped at various scruffy little *dorps* (villages) for petrol, coffee, and ice-cream. At a dot on the map called Noupont, there only seemed to be whites. Benny said, 'Only Boers live here. The blacks aren't that stupid.' We passed through Colesburg, where I'd spent 18 hours waiting for a ride, and crossed into the Orange Free State. My vehicle was falling apart. The indicators had stopped working. The engine temperature gauge had moved into the red. And I got a flat tyre. Once under way again we were stopped by the police. They turned out to be the railway police, checking that we were not contravening their monopoly on transporting goods. Luckily, they didn't ask to see our licences. I didn't have one.

Day became night but we kept on, stopping only for coffee, cakes, and to have a crap. Benny was even more tired than me. He kept falling asleep at our pit-stop tables. I guess he felt he was in some kind of a toughness competition with the English and didn't want to lose. We stopped at a 24-hour roadside cafe, and the whole place was buzzing. There were blacks standing around under lamp-posts, shouting and laughing, and neon lights, and big lorries crashing through. I felt like I was back in another Africa again. It reminded me of the bus stop in Tanzania.

At midnight we stopped, and I went to sleep across the front seats of the Ford. At 3.30am we were up again, and driving on. At daybreak we could see the massive towers of the refinery plant, its chimneys flaring excess gas. Talk about satanic mills. The road was filthy with coal dust. There were black puddles, and the rubbish dumps by the side of the road were smoking non stop. The air was hot and raw. It was an ugly, industrial, dreary place, despite being one of the country's main weapons against international sanctions. When we finally got to Secunda, our destination, we drove to a residential area. It was also a dreadful place – a kind of white man's Soweto, without the football, the *shebeens*, and the laughter.

Benny had agreed to pay me a paltry 25 rand, but in the end he only had 15 with him in cash. That's life. I needed to get to Johannesburg to collect some of my other money, and to see some of my friends, before I headed for Durban. The petrol station had a shower so I cleaned up, had a shave, and got back on the road. (First rule of hitchhiking, 'Look presentable, and don't smell.' Second rule, 'Face the driver, so they can see your face, and smile.') A big BMW stopped immediately, and an American nuclear engineer (interesting) gave me a ride. He told me about the South African nuclear program (for electricity, he said, rather than bombs, though I thought there was a connection.) He compared the place to America, and particularly the American South. This was the early 1980s, when the southern US and South Africa were not that different. He said that although the laws had changed in the US, the southern mindset was still largely one of segregation.

He dropped me off in a Johannesburg suburb, and before I even had time to stick out my thumb, a white, underworld family had stopped. There was lots of swearing, and open talk about robberies and beating people up. They dropped me off in Hillbrow. My guess was they knew my criminal neighbours across the street, but I kept my mouth shut.

Hitching out of Johannesburg again was tough. I'd started at dawn, but in the end I had to take buses to the edge of town. A VW camper van stopped that had a special three-litre engine. We batted along at 140kph, but the radiator didn't match the engine, so there were enforced periods of rest while we doused it down and waited for the steam to subside. The drive through the Drakensburg Mountains, via Van Reenen's Pass, was also dramatic, especially when being driven by a Zimbabwean with an apparent death wish.

One of my mum's thousands of contacts around the world was a family in Pinetown, outside Durban. They were relatives of Charles Dickens. I stopped there and taught their kids to swim before moving on to the steamy port city that was Durban itself.

My adventures on the African mainland were drawing to a close, but there was still one more to be had. On Saturday afternoon I went to the Greyville racecourse. In an air-conditioned pub I struck up a conversation with a cheerful black South African woman (was there any other type?). She was from Natal, and a Zulu. After a few drinks we got to know each other a lot better than I'd originally planned. It was illegal under the Immorality Act, but I felt both delighted and gratified when we emerged from the bushes behind the Standard Bank.

In Durban I was staying with Hywel, who I'd first met in Spain 18 months before, when we'd stumbled around Morocco together. Then we'd been 'just off the boat', as it were; he was now settling down to life at the university. Compared to the land around Johannesburg, Natal was quite rural. Driving around in Hywel's family car, I saw people in bright tribal dress, shouting, smiling, and waving, I felt like I was back in the Africa. I loved the place.

I also tried surfing, and nearly drowned. The waves didn't look very big, but they tumbled me over, and in the murky waters, I couldn't tell which way was up. It was very scary.

I wanted to work my passage by ship. I thought this would be way cooler than flying. I thought it would be cheaper too. Down at the port, I checked at the harbour master's office on what ships were headed for India. My plan was to speak to a captain, or a first mate, about getting a free ride in exchange for my labour. I thought my oil rig experience would help. After all, I was jolly good at painting complex, hot bits of machinery, and I was tops with mops. Nothing seemed to be going in my direction for a couple of weeks. The nearest I could get was Singapore.

Since the start, airlines have been going bankrupt. It's a mystery to me why we're not prepared to pay enough to keep them properly maintained and up in the sky. By that logic, Air Mauritius won't be going bust anytime soon. The ticket from Durban to Mumbai via Mauritius was astonishingly expensive. It was insult

A tourist shot with a Zulu girl in my trusty M&S sweater. I still have the ostrich shell necklace.

added to injury. Not only had I been humbled by not being able to work my passage on a boat. I had to pay though the nose for an air ticket, too. But I bit the bullet. I had no choice.

The normal way to arrive in South Africa was via an airport like Jan Smuts in Johannesburg. Since South Africa was diplomatically cut off from the rest of Africa. Nobody really arrived at the land crossings. When I'd shown up on the Botswana-South West Africa border, the fellow there had slapped a one-year stamp in my passport. The immigration people in Durban went ballistic, 'You should only have got three months!' they shouted. It wasn't my fault.

I flew first to Mauritius. It was a relatively short flight. As Africa dropped away below me, the lights of Durban receded, and we headed out over the black sea.

To get back into the swing of things, I hitchhiked from the airport in Mauritius into the capital of Port Louis. I did so out of principle. I did it because it could be done. The bus fare was only 20 cents.

The hotel I found was infested with cockroaches. There was no air-con, and it smelled. I was home.

Epilogue

Mauritius

Antoine, from my university days, was suave and French and never short of a penny. He had immaculate taste. I think he even owned a jacket and tie. He did pretty well with the English girls, too. As I recall, he was reading accounting (rather infrequently). I was captain of the tennis team, and he was my partner. We were good friends, and partied together a lot. I say French, but he actually came from Mauritius.

The Port Louis telephone directory gave me lots of references to his family name, and there were various companies with it, too. This was clearly no coincidence. It probably explained his wealth, and his tie. Antoine himself, I was eventually to discover, was away, but his family invited me to their beach house for the weekend, which is when he was due back. They also planned to do some deep-sea fishing.

I'd already checked in to a squalid, mosquito-and-cockroach-infested dump, and had begun to know the island. The President Hotel cost a pittance, but I did have my own shower and toilet. After the second night I also had a fan and a mosquito coil. My flip-flops came in handy for whacking the shiny brown scuttlers (my reactions were pretty quick in those days, so the body count was high). Having my own toilet meant having my own cockroaches.

What a varied place Mauritius was. There were Chinese pagodas, Hindu temples, Christian churches, and British botanical gardens. There was also French money. Surprisingly, it had been a British colony until its independence in the 1960s. The Brits had taken it off Napoleon in 1810, but there were few signs of

British influence. I guess they'd just wanted the sugar. They certainly hadn't taught the locals much English. Everyone spoke a bastardised version of French, which consisted of poor French, with lots of English, African, and Asian words thrown in. English was the official language, but nobody seemed to use it much.

The place looked poor. Its economy was based on sugarcane, and a Club Med. With its rusted corrugated iron roofs, and posters peeling off the walls, it had a Caribbean-voodoo feel.

Most of Port Louis was closed for Chinese New Year. Charlie, a French guy from Réunion (a smaller island just to the left of Mauritius) told me about his trade in high-value seashells. Some of them, he said, were worth hundreds of dollars. There was also lots of curry. One of the restaurants had an aging, handwritten sign in French above the door that, roughly translated, read, 'It is forbidden to talk about religion or politics in here.'

The island was volcanic and covered in vegetation. The view from one of the crater rims took in most of it. There were lots of micro-climates as well. The beaches were like the ones in holiday brochures. They had white sand, turquoise seas, low reefs, designer palm trees (at just the right angle), and a white, hot sun that soon turned me into the classic English lobster.

I was completely socially outclassed at Antoine's family beach house at Trou-aux-Biches. I forgot to wear the proper shirt to lunch, and foolishly offered to do the dishes. Of course, they had a million servants hovering around. I was sorry to see how the happy-go-lucky Antoine of our university days had been replaced by a serious, seemingly middle-aged man. He was the chair of the family business. He certainly didn't look like he had much fun these days.

Sadly, the deep-sea fishing didn't produce any Hemingway moments. There are no photos of Chris Price beside a massive marlin he'd just taken six hours to haul in. We did catch 15kg of bonito – a sort of baby tuna – and I didn't get seasick. The latter was a big plus.

Mauritius, as I said, was a real mixture, but for me it was mainly a way-station between travelling in Africa and travelling in what the west calls Asia.

I was soon on my way – to Bombay.